Public Opinion, Public Policy, and Smoking

Public Opinion, Public Policy, and Smoking

The Transformation of American Attitudes and Cigarette Use, 1890–2016

Thomas R. Marshall

LEXINGTON BOOKS
Lanham • Boulder • New York • London

Published by Lexington Books
An imprint of The Rowman & Littlefield Publishing Group, Inc.
4501 Forbes Boulevard, Suite 200, Lanham, Maryland 20706
www.rowman.com

Unit A, Whitacre Mews, 26-34 Stannary Street, London SE11 4AB

British Library Cataloguing in Publication Information Available

Library of Congress Cataloging-in-Publication Data

Names: Marshall, Thomas R., 1949- author
Title: Public opinion, public policy, and smoking : the transformation of American attitudes and cigarette use, 1890–2016 / Thomas R. Marshall.
Description: Lanham : Lexington Books, 2016. | Includes bibliographical references and index.
Identifiers: LCCN 2016021004 (print) | LCCN 2016029192 (ebook) | ISBN 9781498504324 (cloth : alk. paper) | ISBN 9781498504331 (Electronic)
Subjects: LCSH: Smoking--Government policy--United States--History. | Antismoking movement--United States--History. | Smoking--Public opinion--United States--History. | Public opinion--United States--History.
Classification: LCC HV5760 .M38 2016 (print) | LCC HV5760 (ebook) | DDC 362.29/65610973--dc23
LC record available at https://lccn.loc.gov/2016021004

∞™ The paper used in this publication meets the minimum requirements of American National Standard for Information Sciences Permanence of Paper for Printed Library Materials, ANSI/NISO Z39.48-1992.

Printed in the United States of America

Contents

List of Figures

List of Tables

List of Abbreviations

AMA	American Medical Association
CDC	Centers for Disease Control and Prevention
CTR	Council for Tobacco Research
FCC	Federal Communications Commission
FCTC	Framework Convention on Tobacco Control
FDA	Food and Drug Administration
FTC	Federal Trade Commission
TIRC	Tobacco Industry Research Committee

Preface

Public Opinion, Public Policy, and Smoking aims to fill a gap in our understanding of public policy and cigarette smoking: what did Americans actually believe and prefer that the government do about cigarette smoking over the last two-thirds of a century? The literature on the politics of smoking and the health risks of cigarette smoking is by now extensive. Far less published work examines how American public opinion has viewed, influenced, and reacted to the many long-running policy disputes over cigarette smoking. I hope that this book will help to fill in this gap.

Americans' views on smoking have changed greatly since the mid-1900s. So, too, has American public policy toward smoking. Since the 1930s pollsters have asked over five thousand poll questions tapping the public's beliefs and preferences toward smoking and public policy. These poll questions provide the basis for this book. I gratefully acknowledge the many authors, polling firms, and databases upon which work I have relied. Without their efforts this book would not have been possible. The interpretations herein and any errors are my own. I thank the students in my public opinion classes for inspiring this project. For their many helpful efforts, criticisms, and suggestions, I thank my colleagues and the political science departmental and library staff at my university, the reviewers of my articles and papers, and the editors and reviewers of this book.

ONE

Of Public Opinion, Public Policy, and Smoking

That cigarette smoking presents a serious economic and health danger to American society can scarcely be in question. Nearly one in six Americans still smokes cigarettes. The estimated economic costs of cigarette smoking within the United States now exceed $300 billion a year. Nearly $170 billion results from direct medical care costs for adults and more than $156 billion results from lost productivity due to premature death and exposure to secondhand smoke. These costs represent roughly one dollar of every twelve dollars that Americans spend annually on health care (Xu et al. 2015). About three-fifths of these health care costs are paid by public funds. An estimated 480,000 Americans die prematurely from cigarette smoking each year, including nearly 42,000 premature deaths from exposure to secondhand smoke. This equals about one in five deaths annually within the United States. Over the last half century over twenty million Americans have died prematurely from tobacco usage. Worldwide, the annual mortality rates from tobacco usage are much higher and steadily growing. Worldwide, an estimated six million deaths annually result from tobacco usage and that figure is projected to increase to eight million annually by 2030.[1]

Tobacco control is not a recent issue in American politics. Cigarette smoking became common within the United States over a century ago. Almost immediately controversies sprung up and since then both American public opinion and public policy on cigarette smoking have changed greatly, continue still to change, and in all likelihood will keep changing for the foreseeable future.

This book considers the complex relationship between public opinion and smoking-related public policy, particularly on two important issues. The first issue is primarily about public opinion. How well-informed and interested are Americans on tobacco-related issues? Are Americans sufficiently well-informed to have any great impact on public policy? Are a large number of American adults attentive to the many past and ongoing policy debates on smoking? Are a large number of adults closely focused on the problem? Have Americans become better informed from the ongoing and wide-ranging public debate over smoking? If so, why and how quickly did the learning process occur? How greatly do Americans support tobacco control policies?

A second and equally important issue is how closely are public opinion and public policy linked? Does American public opinion on smoking-related issues actually influence public policy decisions at the local, state, or national level, and if so, when and how often? Or, alternatively, is American public opinion largely irrelevant on smoking-related public policy-making? In a democratic society this second issue has considerable importance. This chapter describes several linkages that might possibly tie public opinion to public policy. Chapters 2 through 7 review the empirical evidence, and chapter 8 then reconsiders the ties between public opinion and tobacco control policy.

Both these issues can best be addressed by comparing well-conducted public opinion polls with public policy. At one time gauging the mass public's beliefs was largely guesswork. During most of the global experience with tobacco there was no reliable way to measure the opinions of ordinary adults. Only the views of literate and influential people were recorded and even then only occasionally so. During the mid-1930s several pioneering American pollsters devised the earliest modern public opinion polls, thereby making it possible to measure the mass public's attitudes on political and social issues. These polls measured the opinions of all American adults rather than just the views of those who were actively engaged in an issue such as grass-roots activists or the leaders of corporations, associations, and interest groups all of whose views sometimes agree with poll majorities but often do not.

Three types of opinions stand out as especially important: beliefs, images, and preferences. These three areas are equally important but quite different. *Beliefs* include Americans' changing scientific beliefs about the link between cigarette smoking and illnesses. The best-known and most frequently-polled of beliefs include whether cigarette smoking is a cause of lung cancer, heart disease, birth defects, or a host of other serious diseases.

Images include Americans' positive or negative views about cigarette manufacturers or about cigarette smokers. Among the most important images are whether cigarette manufacturers are honest, credible, or concerned about their product's safety. Other important images include whether smokers are annoying, irresponsible, or potentially harmful to nonsmokers. Beliefs and images are not always considered in studies of public opinion and policy changes. However, the evidence presented in this book is that changes in the public's beliefs and images are extremely important in understanding why public policies change. Changing beliefs and images encourage organized challenges to the tobacco industry and predate important changes in tobacco control policy.

Preferences are opinions about what policy measures should be carried out to restrict—or in earlier years, to encourage—cigarette smoking. During the last two-thirds of a century important preferences have included Americans' attitudes toward tobacco control measures such as higher taxes, bans on smoking in public places, restrictions on the sale and advertising of cigarettes, limits on smoking by minors, and compensation for those harmed by smoking. Preferences change and evolve over time, typically following changes in beliefs and images. Public support for tobacco control policies has dramatically changed since the 1950s and still continues to evolve.

Not surprisingly, Americans' beliefs, images, and preferences are of frequent concern to American pollsters who have asked well over five thousand poll questions tapping these attitudes. The vast majority of these poll questions were asked since the late 1940s. Fortunately this was also the time when the growing number of American pollsters improved their polls' accuracy by adopting better and more random-like sampling techniques. Regrettably, only a few poll questions were available before the late 1940s and none at all were available during the first two decades of the 1900s when a vigorous antismoking movement existed.

This book examines many different types of poll questions. Sometimes pollsters repeatedly ask identically-worded poll questions over time, thereby making it possible to track changing attitudes and to study the impact of attitudes and events one after the other. A well-known example would be Gallup's often-asked questions tapping Americans' beliefs on whether cigarette smoking is a cause of lung questions. This important poll series now goes back over six decades. Several other poll series are available over a much shorter duration. Identically worded poll questions that are frequently repeated over time are very useful.

Many of the best studies of public opinion and public policy are based primarily upon trend questions. Yet pollsters far more often ask timely questions only when a new issue arose and is currently under debate, but cease to ask these particular questions once the issue recedes from public debate. As a result, only one or a few poll questions on a policy dispute are available, and all these questions were asked when the controversy was active. These poll questions do not allow opinion trends to be studied over time but are still useful in other ways. Chapters 5 and 6 use these questions to examine how consistent public policy decisions are with timely public opinion. This book uses both trend and timely poll questions to offer a better understanding of the relationship between public opinion and public policy.

Many of the poll questions considered in this book were conducted for the tobacco industry itself. Why these poll questions should be included merits discussion. Beginning in the early 1950s individual cigarette manufacturers and their associations often hired the nation's most prominent pollsters to survey Americans' beliefs, images, and policy preferences. These privately conducted poll questions usefully fill in missing information for time periods and on attitudes missing from publicly-available polls. The industry's polls are often the only poll questions apparently asked on a topic. The industry's pollsters asked many poll questions that ranged well beyond those available in publicly-available polls. The industry's polls and the accompanying reports also offer useful insights into how cigarette manufacturers and their associations sought to craft a public relations strategy.

Fears that the industry's pollsters might give their clients a falsely optimistic view of American public opinion are unfounded. When the industry's privately-conducted polls can be directly compared to publicly-available polls, similar results appear. The industry's pollsters' reports often reported back brutally candid and highly unflattering poll results to their clients. During the 1960s and 1970s, for example, the industry's pollsters reported back on rising beliefs that cigarettes were harmful on declining levels of public trust and confidence in the industry, and on the growing stigma attached to cigarette smoking. The industry's polls are also useful in better understanding Americans' attitudes on several policy disputes over cigarette smoking. Not surprisingly, even the industry's sharpest critics have not hesitated to consider these polls, as does this book.

The poll questions used in this book come from a wide variety of sources over the last three-quarters of a century. Many poll questions were asked by pollsters employed by cigarette manufacturers or by the industry's associations. The results of this polling, although originally kept private, are now publicly available through the legacy tobacco archive's online site. Other poll questions reported in this book were asked by the nation's leading pollsters, were originally made public, and are now available through the online iPOLL Roper archive or elsewhere. Still other poll questions come from surveys conducted by academics or for government agencies and are available from the original reports or published articles which are at best erratically archived.

Because the poll questions used here come from different sources, the amount of polling information available varies. Sometimes the poll questions' original data files are available for analysis, but more often only the overall poll results are still available and few if any demographic or regional attitude breakdowns were reported. When the original data files are not available, the most commonly available groups for which poll results are reported in the archived reports are age groups, men and women, or smokers versus nonsmokers. As a result, this book necessarily pays more attention to nationwide (or collective) public opinion than to demographic, income, educational, or regional variations in opinion. Considering demographic and regional variations in attitudes is indisputably useful in understanding attitudes (e.g., Berinsky 2004; Brodie, Deane, and Cho 2011; Gilens 2005, 2012a, 2012b) but this information is not consistently available. The polls reported in this book are "cross-sectional" surveys—that is, each survey relies on a newly-drawn sample of respondents. Regrettably, panel studies—that is, surveys that interview the same adult respondents at least twice—are very expensive and not available on tobacco-related topics. Nor, except for scattered split-ballot experiments,[2] is this book primarily based on relatively recent and useful experimental approaches (e.g., Gilens 2002; Gollust and Lynch 2011) to understanding public opinion.

Public policies include a wide variety of tobacco-related government decisions that in some way affect cigarette smoking. These policies have changed dramatically over time. During the early 1900s anti-cigarette activists succeeded in passing many new policies to discourage cigarette smoking, although with only temporary success and chiefly so at the state and local level. From the mid-1920s through the 1950s most public policies encouraged the tobacco industry and cigarette smoking. Since then tobacco control advocates have often, if not always succeeded in enacting new policies to discourage cigarette smoking. During the 1960s and 1970s these new policies were only modest in scope. In 2009 a new federal regulatory regime for cigarettes at the U.S. Food and Drug Administration was finally enacted.

The American political system is unusually open to seeking activists seeking favorable policies from different levels of government (Courtwright 2005; Nathanson 1999, 2007; Risse-Kappan 1991). This has often proved to be very useful to tobacco control advocates and sometimes to the tobacco industry as well. Important smoking-related policies can occur at the local, state, or federal level, and can occur through legislative action, executive orders, agency decisions, court rulings, or through popular votes in state or local issue elections. Some, but not all tobacco control proposals become public policy. Some, but not all of the tobacco control policies considered in this book are well-known. Not surprisingly, pollsters may ask many poll questions tapping public opinion on high profile issues. Most tobacco control proposals are low profile and attract only a small amount of media, little public attention, and only a single poll question or even none at all.

LINKING PUBLIC OPINION AND PUBLIC POLICY

Of the two issues considered here, the first is how well-informed public opinion is on smoking-related issues, and why and how quickly the public becomes better informed. Whether American public opinion is generally well-informed on policy issues has been much debated. Several early accounts painted a generally negative picture. Walter Lippman (1925) described public opinion as ill-informed and unstable over time. Joseph Schumpeter (1950: 262) was even less flattering to the "typical citizen" whom he characterized as "infantile" and "primitive" and "given over to irrational prejudice and impulse." Early survey research on American elections (Campbell, Converse, Miller, and Stokes 1960; Converse 1964; see also Herbst 2011) described public opinion as unstable and incoherent ideologically. Later accounts offer a more balanced and more positive view (Gilens 2012a; Page, Shapiro, and Dempsey 1987; Page and Shapiro 1992; Shapiro and Jacobs 2011: 720–22). How public opinion on tobacco control issues fit into this long-running debate over citizen competence is considered at length below.

The second issue is whether and how greatly does public opinion influence tobacco control policy-making? A large and steadily growing literature has examined why, when, and how greatly public opinion influences public policy-making—and sometimes the reverse. Many studies suggest that public opinion has a strong, if imperfect impact on public policy decisions. Shapiro (2011) and Manza and Cook (2002) recently summarized this literature. Five conclusions stand out. First, when polls can be timely compared to policy decisions, wide variations exist across policy areas but, overall, timely poll majorities and policies agree roughly at the rate of three to two or two to one (Monroe 1979, 1998; Gilens 2005; Mayer 1992).[3] Second, where the poll support for a policy is rapidly changing, policy changes typically follow within a few years (Stimson, MacKuen, and Erikson 1995). Third, changes in policy reflect not only changing attitudes toward that particular policy, but also changes in Americans' liberal-versus-conservative national mood (Stimson 1999). Fourth, public opinion more often and more greatly influences public policy-making than the reverse (Page and Shapiro 1982, 1983). Fifth, although the political influence of interest groups and of stakeholders is difficult to separate from public opinion, where this can be done, the influence of public opinion on policy-making remains significant and the influence of interest groups and of stakeholders is considerably less than at first might appear (Burstein 1998, 2003, cf. Gilens and Page 2014). Whether the impact of public opinion upon public policy is growing over time remains in dispute (Quirk and Hinchliffe 1998; Monroe 1998; Shapiro and Jacobs 2011).

How exactly public opinion and public policy come to agree can be explained in several different ways. Half a century ago V. O. Key (1961) suggested that public opinion operated as an effective outer bound for policy debates: "(P)roposals that depart too far from the general understandings of what is proper . . . can scarcely expect to attract serious attention (at 552)." Public opinion does not usually dictate the specifics of policy but instead operates as an area of a "permissive consensus" within which policy debate occurs (Key 1961: 552–55). To Key (at 11, 531) relevant public opinion was not narrowly limited to the "substantive issues of public policy." Also important are a broad range of politically relevant views such as the images of interest groups and lobbyists and attitudes about the proper role of government. Key did not view public opinion as inevitably stable over time. American attitudes sometimes change quickly in response to high-profile, important events such as the Great Depression or World War II. In Key's view of public opinion as forming a "permissive consensus" visionaries who are too far ahead of current public opinion and reactionaries who wish to return to the status quo ante will seldom succeed in making public policy to their satisfaction. In another such argument Paul Starr (1982: 288–89) argued that strong public opposition to socialism during the Cold War era helps to explain why no national health care plan was passed at that time. Weaver (2002) and Burstein (2002) offer other examples.

Several other views have emerged since the time that Key argued public opinion formed an outer boundary for public policy-making. An important explanation is the "electoral connection" between public opinion and public policy.[4] In this model candidates, officeholders, and political parties take positions on issues and make campaign promises with future elections in mind. Supporting a popular position helps to win extra votes in an upcoming election or at least to gain momentary favorable publicity. When high quality polls are affordable and widely used, politicians can gauge current public opinion fairly easily and weigh the possible benefits. Taking popular positions is especially important for politicians when the outcomes of future election are uncertain, when the balance between the political parties is close, and when public opinion on an issue is clear, salient, one-sided, or rapidly changing (Peterson 1993). In this linkage model whether a candidate or officeholder's support for an issue is longstanding and sincere or simply recent and strategic is largely irrelevant. Further, candidates and officeholders who promise a position typically carry through with their promises, once elected. When newly-elected politicians, particularly presidents, replace a predecessor who held different views, public policy can change dramatically and often in such a way that public opinion and public policy will finally become consistent (Oberlander and Lyons 2009). In one version of this argument, even politicians who are unsympathetic to an issue may offer strategic modest policy concessions in response to public opinion. The electoral connection is a well-documented and well-supported argument linking public opinion to public policy.

While the candidate-centered electoral connection argument is often examined, another electoral connection linkage is also important in tobacco control policy-making. Nearly half the American states and thousands of cities and counties allow direct issue elections, commonly called initiatives and referendums. This electoral connection receives too little attention, in part because polling data are less readily available at the state and local level and in part because most accounts of the electoral connection focus on federal-level American politics where direct issue elections do not exist. State and local issue elections are important in tobacco control policy-making. Over the last four decades tobacco control advocates often turned to issue elections. Occasionally so has the tobacco industry. Chapter 4 examines this linkage.

Public opinion and tobacco control policy are linked in still other ways. Many important tobacco control policy decisions in this country are not made by elected officials but rather by bureaucrats, by appointed state judges, or by life-tenured and appointed federal judges. Here the candidate-centered electoral connection argument fits less well. An alternative argument is that both bureaucrats and judges sense, share, and act on widely-held attitudes. In the sense-and-share view even public officials who are not elected often make decisions that follow and reflect dramatic news stories and rapid changes in public opinion. In part this occurs because popular decisions by agencies and courts last longer, are less often overturned, and are more widely accepted than are unpopular decisions. In part this occurs because bureaucrats and judges defer to the wishes and to the policies of elected officeholders whose decisions often reflect current public opinion. In part this occurs because elected officials can over time make new appointments to the agencies or to the bench, thereby bringing the agencies and the courts back into line with public opinion. How well elected officials, bureaucrats, and judges, respectively, represent majority public opinion on tobacco control is an empirical question that can be investigated. Chapters 5 and 6 provide evidence on this linkage.

In several accounts public opinion does not simply influence public policy; the reverse also occurs when public officials successfully influence (or "manipulate") public opinion. Public officials, particularly so American presidents, try with varying degrees of success to sway public opinion in favor of their preferred policies. The increasing availability of polls and focus groups helps officeholders to measure public concerns and to define effective public relations messages and strategies. When these efforts succeed, poll majorities agree with public policy but not because public opinion had any causal influence on policy.

The manipulation model is best tested with polling data taken before and then after such efforts are made. If the polls regularly and quickly shift in favor of a public official's efforts, then the manipulation model is supported. The evidence on this model is mixed, modest, and sometimes negative. Several studies show that poll support reacts negatively, not supportively to major policy decisions. In Wlezien's (1995) and Soroka and Wlezien's (2005, 2009) well-known "thermostatic" studies, poll support for federal spending usually reacts negatively to recent changes in spending on domestic and particularly on foreign policy. Stimson's (1991, 1999) studies of over-time changes in the American public's liberal-versus-conservative national mood also shows public opinion moving away from recent election outcomes and policy shifts. A study of polls taken before versus after important events suggested that popular presidents—that is, those whose approval ratings were currently over 50 percent—can favorably move public opinion about half a percentage point per news-reported comment. Popular presidents can reasonably expect a five to ten percentage point poll change in their favor over several months by repeatedly pressing for an issue in speeches, statements, and appearances (Page, Shapiro, and Dempsey 1987: 32–34; Page and Shapiro 1984). Unpopular presidents, however, cannot produce positive poll shifts in favor of their favorite positions.

The term "manipulation" clearly has a pejorative tone and may imply that the American public is quickly and easily influenced. Most accounts suggest this is not the case. In an early and influential study by Page, Shapiro, and Dempsey (1987) there was no evidence that interest groups, federal court decisions, members of the president's party or of the opposition party, or foreign leaders could regularly manipulate American public opinion on specific issues. Jacobs (1992) argued that top British and American political leaders used polls to manage public opinion, but often found themselves constrained by poll results. In Druckman and Jacobs' (2015) recent study of White House efforts to influence public opinion, presidents often try to manipulate public opinion. Presidents can sometimes successfully raise the visibility of their favorite issues and focus attention on their own personal skills. Yet presidents were less successful in shifting Americans' policy attitudes. In Edwards' (2003) well-turned phrase the White House's best efforts often fall on "deaf ears" (cf. Cavari 2012). In another example the U.S. Supreme Court's decisions do not typically result in increased poll support for those decisions (Marshall 2008). In the Page, Shapiro, and Dempsey study only scientific and nonpartisan experts and news commentators could successfully shift public opinion on specific issues and in magnitude by about three or four percentage points per news-reported statement.

Does the manipulation model accurately describe tobacco control policy-making? A considerable amount of polling evidence on Americans' changing scientific beliefs is available, as is some polling evidence on image attitudes. On the public's policy preferences the polling data are more limited since identically worded poll questions both before and after an event are seldom available. The evidence suggests that successful attempts to manipulate American attitudes on tobacco control issues are rare. U.S. presidents have never so succeeded, mostly because few presidents have tried. By far the single most dramatic instance of a favorable short-term poll shift on Americans' scientific beliefs occurred after the 1964 Surgeon General's advisory committee issued its landmark report on the lung cancer and heart disease risks of cigarette smoking.[5] However, Americans' attitudes at the time shifted surprisingly little on preferences for government action. During the early 1990s public awareness of the risks of secondhand smoking grew quickly as a result of Congressional hearings, a major lawsuit, and media-reported exposes. During the late 1970s and 1980s the tobacco industry enjoyed some success in reducing early poll support for state and local tobacco control ballot measures. Sometimes the industry's success at producing poll shifts was sufficient to defeat these ballot initiatives, sometimes not.

These examples of successful short-term manipulation of public opinion are exceptions to a general pattern. Grass-roots tobacco control activists, media coverage, and new scientific evidence usually have a slow, long-term impact on Americans' smoking-related attitudes. Public beliefs about the health risks of smoking and support for limits on cigarette smoking typically grow very slowly over time and in some time periods not at all. The tobacco industry's image similarly deteriorated slowly and steadily. Instances of successful short-term manipulation of public opinion on smoking-related issues are rare. Dramatic poll changes in Americans' beliefs, images, and preferences occur, but are typically slow and long-term.

Several studies of public opinion and public policy look beyond whether public policy reflects overall (or collective) poll results and examine how well policy-making reflects the views of different population groups, particularly rich versus poor Americans (Bartels 2008; Gilens 2005, 2012b; Gilens and Page 2014; Rigby and Wright 2010; cf. Wlezien and Soroka 2011, Ura and Ellis 2008; see also Campbell 2012). Majorities of both wealthy and poor Americans frequently hold similar policy views and their views often change in tandem (Enns and Wlezien 2011, Enns 2015, Erikson 2015). When wealthier and poorer Americans differ in their views, on most issues and in most years public policy better reflects the opinions of wealthy Americans than of poor or middle-class Americans.

This linkage is sometimes described as "coincidental representation" and serves as a useful reminder, first, that mere agreement between the polls and public policy does not prove causal influence and, second, that some groups may be better represented than others. Here coincidental representation is explored in two ways. Chapter 5 suggests that when the wealthy and poor differ in their views about tobacco control policy, the views of the wealthy mostly prevail. Such instances are relatively rate and comprise about one-sixth of these fifty-nine federal-level tobacco control policy decisions. Chapter 5 also offers statistical evidence that both mass public opinion and the tobacco industry influenced tobacco control decision-making at the federal level. Chapter 6 examines a different example of coincidental representation based on the lawsuits brought by sick or dying smokers against cigarette manufacturers. Nationwide public opinion did not support these lawsuits and until recent years all these lawsuits failed. Mostly this occurred because these lawsuits were too expensive to bring to trial, not because nationwide public opinion was brought directly to bear.

The final linkage model considered here links public opinion and public policy but takes a different and longer-term view. Here critical events that were unforeseeable in advance can lead to important changes in both public policy and in public opinion. Baumgartner, DeBoef, and Boydstun's (2008) careful examination of the death penalty provides a recent example. During the 1980s and 1990s several small-scale "innocence projects" began to challenge a few specific death penalty sentences. At first housed in faith-based ministries or in law schools, these innocence projects successfully overturned several death penalty or life imprisonment sentences for prisoners who had been convicted after faulty police investigations, false confessions, or flawed courtroom procedures. Within a few years these efforts led to the rise of a new "frame" for journalists' stories about the death penalty, one that focused on evidentiary and procedural flaws. During the mid-1990s several state and federal appeals courts handed down rulings that limited the number of death penalty sentences; prosecutors sought and juries handed down far fewer death penalty sentences; a newly-passed federal law changed procedures for handling DNA evidence and the qualifications required of defense counsel; and several new state laws and decisions by sitting governors restricted or even barred the use of the death penalty. By the mid-1990s the number of death penalty sentences imposed annually in this country fell dramatically. Since the mid-1990s poll support for the death penalty declined modestly and slowly at the rate of about 1 percent annually. These changes are noteworthy since early efforts to reduce the frequency of or even to eliminate entirely the death penalty were initiated by small, local, poorly-funded groups rather than by high-ranking judges or politicians or wealthy individuals or corporations. Even so, within two decades these efforts reached a "tipping point"[6] and the ensuing "social cascade" led to important changes in media coverage and in public policy and to a marked reduction in the number of death sentences either imposed or carried out.

The tipping points and the ensuing social cascades for the innocence movement and for tobacco control are in some ways similar but in other ways are quite different. In both cases change were initiated by relatively powerless grass-roots movements and by a few legal or scientific experts, not by high-ranking politicians or powerful business interests. In both cases the news media used early evidence to construct a new narrative or frame in its news coverage. In both cases grass-roots advocates sought out a wide variety of friendly policy-making forums (or venues) rather than focusing their efforts on a single policy-maker such as Congress. For the tobacco control movement Americans' beliefs and images changed much more rapidly than did public policy; for the innocence project the reverse was true. For innocence projects the policy outcomes often involved specific individuals' death penalty and long prison sentences; for the tobacco control movement the ends were more generally applicable public policies. The innocence project moved through its social cascade process more quickly than did the tobacco control movement.

On tobacco control public opinion has its greatest impact not immediately, but as public opinion grew heavily one sided and better informed; then for changing public opinion to spin off a growing number of activists, organizations, and politicians who took up the cause; then when early and often local or state-level policy successes recognized the issue's importance and reinforced public beliefs, thus encouraging further efforts and wider coalitions. Only by the 1990s and the early 2000s, when Americans' knowledge on the harm of smoking was by any ordinary standard common knowledge, did important trial lawyers and state attorney generals enter the fray. By the late 1990s and early 2000s the transformation of American opinion and a steadily growing number of policy and legal challenges led some within the cigarette industry to believe that the strategy of denying the harm of smoking and fighting any and all regulation was implausible and excessively risky; rather, the safer strategy was to seek manageable federal regulations.

These important changes in public opinion and public policy occurred in a sequenced way that played out over six decades. As this social cascade occurred, smoking prevalence declined although was sufficiently common that the issue remained familiar to Americans. Underlying this book is the argument that public opinion becomes important in policymaking as it is transformed. The impact of public opinion is not well understood by simply comparing individual poll questions with policy decisions. Instead, poll questions should be considered as public opinion evolves over time and around important events. Public opinion is not static, but rather dynamic and sequential. When an issue is newly arisen—or as with tobacco control during the 1950s and early 1960s, newly rearisen—the public is not yet well-informed or agreed on proper policies. Mass public opinion is then relatively unimportant, largely irrelevant, and easily ignored or outmaneuvered by lobbyists, interest groups, and stakeholders, and policy-makers.

As the public's beliefs, images, and policy preferences evolve, this changes. Individual activists and advocacy groups emerge and press for a steadily broader range of restrictions and to seek out a friendly forum for their complaints. On tobacco control individual activists, small local groups, and the occasional reporter were typically the first to appear. Most of these activists followed, not preceded important changes in public opinion and acted consistently with recent poll changes. As this happened public opinion did not remain merely inchoate. Within a few months or years large and rapid changes in public opinion spun off a number of activists and organized groups who took action. Conceded, these activists and groups were not always immediately very successful. Their early actions were often poorly organized and poorly funded, amateurish, modest in vision, purely local, and led to no changes of great importance. Even so, these efforts transformed mere poll shifts into an organized and lasting movement and sustained what might otherwise have been only transient poll shifts.

Larger and more formally organized interest groups and stakeholders became active only in later years. Not all activists, interest groups, stakeholders, and policy-makers active in tobacco control fit this model, but many do. Chapter 3 so describes organized efforts beginning during the 1950s to make students more aware of the dangers of cigarette smoking and the "fairness doctrine" during the 1960s. Chapter 4 so describes efforts during the mid-1970s to use statewide and initiative elections to raise cigarette taxes and to ban cigarette smoking in public places.

Not all research finds that mass public opinion has much influence on public policy-making. Many public policies simply do not agree with timely-measured public opinion. Studies that compare public policies with timely public opinion polls consistently report that at least a third of policy decisions disagree with current poll majorities (Monroe 1979, 1998; Marshall 1989, 2008). Policy decisions that are of little interest to the public especially often disagree with the polls. So are policies that require basic political change, such as political reforms or constitutional amendments. Nor do small poll shifts, over time, reliably lead to policy changes (Page and Shapiro 1983). Some recent research suggests that the linkage between public opinion and public policy virtually disappears once the positions of interest groups and the preferences of wealthy Americans are taken into account (Bartels 2008; Gilens 2005, 2012b; Gilens and Page 2014; Rigby and Wright 2010).

Some authors, for example, argue that public opinion has little influence on health care financing plans. Marmor (2000: 75–76) describes the enactment of Medicare as an example of "the comparative irrelevance of mass public opinion in federal policymaking." The designers of Medicare did not seek out public opinion polls on Medicare's many details and felt satisfied by broad public support for the program's goals. Himmelfarb (1995) describes how poorly-designed poll questions encouraged the passage of the 1998 Medicare Catastrophic Coverage Act, but within two years Congress repealed nearly all that act's provisions. Oberlander (2003: 96–99, 140–45) argues that despite broad public support for establishing and keeping the Medicare program, mass public opinion was otherwise not important in the program's continued operation or in efforts to expand Medicare benefits. The public was too little informed and too seldom engaged to influence the Medicare program's operations. In these well-known accounts mass public opinion has little influence on policy for several reasons. The policy details are unusually complex; involve expensive and ongoing tradeoffs between stakeholders and interest groups; are constrained by financial realities; and are bargained out in the back rooms of the federal agencies, the White House, and Congress (Marmor and Oberlander 2011; Marmor, Oberlander, and White 2009; Oberlander 2010; Steinmo and Watts 1995; cf Jacobs 1993a, 1993b). Mass public opinion is too poorly informed and too unstable over time to have any great influence on policy-making.

Public opinion may not have much influence on public policy for still other reasons. Key policy-makers and the public sometimes hold very different views about important policy issues (Cook and Barrett 1992). Top policy-makers sometimes badly misperceive what Americans' current policy views are (Kull and Destler 1999; Kull and Ramsay 2002; cf. Jacobs, Lawrence, Shapiro, and Smith 1998). Top policy-makers, particularly presidents, may also try to use their polls more to manage and influence than to reflect public opinion (Jacobs and Shapiro 2000). Public policy may lag years or even decades behind the polls (Oberlander 2003: 43–53). In these accounts mass public opinion merits little attention, provides only a very general direction for policy change, and is of minor and indirect importance in policy-making. Except for establishing the outer boundaries for policy-makers—for example, in ensuring that popular programs, once enacted, are not repealed or cut back (Oberlander 2003: 140–41; Oberlander 2007b)—public opinion seems to be of relatively little importance (Derthick 1979: 183, 204–05; Himmelfarb 1995: 3; Oberlander 2003: 96–99, 140–45).

Public opinion also receives short shrift when the available poll questions are poorly worded, when few if any reliable public opinion polls are available, or when early polls poorly predict public reactions once a policy is proposed, debated, or enacted (Himmelfarb 1995: 56–72; Jacobs and Mettler 2011; Magleby 1989: 106–14; Meranto 1967: 43–50; Oberlander 2007b, 2003: 98–99, 172–73; Marmor, Oberlander, and White 2009; Skocpol 1996: 74–76). In these instances the available poll questions seldom yield more than a dim or even inaccurate outline of current public opinion (Derthick 1979: 183, 189; Himmelfarb 1995: 3, 54–60; Oberlander 2003: 140–45; Schiltz 1970: 29–49; Starr 1982: 273). In historical accounts of policy-making both the leanings and the impact of public opinion are particularly difficult to assess. This is a wholly unavoidable problem before the mid-1930s since reliable public opinion polls did not then exist (Skocpol 1992). Chapter 2 below faces this dilemma; before the mid-1930s public opinion on tobacco control issues can neither reliably be measured nor estimated (cf. Karol 2007). This problem did not simply disappear in the mid-1930s when public opinion polls originated. In the absence of reliable polls social movements, groups with a mass membership, professional associations, lobbyists, reformers and intellectuals, church leaders, journalists, politicians, party platforms, election results, corporations, unions, and stakeholders serve as uncertain and imprecise surrogates for mass public opinion (Herbst 2002).

These pessimistic conclusions about the limited importance of public opinion do not fully describe the relationship between public opinion and tobacco control policy-making. Nor do all accounts of health care agree with these conclusions. Several accounts suggest that when public opinion is clear and unchanging, the opposition of stakeholders and interest groups can be overcome (Peterson 1993, Jacobs 1993a). For five important reasons public opinion plays a more important role in tobacco control policy-making than it does on specifics of health care financing. A first difference is that public policy-making on cigarettes is relatively simple, at least compared to major social welfare programs or health care financing. Very often a new tobacco control measure "simply" involves a tax increase on cigarettes, a new restriction on smoking in public places, a tighter restriction on cigarette advertising or sales, or a subsidy to tobacco farmers. Antismoking advocates usually press for these policies one at a time rather than in a complex and far-reaching package. Further, the financing issues involved in tobacco control are far less complex than those involved in health care financing proposals. For example, per-pack tax increases yield additional revenue to the federal or to a state government at the expense of cigarette manufacturers or smokers. In tobacco control there is seldom a complex, ongoing set of financial gains and losses among major companies and stakeholders. For the growing number of nonsmokers a new tobacco control policy usually involves no obvious personal costs and no immediate or long-term financial gains except for a small gain in public revenue.

This is not to say that tobacco control policies do not impose costs and benefits. Clearly they do. Television networks and station owners lost lucrative advertising revenue when the 1971 broadcast ban was imposed. So did outdoor billboard companies or manufacturers of cigarette vending machines when restrictions on cigarette advertising and sales were imposed on those businesses in later years. Even so, the financial costs and benefits are fairly simply computed and mostly soon incurred. To an ordinary citizen these costs are negligible and indirect. Similarly, a ban on smoking in public places or in workplaces imposes both costs and benefits. Smokers may be inconvenienced but by smoking less and less often, smokers save money and enjoy better health. Bar and restaurant owners may lose business or fear doing so. Employers of smoke-free workplaces benefit from lower health care costs, fewer work interruptions, and reduced absenteeism. Nonsmoking employees benefit from cleaner air and fewer illnesses. These costs and benefits are neither negligible nor illusory, but they are not as complex as the cost calculations involved in major health care financing schemes.

Nor are large new agencies usually created by new tobacco control measures. Per-pack tax hikes are simply added to existing and long-collected taxes. Bans on cigarette smoking in the workplace or in public places require little additional policing and no new agencies. An exception is the 2009 federal tobacco control bill that created a new regulatory oversight within the U.S. Food and Drug Administration. However, the 2009 bill's financial costs were relatively slight and borne by cigarette manufacturers and the new administrative structure so far remains small. In short, tobacco control is a relatively simple policy area compared to new health care plans such as the Affordable Care Act or major social welfare programs such as Social Security.

A second important reason why public opinion is important in tobacco control policy lies in the multiple forums involved. Sometimes important tobacco control policies are fashioned (or else discarded) through Congress, the federal branch long perceived as the most tobacco friendly of any policy-makers. Yet tobacco control supporters often sought remedies outside Congress in settings where the antismoking agenda would be more favorably received. During the 1950s this meant taking antismoking education to the schools. In 1964 the U.S. Surgeon General's office issued the first high-profile federal report on the health dangers of cigarette smoking. During the 1950s and 1960s federal agencies such as the Federal Communications Commission or the Federal Trade Commission proposed limits on cigarette advertising. During the late 1970s and thereafter advocates turned to state and local referendums and initiatives to raise cigarette taxes and to ban smoking in public places. During the 1990s a major lawsuit was pressed against cigarette manufacturers and an unprecedented legal settlement achieved in favor of the states. The availability of multiple forums gave tobacco control advocates options to pick and choose a policy-making forum in which public opinion would be more influential. The availability of multiple forums did not guarantee that that public opinion and tobacco control policies would agree, but did increase the odds of that happening (Jones, Bradley, and Oberlander 2014).

A third reason why public opinion plays an important role in tobacco control policy is the familiarity of cigarette smoking itself. By the time that the modern tobacco control movement originated during the 1950s and 1960s cigarette smoking was long established and widely familiar to Americans. Nearly half of Americans then smoked cigarettes. Virtually all Americans encountered cigarette smoking on a daily basis. Proposed tobacco controls required Americans to have no special knowledge and to make no abstract calculations about future costs and benefits. The American public was already long exposed to cigarette smoking and was well familiar with the product itself, if not fully so to the health dangers of smoking.

Public opinion also plays an important role in antismoking issues for a fourth reason—the relatively long time frame involved in tobacco control efforts. Beginning in 1950 scientific evidence quickly mounted on the health risks of smoking. The 1964 Surgeon General's advisory committee report summarized that evidence had caused a rapid increase in the percentage of Americans who understood that cigarette smoking was a cause of lung cancer and heart disease. By the end of the 1960s two-thirds of Americans linked cigarette smoking to lung cancer. Thereafter these beliefs steadily increased at the rate of about 1 percent annually until the 1990s when over nine-tenths of Americans linked cigarette smoking to lung cancer.

The modern debate over tobacco control policies mostly occurred well after public opinion had grown better informed and more one-sided. As the health risks of smoking became widely understood during the 1960s and 1970s, another important transformation of public opinion occurred: the image of cigarette manufacturers and of smokers rapidly deteriorated. By the mid-1970s these poll changes spawned many grass-roots anti-smoking activists and groups who turned their efforts to statewide and local elections, to state legislatures, and to city councils to impose higher taxes or bans on cigarette smoking. By the 1990s these groups had achieved a considerable, if yet far from complete success. In short, by the time that most public policy challenges to cigarette smoking arose, the public was already better informed about the health risks involved in smoking and already viewed cigarette manufacturers or smokers unfavorably.

Finally, the impact of public opinion on tobacco control policy may be enhanced due to the large number of polls publicly available. Since the late 1940s American pollsters have asked well over five thousand poll questions on cigarette smoking and tobacco control. Not all poll questions were made public and not all such policy issues were well-polled. Yet many prominent pollsters made their poll questions quickly and publicly available and the general conclusions were readily available to policy-makers. Americans' beliefs about the health dangers of smoking are the most frequently polled; image and stigma often so; and specific policy areas sometimes so. Since the 1960s elected politicians, bureaucrats, and judges nearly certain have known that the American public believed that cigarette smoking was a serious health danger and that cigarette manufacturers had a poor public image. Supporters and opponents of tobacco control alike could often know of the same poll results. In many cases policy-makers would have timely known of public attitudes toward specific tobacco control issues then under debate. The widespread availability of polls not only helps to understand the relationship between public opinion and tobacco control policy, but also facilitates that linkage.

Most linkage studies focus on one particular linkage model such as the manipulation model (Domhoff 2002, 2013; Schlozman, Verba, and Brady 2012), social cascades (Baumgartner, DeBoef, and Boydstun 2008), or coincidental representation (Gilens 2005, 2012b). Tobacco control, however, is an extremely complex and even "messy" policy area. Many different political actors have battled for many decades over many different policy proposals and in many different policy-making forums. Some tobacco control proposals become policy, some proposals do not. Not surprisingly, the evidence offered later in this book suggests that no single linkage model fully describes the complex relationship between American public opinion and tobacco control policy. Chapter 8 returns to this issue.

THE PLAN OF THIS BOOK

As the foregoing suggests, public opinion sometimes influences public policy. Sometimes public opinion is influenced by public policies or by public officials, activists, or interest groups. The relationship is not static but rather dynamic and sequenced. The next six chapters examine the evidence linking public opinion and public policy on smoking. The final chapter reconsiders the evidence.

Chapter 2 reviews the first two of five historical stages. The first stage lasted from the 1890s to the mid-1920s when cigarettes became a popular consumer product. Almost immediately a vigorous anticigarette movement sprang up and raised complaints about both the health and moral effects of cigarette smoking. This movement enjoyed some temporary success at the state and local level, but ultimately failed to enact any lasting public policies. The anticigarette movement did not win support from the medical profession, faded away before strong scientific evidence arose about the harm of cigarette smoking, lacked allies in the federal agencies, and suffered from the military's demand for cigarettes during World War I. By the late 1920s the movement largely disappeared, leaving behind little by way of tobacco control policies but at least a modest and lasting impact on public opinion.

During the second stage cigarette manufacturers enjoyed a "golden age" with no well-organized popular opposition, steadily rising sales, only scattered scientific studies and media reports on the harm of cigarette smoking, and only occasional and minor challenges from the Federal Trade Commission. An "iron triangle" of tobacco growers and manufacturers, friendly federal agencies, and helpful members of Congress protected the industry's interests. Pollsters depicted an American public that was skeptical of the industry's honesty and that perceived cigarette smoking as harmful. Yet absent a high-profile critical event, greater media attention, stronger scientific evidence, or clear support from leading medical associations, public unease did not coalesce into a serious challenge to cigarette manufacturers. Health activists concerned over the issue focused largely on the schools. By 1962 public opinion was little better informed, more closely focused, or more favorable toward dramatic policy change than it had been in 1950 when the scientific evidence on the harm of smoking began to mount. Not surprisingly, elected officials largely ignored the issue.

Chapter 3 focuses on the third stage and on when, why, and how greatly Americans came to understand the dangers of cigarette smoking. During the 1950s growing scientific evidence and media attention had raised very little public knowledge of the link between cigarette smoking and lung cancer or heart disease. Public opinion does not inevitably react to new information if that new information is offset by seemingly-contradictory messages such as well-funded industry reassurances of concern, new products such as filter cigarettes, and inconsistent federal policies. A crystallizing event, heavy news coverage, and a reputable endorsement are needed to raise public awareness of health risks. The January 1964 report of the U.S. Surgeon General's advisory committee on smoking was that event. The 1964 report unequivocally linked cigarette smoking to lung cancer and to several other deadly diseases, commanded unprecedented media attention, and led to a rapid, dramatic, and sustained growth in public beliefs on the health risks of cigarette smoking. No other event equaled that report's immediate impact on public knowledge about the ills of smoking. Only the exposes, lawsuits, and Congressional hearings of the 1990s came close to doing so. Absent such high-profile events public awareness about the health risks of cigarette smoking increases only slowly and sometimes not at all.

Public knowledge is only a first step toward policy change. At first Americans' increased knowledge of the health risks of smoking came without any great increase in poll support for serious policy change. Even so, several tobacco industry critics were embolden to press their complaints against the tobacco industry's advertising and disclosure practices. In 1965 an otherwise tobacco-friendly Congress conceded the first mildly-worded mandatory warning label on cigarette packages. In 1967 the Federal Communications Commission required broadcasters who aired cigarette advertisements also to air unpaid anti-smoking commercials. For the first time rapid changes in public opinion, admittedly somewhat indirectly so, had led to modest changes in federal policy.

Chapter 4 explores a slightly later fourth transformation of public opinion. As Americans came better to understand the health risks of smoking, within the next decade two other important changes in public opinion occurred. The tobacco industry's image rapidly worsened and then continued to worsen for many more years until cigarette manufacturers stood out as a pariah among industries. The image of smokers also worsened as cigarette smoking emerged as a stigma. These changes lagged a few years behind rising public beliefs on the health risks of smoking, but both shifts were well underway by the 1970s. The tobacco industry closely tracked these changes and sought to reframe cigarette smoking in more positive ways but failed to reverse these trends. During the mid- to late 1970s the industry's image deteriorated and the stigma of smoking increased. A growing number of state and local tobacco control activists sought voter-approved cigarette tax hikes and bans on smoking in public places. Although at first enjoying little success, these efforts became more successful as antismoking activists grew more skillful at campaigning and as Americans grew steadily better informed about the health risks of smoking, more negative toward smokers, and more hostile toward cigarette manufacturers.

Chapter 5 turns to the relationship between public opinion and tobacco control proposals at the federal level. Since the 1960s dozens of tobacco control policies have been debated in Congress and the White House, at the federal agencies, and in the federal courts. Some, but not all of these proposed tobacco control policies were far-reaching. Some, but not all these proposals enjoyed majority poll support. Some proposals succeeded, others failed. Chapter 5 compares fifty-nine tobacco control proposals with the polls and suggests several conclusions. Not surprisingly, a strong status quo bias appears in tobacco control policy-making just as it does in other policy areas. Tobacco control policies typically lag behind, not lead public opinion. As expected, the chances that a newly-proposed tobacco control measure will pass depends in part upon the tobacco industry's position. Timely public opinion on the issue is also important. Public opinion influences federal policy-making much more than the reverse; once enacted, federal tobacco control policies have a small positive effect on public opinion. The most far-reaching of federal tobacco control policies—the 2009 tobacco control bill—was enacted only long after public opinion became well-informed about the risks of cigarette smoking, after the industry's image deteriorated, and after the stigma of smoking was well-established.

Chapter 6 turns to tobacco litigation, an area in which public opinion might possibly be thought to have little influence. Neither federal judges, jurors, nor most state judges are closely tied to public opinion through an electoral connection. Even so, most tobacco litigation outcomes agree with timely nationwide polls. Public opinion consistently opposed both lawsuits brought by individual smokers and class action lawsuits, and very few such lawsuits succeeded. Nor are the polls favorable toward smokers' lawsuits brought in the future. On these lawsuits the opinion-to-decision linkage is more coincidental than causal; most such lawsuits failed because of the heavy financial costs imposed on plaintiffs or because of adverse legal precedents. The few successful lawsuits brought by individuals occurred only after the industry's credibility reached its lowest and public knowledge of the health risks of smoking was at its highest. Public opinion toward government-sponsored lawsuits has been more closely divided as were the outcome of these cases. Arguably, negative public opinion in part led the industry to settle on the 1998 Master Settlement Agreement, thereby avoiding sustained negative publicity and the risks of continued litigation. Chapter 6 also suggests that tobacco litigation had little affect on American attitudes about health risks, industry image, or the stigma of smoking.

Chapter 7 considers contemporary public opinion and public policy on cigarette smoking during the fifth stage of tobacco control policy-making. By the early 2000s public awareness of the health risks of smoking was very high and the image of cigarette manufacturers of smokers very poor. After nearly half a century of enacting only modest and occasional regulations, Congress in 2009 finally passed and the President signed a major tobacco control bill. A growing international movement to limit by treaty the harm of smoked tobacco emerged, but in effort this the United States did not participate. An American end-of-smoking movement developed and offered a wide variety of new tobacco control policies, some of which enjoyed majority poll support. As chapter 7 notes, poll support for end-game tobacco control policies is quite mixed. At the extreme only about a quarter of Americans favor prohibiting cigarette smoking. Nor has tobacco control recently ranked highly as a priority health issue for Americans, shown increasing poll support, successfully replaced its high-profile leaders, or sustained high levels of media coverage. Under these conditions tobacco control and public opinion are far from becoming a finally settled issue. Chapter 8 reevaluates the evidence and reconsiders the linkage models between public opinion and tobacco control policy.

NOTES

1. These figures are taken from Centers for Disease Control and Prevention reports, particularly *The Health Consequences of Smoking—50 Years of Progress*. 2014. Rockville, MD: U.S. Department of Health and Human Services—Public Health Service.
2. A split-ballot sample randomly assigns one question wording to one group of respondents while another group or groups of respondents within the same survey receive a differently worded question. Chapter 7 reports an example.
3. Burstein (2006) and Page (2002) caution that the impact of public opinion upon public policy may be overstated for several reasons, particularly because polls are more often available on high salience political issues and because public officials are more attentive to public opinion on high, rather than low salience issues.
4. The model was originally offered by David Mayhew (1974). Sulkin (2011) recently reviewed the evidence.
5. Whether the 1964 report's impact should be credited to presidential efforts is arguable, but doubtful. President Kennedy authorized the report but apparently in response to an unexpected question at a 1962 press conference, was not involved in the advisory committee's efforts, and was assassinated before the report was released. His successor, Lyndon Johnson, took no public position on the report.
6. The 'tipping point' refers to a point in time at which the public's understanding has sufficiently changed to cause changes in individual or collective behavior or in public policy which then cause further changes in behavior and policy. Early studies of tipping points often focused on social problems or consumer behavior rather than on public policy-making (Crane 1991; Granovetter 1978; and Schelling 1971). For an example in tobacco control policy see Baumgartner and Jones (1993).

TWO

In the Beginning

Within the United States cigarettes are now heavily regulated, heavily taxed, and widely viewed as harmful. Yet the relationship between cigarettes, public opinion, and public policy has greatly changed over the last century and continues to change. Whether tobacco is a dangerous and undesirable product is a long-standing issue. Europeans first discovered tobacco five centuries ago when they overwhelmed the Western Hemisphere's Indian tribes and nations. American Indians had cultivated tobacco, usually nicotiana rustica or nicotiana tabacum, for four to eight thousand years before European explorers arrived in the Western Hemisphere.[1] By the time of Christopher Columbus' voyage in 1492, tobacco was cultivated, used, and traded throughout the Western Hemisphere. American Indians used tobacco in many ways and for many purposes. Indians inhaled tobacco as snuff; drank it as a tea by the mouth or as a liquid through the nose; ate it; chewed or sucked it; boiled it into syrups or jellies to be licked, drunk, or eaten; applied it as a poultice; rubbed it onto the gums; took it as an enema; used it as an eye drop; blew it as smoke; and spit or smeared it onto the body. A common practice was to smoke tobacco in pipes or in a roll of corn husks, sugar cane, or banana leaves.

Many uses of tobacco were medicinal. Tobacco was used as an analgesic or as an antiseptic to relieve headaches, asthma, rheumatism, and fever; as an insecticide on plants; as a juice on the skin to kill lice or parasites; or as a paste or a liquid to treat toothaches, earaches, rashes, hemorrhages, infections, wounds, snakebite, or gout (Stewart 1967: 231–33; Wilbert 1991; Winter 2000). Tobacco smoke was blown across sick people to protect them from disease, to identify a disease's location, or to placate and draw out malignant spirits. Tobacco relieved hunger, thirst, fatigue, and the pains of childbirth. Used heavily, tobacco induced hallucinations and visions, an important way to contact the spirit world (Norton 2008: 54). Used too heavily, as during initiations for shamans, tobacco could cause death. Flavors or additives such as burned ashes, seeds, lime, insects, or hallucinogenic plants were blended with tobacco to enhance its potency and to cause hallucinations (Goodman 1993: 20–23). Tobacco had other practical and religious uses. Many tribes and nations used tobacco ceremonially to open trade negotiations with outsiders, to facilitate council meetings, to initiate the young into adult life, to signal the start of wars, or to propitiate the spirits. For many Indians using tobacco simply made life more comfortable and pleasant (Furst 1976: 29; Winter 2000: 3–6; Norton 2008: 98–102).

Other than recognizing its immediate deadly potential when used too heavily in ceremonies, there is no evidence that pre-contact Indians saw any harm in using tobacco (McCullen 1967; Winter 2000). American Indians viewed positively some results of heavy tobacco usage, such as visions, hallucinations, dimming vision, and voice changes, as a method to engage in ecstatic intoxication and to contact the spiritual realm (Furst 1976). Indians' long experience with tobacco allowed them carefully to limit the dangers of heavy tobacco use during religious rituals. Since the pre-contact Indians' life span averaged only twenty to thirty years and seldom exceeded forty years for those who survived childhood (Alchon 2003: 41; Crawford 1998: 53, 63–78; Livi-Bacci 2007: 9–28, 43–49) even those who used tobacco regularly normally died of other causes.[2] After 1492 wars, displacement, forced labor, and the frequent epidemics of smallpox, measles, malaria, influenza, typhus, yellow fever, scarlet fever, plague, typhoid fever, mumps, dysentery, hepatitis, diphtheria, pleurisy, venereal syphilis, and cholera that followed contact with Europeans greatly reduced the Indians' population and made tobacco-related illness trivial in comparison (Alchon 2003: 43–45; Gibson 1964: 141; Livi-Bacci 2007: 43–47; Ubelaker 1992: 169–97; Verano and Ubelaker 1992).

To the Europeans who poured into the Americas, tobacco was only one of many new agricultural products—among the others corn, coca leaves, potatoes, turkeys, chili peppers, quinoa, beans, gourds, sarsaparilla, tomatoes, squash, yams, cassava, cacao, cotton, dyes, pelts, fish, nuts, and fruits—as well as silver and gold in startling quantities (Langer 1975; Sauer 1993; Stone 1984). When Christopher Columbus reached the Bahamas and Cuba in October 1492, Europeans first observed tobacco smoking (Norton 2008: 49–50). The earliest European explorers used tobacco as a pain killer against syphilis, but otherwise typically scorned it as shamanistic (Norton 2008: 58, 85, 105) or even as depraved, heretical, and demonic (Martyr d'Anghiera 1516; Furst 1976: 19–21). Europeans' contacts with the Aztecs and the Incas, two far wealthier Indian nations, showed that tobacco was widely used. Yet except for snuff, tobacco remained for some time a product of little interest in Europe or the new Spanish colonies.

During the 1500s many Europeans came to view tobacco as a useful medicine (Norton 2008: 84–90; Courtwright 2001: 70–72; Hughes 2003) or even as a wonder drug (Stewart 1967: 233–39). By the mid-1500s tobacco seeds were sent to Spain and Portugal where royal gardeners initially grew the plant for its striking appearance. Within a few decades tobacco plants were widely cultivated and used as snuff or to make ointments. A Spanish doctor, Nicolás Monardes (1571), declared that tobacco was helpful for breathing problems, bad breath, overeating, kidney stones, animal bites, wounds, cancer, headaches, gout, intestinal worms, female diseases, and parasites.[3] Accounts of the time described tobacco as a useful narcotic or painkiller, as a protection against bubonic plague or yellow fever, or as a remedy for fits, gangrene, gout, halitosis, intestinal worms, madness, or tooth decay. A few accounts cautioned that tobacco was not a panacea, and that using tobacco had harmful side-effects (Stewart 1967: 233–44). By the early 1600s many Europeans were using tobacco as a recreational drug by snuffing or smoking it (Kiernan 1991; Mancall 2004; Menard 1985; Shammas 1994).

By the 1700s Italian, Portuguese, French, Spanish, Dutch, and English merchants and sailors had spread tobacco across the globe (Bethencourt 2005; Gordillo 2005; Kellman 2005; Klooster 2005; Norton 2008: 161, 257–59; Courtwright 2001: 148–51). Tobacco could be stored and shipped long distances without spoilage and once introduced to a region, usually became widely popular—no small benefit for Europeans who produced few trade goods that Asians and Middle Easterners desired. In Japan smoking tobacco became popular among the samurai and the court. In China tobacco was used to protect against malaria, to prevent indigestion, to kill lice, to suppress hunger, and to stimulate the imagination (Dikötter 2005). In the Middle East tobacco was sometimes thought to be an aphrodisiac or a miracle drug. In Southeast Asia children who smoked tobacco were believed to become calmer and stronger. In Africa tobacco joined cannabis as a means to produce happiness and a sense of well-being. Polynesians and native Australians used tobacco to induce trances; to protect against hunger, thirst, and exhaustion; and to facilitate trade. Tobacco was not only widely used; it was consumed in several different ways. In Asia tobacco was typically smoked in pipes or small cigars. In Persia and Russia the water pipe was popular. In South America and Spain cigars predominated, although women and the clergy typically snuffed. In England, Holland, and France, snuff and pipe smoking were common. Global commerce in tobacco seeds led to crops being grown in Turkey, India, Brazil, Venezuela, Holland, France, Cuba, Virginia, Maryland, Australia, China, Ukraine, and elsewhere (Goodman 1995).

Despite tobacco's growing popularity, from its earliest appearance some saw tobacco as undesirable or even dangerous. In 1583 a religious decree in Lima, Peru banned priests from smoking or snuffing tobacco before or during the mass (Norton 2008: 131, 231–36). To English Puritans tobacco smoking contaminated the human body, encouraged idleness and extravagance, and led to irreligion (Harley 1993: 32). Some critics argued that tobacco suppressed sexual appetites and interfered with reproduction (Norton 2008: 199; Rogozinski 1990: 50–51). In 1604 King James I of England wrote a scathing, if ineffective pamphlet arguing that tobacco was medically harmful, addictive, costly, decadent, and encouraged licentiousness and sloth (James I 1604; Wagner 1971: 11–13; Harley 1993; Courtwright 2001: 56–59, 70–71). A few critics even saw tobacco as a form of sorcery, heresy, or witchcraft (Klaits 1985; Norton 2008: 221–23, 257–59, 278 at n. 450; Wagner 1971: 12).

During the 1600s several rulers banned tobacco smoking either on religious or political grounds or because of fire risks. The most severe penalties for smoking included imprisonment, asset confiscation, mutilation, exile or even death (Barth 1997: 17–21; Proctor 1997: 176–77). Still other tobacco-using rulers relaxed the rules against smoking because of their own habits (Courtwright 2001: 193) or because of the enormous popular demand for tobacco, and encouraged reliable and affordable supplies; licensed its production, commerce, and distribution; regulated its price; and taxed tobacco as heavily as possible. In 1606 the cash-strapped Spanish government restricted where tobacco could be grown in the Caribbean, then issued a royal decree allowing only the Spanish government to buy New World tobacco for export, then in 1636 established a royal tobacco monopoly in Castile (Norton 2008: 151–56, 143–45, 201–09). Many other governments also saw tobacco as a lucrative source of tax revenue, notwithstanding widespread smuggling and tax evasion.[4]

As early as the 1600s a few physicians described cases of tobacco smoking, chewing, or snuffing that led to illnesses such as nasal, oral, stomach cancer, impotence, frigidity, sterility, licentiousness, gluttony, loss of hearing or smell or sight, or problems with pregnancy or child development (Norton 2008: 199, 236–37; Harley 1993: 35–38, 48).[5] By the early 1700s few doctors any longer viewed tobacco as a miracle drug (Norton 2008: 234–40) although tobacco was used in medicine until the mid-1800s and as a folk remedy even longer (Kell 1965; Silvette, Larson, and Haag, 1958; Stewart 1967; Walker 1980). By the mid-1800s most doctors neither viewed tobacco as medically helpful nor viewed the "moderate use" of tobacco as harmful (Stewart 1967; Walker 1980).

What most people during these early times believed about the benefits or dangers of tobacco or of smoking is impossible to know with any great precision. Most adults seldom saw doctors and left no written accounts on their views. No reliable surveys exist of public attitudes. Rulers, priests, courtiers, merchants, or doctors had different experiences with tobacco than did ordinary people.[6] Nor had medical experts reached a consensus about tobacco. Some doctors and scientists praised tobacco, but others condemned it. Tobacco's critics freely mixed religious, moral, and health arguments. During the first four centuries of the global experience with tobacco, the weed (or drug or herb, depending on the observer) was widely used and in many different ways. Further, tobacco's many ingredients were poorly understood; nicotine, for example, was not isolated and identified chemically as a poisonous alkaloid until 1828 (Stewart 1967: 244; Proctor 1999; Santora and Henningfield 2005).[7] Nor was tobacco a pressing health issue. Infectious diseases, deaths at childbirth or in childhood, wars, and hunger killed vastly more people than did tobacco smoking, chewing, or snuffing. Until the 1800s post-mortem autopsies were seldom performed and until the 1900s chronic diseases were little understood (Kovach 2009: 33–42). During these times short life expectancies and early death meant that even heavy tobacco users seldom died of its long-term consequences.[8]

THE RISE OF CIGARETTES

By the late 1800s when cigarettes became popular, tobacco was already a major crop, long grown and widely used in North America. In 1612 tobacco growing began in a modest way in Virginia's Jamestown Colony when the first commercially successful tobacco seeds were planted. That crop was shipped to London in 1613 (Gately 2001: 69–76). By 1618 Virginia farmers grew twenty thousand pounds of a fragrant, light colored tobacco, Orinoco, chiefly for export. A decade later Virginia farmers shipped nearly half a million pounds abroad (Tilley 1948: 3–36). By 1700 Virginia farmers exported nearly thirty-eight million pounds annually. Farmers in Maryland, elsewhere along the Atlantic Coast, and further inland soon joined the trade (Menard 1980). By the mid-1700s tobacco exports were worth almost half of the North American colonies' exports. During the American Revolution colonialists bargained tobacco for war loans.

Cigarettes gained popularity only slowly. Until the late 1800s Americans typically chewed plug, used oral or snuff tobacco, smoked pipes, or chewed or smoked cigars (Rogozinski 1990: 46–49, 123–28). Plug or chewing tobacco was particularly common among Americans until the early 1900s when its dirty image and the health risks of spitting led to a decline at least in urban areas (Abrams 2013). Cigars were typically chewed or smoked almost entirely by men, and became common in the United States during the mid-1800s when prominent public figures such as Ulysses S. Grant and Mark Twain popularized their use (Robert 1952: 96–104; Wagner 1971: 14–31). Although some Europeans already smoked cigarettes, they were not yet widely smoked in the United States. During the early 1800s Spanish women working in Seville's tobacco factories smoked papelotes, thin paper wrappers filled with scrap tobacco, a practice immortalized in Bizet's 1875 opera, *Carmen*. During the mid-1800s smoking tobacco in paper wrappers spread to France, Great Britain, and elsewhere in Europe (Gately 2001: 178–86; Tate 1995: 19–20). The practice grew more popular after the friction match was invented in 1827[9] and after contacts between English, French, Russian, and Turkish troops during the 1853 to 1856 Crimean War.

Until the late 1800s cigarettes were hand rolled; were typically imported and expensive; suffered from a decadent, European, and effeminate image; and were not widely smoked within the United States. The *New York Times* once editorialized that "the decadence of Spain began when Spaniards adopted cigarettes."[10] Cigarette smoking was largely confined to immigrants, the urban poor, boys, and a few upper class women (Sobel 1978; Segrave 2005). Cigarettes were imported into the United States before the Civil War, but heavy taxes handicapped their popularity until taxes were reduced in 1868. Federal taxes then rose and fell several times until 1901 (Tennant 1950: 15–17, 35; Licari 2005). During the Civil War (1861–1865) many soldiers smoked hand-rolled cigarettes, but cigarettes still won little mass appeal (Elliot 2005; Sobel 1978: 14–15). In 1875 only forty-two million cigarettes were sold. By 1877 that number rose to 150 million (Sobel 1978: 16–42).[11] By 1888 some 2.2 billion cigarettes were sold but even that figure was smaller than the 3.6 billion cigars sold that year.

Cigarettes became commercially successful only after 1881 when James Bonsack, a young Virginia inventor, patented a machine for mass producing cigarettes. By 1884 a fully operating Bonsack machine could turn out 120,000 cigarettes a day compared to no more than three thousand a day by an experienced hand roller (Sobel 1978: 31; Wagner 1971: 37). Bonsack machines vastly increased cigarette output, reduced labor costs, helped a few large and well-financed firms to dominate the industry, encouraged heavy advertising to create a mass demand, and increased manufacturers' profit margins (Tennant 1950: 17–19; Tilley 1948: 568–75). Cigarettes' rising popularity also benefitted from the aggressive tactics of James Duke's firm which used newspaper and billboard advertising, price-cutting, coupons, rebates, and even pictures of scantily dressed "actresses" enclosed in its cigarette packages (Tennant 1950: 20–25; Robert 1952: 142–45; Winkler 1942: 47–67). Some manufacturers introduced sweetened blends of tobaccos to broaden their cigarettes' appeal to the many potential consumers who already used plug chewing tobacco. Rising demand by urban and immigrant Americans also aided the industry's steady growth (Rogozinski 1990: 49–53).

From 1890 until 1911 a tobacco trust, the American Tobacco Company, dominated cigarette manufacturing, largely as a result of James Duke's relentless pressure.[12] Over its twenty-one year lifespan the tobacco trust kept the cigarette business profitable by limiting advertising costs, avoiding price wars, keeping prices low, promoting sales abroad, buying tobacco at favorable prices, and undercutting any remaining competitors (Winkler 1942: 113–64, 190–245; Courtwright 2001: 112–24; Tate 1995:

23–32). After prolonged litigation a United States Supreme Court ruling, *United States v. American Tobacco Co.* (1911), declared that the tobacco trust was an illegal monopoly under the Sherman Antitrust Act.[13] Upon the trust's dissolution the three largest successor companies became the American Tobacco Company, Lorillard, and Liggett & Myers. R. J. Reynolds and several other small companies followed in size (Tennant 1950: 57–63; Sobel 1978: 56–60).

Until the early 1900s, despite the tobacco trust's best efforts cigarette smoking remained only modestly popular. By 1910 cigarettes made up only 3 percent of tobacco product sales, by weight, about the same as oral and nasal snuff and far less than chewing tobacco and cigars. By 1920, however, cigarettes' share of all tobacco products rose dramatically to 16 percent, then to first place with 36 percent in 1930, to 49 percent in 1940, and to 72 percent in 1950. The rise in annual per capita consumption was equally dramatic: only 8 cigarettes per capita in 1880; only 35 in 1890 and 1900; then 94 cigarettes per capita in 1910; 419 in 1920; 972 in 1930; 1,370 in 1940; and 2,479 cigarettes per capita in 1950 (Rogozinski 1990: 123–28; Segrave 2005: 10). The 1950 figure represented nearly 352 billion cigarettes (Tennant 1950: 3).[14] By 1950 nearly half of American adults smoked cigarettes; an average smoker smoked nearly 250 packs of twenty cigarettes a year.

THE ANTI-CIGARETTE MOVEMENT

During the late 1800s and early 1900s the growing popularity of cigarettes coincided with a wave of protests against dangerous products, unscrupulous business practices, and unhealthy living conditions. The anti-cigarette movement was an active if ultimately unsuccessful part of this wide-ranging reform movement.[15] From the 1890s until the early 1920s anti-cigarette reformers organized rallies; lectured schools, youth groups, and adults; lobbied Congress, state legislatures, and city councils; filed lawsuits; engaged in street confrontations and disturbances; published magazines and pamphlets; popularized anti-cigarette phrases such as "coffin nails"; and pressured public figures to stop smoking, among them President Warren G. Harding, presidential daughter Alice Roosevelt Longworth, and First Lady Edith Wilson (Dillow 1981; Segrave 2005: 78–81, 214; Tate 2005).

Most anti-cigarette reformers had backgrounds in religion, education, or business, not in medicine. Perhaps not surprisingly their complaints freely mixed together moral, economic, and health issues.[16] To these reformers cigarettes led to sloth, licentiousness, nervousness, and dropping birth rates. Cigarettes were a gateway to marijuana, alcohol, morphine, and cocaine (Segrave 2005: 9, 129; Tate 1995: 59–65; 1999: 46–50; Walker 1980). Smoking took too much of family incomes.[17] Cigarettes were rumored to be spiked with opium, and cigarette papers were claimed to be laden with arsenic (Tate 1995: 60–65; 1999). Cigarettes were said to damage the throat, digestion, and mucous membranes (Segrave 2005: 128), and to cause cancer of the mouth or throat. Pregnant women who smoked bore sickly children (Segrave 2005: 129–30). Cigarette smoking damaged a woman's moral standing and public image and led women to acquire "tobacco face," a pallid and sagging complexion, twitches, and blank eyes (Segrave 2005: 110, 176–77, 210).

The anti-cigarette movement had widespread grass-roots support and among church groups. Among the most vocal anti-smoking groups were the Women Christian Temperance Union (WCTU), the Young Men's and Women's Christian Association (YMCA and YWCA), and the Anti-Cigarette League (Engs 2000; Tate 1995, 1999). Methodists, Presbyterians, Baptists, Seventh-Day Adventists, and Mormons were all large denominations well-known for opposing cigarette smoking. These denominations' grounds for opposing cigarette smoking varied considerably and included a variety of religious, health, and family objections. Leading Methodists viewed tobacco usage as medically harmful to the body, as financially costly and as a drain on family finances welfare, as a cause of idleness, and as a distraction from improving one's moral character (Judy 1904). To religion-based temperance advocates tobacco, alcohol, and gambling—and to some reformers dancing and theatre-going—all posed a danger to a sound family life. An early Presbyterian leader (Hill 1908) wrote that tobacco usage was more harmful to health than was liquor; tobacco weakened the intellect, demoralized the character, and led to crime: "first, cigarettes; second, beer and liquor; third craps; fourth, horse racing (and) gambling on a bigger scale; fifth, larceny; sixth, state prison." Among Seventh-Day Adventists opposition was based on the religious admonition that the human body is a "temple of the Holy Spirit" and the belief that using alcohol and tobacco weakens the ability to witness for God and to provide a good example to others, particularly children (Rosten 1963: 182–83). Opposition to tobacco usage among Mormons dates back to a revelation received in 1833 by Latter Day Saint founder Joseph Smith that rebuked tobacco usage; a ban on tobacco chewing and smoking is included in the Doctrine and Covenants, commonly known as the Word of Wisdom.

Several important industrialists and business leaders supported the anti-cigarette movement. Industrialists Henry Ford and Thomas Edison were prominent anti-cigarette enthusiasts as was the health advocate and cereal magnate John Harvey Kellogg (Ford 1916). Many industrial firms, retailers, public schools, and local governments refused to hire cigarette smokers (Tate 1999: 54–56). Lucy Page Gaston, a social reformer from Chicago and the best-known anti-cigarette reformer, founded the Anti-Cigarette League in 1899. Until her death in 1924 Ms. Gaston spent her considerable energies in organizing, publicizing, and lobbying to ban cigarettes. Whether or not the anti-cigarette movement ever won majority support from the American public is unclear since accurate public opinion polls were not then available.[18]

Even conceding their tendency to mix moral, medical, and economic charges against tobacco, anti-cigarette reformers raised many of the same complaints that would reemerge several decades later, among these charges the dangers of passive smoking[19] and the danger to unborn children.[20] Luther Burbank, a well-known scientist, argued that smoking had long-term delayed effects: "Tobacco kills. . . . Smokers do not all drop dead around the cigarette lighter in tobacco stores. They go away and years later, die of something else."[21] Anti-cigarette reformers also charged that cigarette smoking was addictive and that cigarette companies' advertising targeted young people (Burnham 1993: 88, n. 3, 91).

Judged against other reform movements of the times, the anti-cigarette movement enjoyed only limited and temporary success. Unlike the temperance movement, the anti-cigarette movement failed to pass a constitutional amendment to limit smoking. Unlike the movements for minimum wages, maximum working hours, overtime pay, banking regulation, or for a ban on child labor, the anti-cigarette movement never passed a federal law to ban cigarettes nor even succeeded in barring cigarettes from the mail. Neither the Pure Food and Drug Act of 1906 nor the Harrison Act of 1914 regulated cigarettes. The U.S. Supreme Court's decision to break up the tobacco trust, ironically, reinvigorated the cigarette industry.[22] The anticigarette movement made little headway with medical organizations which disdained the movement's enthusiastic, unproven, and far-ranging charges (Engs 2000; Tate 1999: 140–45; Burnham 1993: 42–43). At the time doctors were more concerned with licensing protection, medical school accreditation, newly-available medical technologies, and the many new advances in public health. The involvement of health-oriented reformers and activists was increasingly less welcome (Starr 1982: 145–97). Nor did the anti-cigarette movement survive long enough to capitalize on later studies linking cigarette smoking with early death or with lung cancer.

The anti-cigarette movement's greatest, albeit temporary success was at the state and local level.[23] Fifteen states and several cities passed laws banning either the sale, manufacture, or the giving away of cigarettes to adults. Twenty-two other states considered such prohibitions (Tate 1999: 159–60).[24] Nearly all states barred cigarette sales to minors, although few of these bans were ever well-enforced. Bans on cigarette sales to or smoking by adults proved to be unpopular. By the early 1920s most of these statewide bans had been repealed and few states enacted new restrictions. In 1927 the last statewide ban on cigarette sales to adults (in Kansas) was repealed.

World War I transformed the cigarette industry and hastened the anticigarette movement's demise. During the war military and civilian demand for cigarettes rose dramatically.[25] Cigarette production tripled, presenting cigarette manufacturers with serious short-term challenges since key materials such as tin, licorice, saccharin, Turkish tobacco, and cigarette paper became costly and scarce (Tilley 1948: 613). General Pershing famously stated that "tobacco is as indispensable as the daily ration" and called for thousands of tons to be shipped to the front (Tilley 1948: 613). The federal government included cigarettes in soldiers' rations and subsidized sales on military bases. Both the YMCA and the Salvation Army, previously opponents of smoking, organized drives to collect cigarettes for the troops (Sobel 1978: 84; Segrave 2005: 10; Tate 1995: 205–97; 1999: 149; Burnham, 1993: 95; Courtwright 2001: 141–43). Cigarettes underwent an important image change, shedding their lingering image problem as decadent, foreign, and effeminate. Instead, cigarettes were depicted on recruiting posters and won support from civic groups and from the federal government. Cigarettes became patriotic, manly, and American. Previous critics of the cigarette, including the *New York Times*, changed their position (Brandt 2007: 50–54).

During the war the anti-cigarette movement faded and during the 1920s virtually disappeared (Engs 2000; Tate 1995: 375–413). Even so, the anti-cigarette movement left a lasting impact on American attitudes. The generation (or cohort) of Americans exposed to the anti-cigarette movement less often smoked and more often believed that cigarettes were harmful than were those who grew up in later years. Taking the year 1900 as a cutoff, Americans born in or before that year were as teenagers and young adults exposed to the anti-cigarette movement at its most vocal. By comparison, Americans born after 1900 became teenagers and adults during or after World War I when the anti-cigarette movement was in decline or had disappeared. Not until the late 1950s did another generation of Americans reach adulthood at a time when cigarettes were widely criticized. As the polls discussed later in this chapter show, these early learning experiences left a lifelong impact on attitudes.

THE GOLDEN AGE OF THE CIGARETTE

As the anti-cigarette movement faded and as the tobacco trust disappeared, cigarette smoking became steadily more popular. Cigarette manufacturers increased their advertising and promotional efforts and focused on a few major brands.[26] R. J. Reynold's new brand, Camel, rose quickly in sales after it appeared in 1913. By the early 1920s Camel had captured over 40 percent of nationwide sales[27] (Tennant 1950: 75–78; Wagner 1971: 48–51). Liggett & Myers' Chesterfield and American Tobacco's Lucky Strike followed in popularity. Lorillard's Old Gold (introduced in 1926) and other brands trailed far behind. By the early 1920s the modern American cigarette industry had emerged with a few large and dominant firms, heavy investments in machinery and packaging, blended tobaccos, aggressive advertising, a small number of dominant brands, and standardized packages of twenty cigarettes.[28]

Cigarette manufacturers aggressively sought new markets (Borden 1944; Sobel 1978: 91–97). Women soon became a target. During the early 1900s perhaps only 5 percent of American women smoked cigarettes and fewer still did so in public.[29] The anti-cigarette movement claimed that cigarettes harmed a woman's nerves, her looks, her heart, her image, her morals, and her ability to bear healthy children. Some colleges expelled women for smoking. A few women were even jailed for smoking in public (Segrave 2005: 33–34, 72–75). Few brands enjoyed much success at targeting women (Segrave 2005: 25). The number of women smokers grew during World War I and during the 1920s (Pierce and Gilpin 1995; Tate 1995: 298–374; Tinkler 2005; Segrave 2005). By 1919 a few ads depicted women smoking; during the late 1920s this became common (Sobel 1978: 91–97; Segrave 2005: 71, 113–23). Hotels and restaurants more often allowed women to smoke. By the 1930s most colleges allowed women students to smoke (Segrave 2005: 72–73, 92–93, 98–112, 157). Chesterfield's slogan, "Blow Some My Way"; Lucky Strike's "Reach for a Lucky Instead of a Sweet"; and Marlboro's "Mild as May" all targeted women. Moody's Investors Service estimated that by 1929 women smoked 12 percent of all cigarettes.[30] A 1935 *Fortune* magazine survey reported that 18 percent of women said they smoked, compared to 52 percent of men.[31]

Cigarette advertising made both implicit and explicit health claims.[32] The most common health claim was that a brand was mild and did not irritate the throat (Segrave 2005: 52). Old Gold claimed that its cigarettes contained "not a cough in a carload." Lucky Strikes boasted "your throat protection," "no throat irritation, no cough," and "It's Toasted—Your Throat Protection." R. J. Reynolds used the pitch "For Digestion's Sake—Smoke Camels"; claimed that "More Doctors Smoke Camels than any Other Cigarette"; and advertised pictures of a doctor wearing a lab coat. Philip Morris pitched Marlboros, then a premium brand for women, as "Mild as May," and advertised its Philip Morris brand as "The Throat-Tested Cigarette" (Wagner 1971: 72; Sobel 1978; Segrave 2005). Tareyton claimed that "Need of Steady Nerves made them turn to Tareytons, smokers say." The Federal Trade Commission occasionally forced a manufacturer to cut back on such claims, but the FTC's case-by-case enforcement never reined in health-oriented advertising.[33] Cigarette manufacturers also used many slogans that were not health-related, among them "I'd Walk a Mile for a Camel"; "They Satisfy" for Chesterfields; "Call for Philip Morris" using a bellboy's voice in radio ads and displays; and "Lucky Strike Means Fine Tobacco" (Dillow 1981; Petrone 1996; Sobel 1978: 119; Warsh 2005). Many ads simply depicted young, active, healthy, and attractive smokers.

Recognition of the health risks of cigarette smoking developed slowly. By the early 1900s tobacco usage—then mostly pipes, plug, snuff, and cigars—was recognized as a cause of cancer of the throat, nasal passages, the lip, the pharynx, the jaw, the mouth, and the throat, but not of the lung or other organs. Nor was there clear evidence of cigarette smoking's effect on longevity. Early evidence of cigarette smoking's effects on mortality came from insurance company statisticians and a few scientists. A 1931 article linked rising cancer rates to the rise in cigarette smoking (Hoffman 1931). A 1938 *Science* magazine article by Dr. Raymond Pearl, a biology professor at Johns Hopkins Medical School, reported that an average adult white male who smoked heavily died almost eight years sooner than did one who smoked moderately; a moderate smoker died nearly two years sooner than did a nonsmoker (Pearl 1938; Burnham 1989: 14 and nn. 40, 41). The 1938 *Science* article, however, only discussed longevity patterns and not the specific causes of death.

Other evidence linking cigarette smoking to lung cancer came from Germany and the United States during the 1920s, 1930s, and 1940s (Hoang and Samet 2005; Proctor 1997, 1999: 173–247; 2000). By the late 1920s several studies pointed to the high rates of smoking among lung cancer patients (Lickint 1929; Lombard and Doering 1928).[34] Franz Müller's pioneering 1939 research tied smoking to Germany's rising rates of lung cancer by matching a sample of eighty-six recently deceased lung cancer patients (all men) with a control group of eighty-six healthy living men (Müller 1939). Using medical histories, workplace records, and questionnaires sent to relatives of the lung cancer patients, Müller compared the smoking habits of the deceased lung cancer patients with the control group. The lung cancer victims were over six times as likely to smoke heavily and on average smoked more than twice as much tobacco as did the healthy men. Müller concluded that smoking was the "single most important cause of the rising incidence in lung cancer" (Proctor 1999: 191–98).[35] A 1941 American study pointed to the similarity between rising cigarette sales and rising lung cancer rates (Ochsner and DeBakey 1941).[36] A 1943 German study tied smoking to lung cancer, although much less so to other forms of cancer (Schairer and Schöniger 1943).[37] A post-war Dutch study reported similar findings (Wassink 1948). None of these studies, however, received much attention in the American mass media.[38]

These scientific and actuarial studies little influenced the medical community which downplayed the dangers of "moderate" smoking (Blum 2014; Doll 1998: 94–96; Howells 2011: 37–39; Tate 1995: 413–28).[39] Until 1954 the *Journal of the American Medical Association* accepted tobacco advertising.[40] Both *JAMA* and officials of the AMA continued to express skepticism of the smoking-to-cancer link throughout the 1950s.[41] Medical textbooks and medical classes of the time said little about the dangers of smoking or its ties to heart disease, emphysema, or lung cancer (Doll

1998; Porter 1998). If these risks were mentioned at all, it was usually to caution against "heavy" or "excessive" smoking. So, too, was the American Heart Association at the time slow to recognize the health risks of smoking (Burnham 1989).

Exactly why the medical community so long remained indifferent to the health risks of smoking has been much debated. Some critics point to then prevailing medical views that the cause of a disease was immediate and proximate to the disease, not long-term and delayed. The so-called "germ theory" was developed from the study of infectious diseases and long predates the interest in chronic, delayed diseases such as lung cancer (Cantor and Timmerman 2005; Doll 1998; Matthews 2005; Proctor 1999: 183; Parascandola 1998, 2004). Another common medical view was that the agent of a disease should have a one-to-one relationship with the disease that could be demonstrated experimentally in a laboratory setting. "Case control" evidence, such as hospital or post-mortem observations that lung cancer patients were nearly always smokers, did not provide such proof. Further, many smokers did not develop heart disease or lung cancer, and a few non-smokers did (Doll 1998: 93, 101–02). Nor did statistical evidence linking smoking to lung cancer, heart disease, strokes, or emphysema identify the specific chemical or biological connection. To some medical statisticians the practical difficulties of case control studies with sampling, selection biases, control groups, and the different magnitude of reported relationships posed a problem (Berkson 1946, 1955, 1958; Fisher 1957, 1958; Parascandola 2004; Saiger 1960; Susser 1985). Not until the "prospective studies" of the 1950s (discussed below in chapter 3) that followed a large group of adults over time were these concerns largely overcome.[42] Some researchers were skeptical about the wide range of diseases linked to cigarette smoking, arguing that that no single agent was likely to cause such a large number of illnesses (Parascandola 2004: 252–53). Further, the particulate components of smoked tobacco, commonly called tars, and their effect on human cells were poorly understood (Burnham: 1989: 17; Rosenblatt 1964). Some researchers argued that rising lung cancer rates were due to air pollution, road asphalt, gasoline fumes, viruses, food preservatives, workplace exposure to chemicals or radiation or dust, x-rays, genetics, or to "soft living" (or in other versions, to the stresses of modern living). To some scientists the apparent rise in lung cancer rates was simply due to better diagnoses and more frequent autopsies (Proctor 1999: 53–54, 67–68, 126, 181; Rosenblatt 1964: 413; Patterson 1987). Most cancer doctors and clinics spent little effort in explaining the origins of cancer, instead focusing their efforts on treating the disease as well as they could, typically by early diagnosis and surgery (Patterson 1987).

Still other explanations abound for the medical community's indifference. Some doctors felt that warning patients against smoking would make them unpopular (Riis 1950). Doctors who themselves often smoked cigarettes were fatalistic or slow to recognize smoking's risks (Proctor 2011: 309).[43] Lung cancer was recognized as early as 1815 but was rarely diagnosed before the early 1900s and often so only post-mortem (Goodman 1993: 123–26). During the early 1900s stomach and breast cancer were much more commonly diagnosed than lung cancer (Adler 1912; Proctor 1999: 42, 180). The U.S. Public Health Service focused its efforts on infectious or communicable diseases, such as yellow fever, influenza, hookworm, Rocky Mountain spotted fever, typhoid, malaria, trachoma, leprosy, and venereal diseases (Mullan 1989; Susser 1985). Many doctors distanced themselves from the moralistic, often vague claims of the hygiene and anti-cigarette movements[44] and avoided lecturing their patients about the dangers of smoking since few immediate health risks were apparent (Burnham 1989: 5–13; Proctor 1997). From the late 1940s through the mid-1960s the AMA was engaged in a prolonged fight against "socialized medicine" in the form of government-run Medicare and Medicaid plans and was unwilling to start a fight with cigarette manufacturers and retailers or with otherwise-friendly members of Congress from the tobacco-producing states. Cigarette companies advertised heavily in medical journals just as they did in other magazines and newspapers. None of these explanations are mutually exclusive.

If the medical community mostly ignored the hazards of smoking, the federal government was unabashedly pro-tobacco and pro-smoking. The Food and Drug Act of 1906 ignored tobacco entirely.[45] Cigarettes could be sent through the mail even to states that banned cigarette sales to both adults and minors (Segrave 2005: 89, 92). During World War I nearly five million American troops received cigarettes through their rations, cigarette drives by civilians, and subsidized prices on military bases.[46] During and after the Great Depression of the 1930s, the federal government's Agricultural Adjustment Act raised tobacco growers' incomes and farm values by fixing acreage limits, reducing tobacco surpluses, setting target prices for tobacco, providing loans against surplus production, and by preventing farmers who had not previously grown tobacco from doing so (Badger 1980: 189–235; Rowe 1935). In 1939 Congress set up an export corporation to buy surplus tobacco and sell it abroad (Whelan 1984: 97–98).

During World War II the federal government declared tobacco to be an essential crop, exempted tobacco farmers from the military draft, and generously supplied sixteen million American troops with cigarettes (Gately 2001: 256–68; Sobel 1978: 126–46; Volanto 2005).[47] Unlike sugar, tires, gasoline, meat, coffee, butter, canned goods, and shoes, tobacco was not rationed for civilians.[48] Price controls notwithstanding, tobacco companies were sometimes allowed to raise the price per pack. Consumer demand for cigarettes rose spectacularly. The number of cigarettes manufactured rose from 180 billion in 1939 to 400 billion in 1946 (Sobel 1978: 127). Wartime leaders such as President Franklin Roosevelt and General

Douglas MacArthur smoked. After World War II the federal government encouraged or at least tolerated massive tobacco sales and shipments abroad, particularly to Western Europe. For a time cigarettes were included in American post-war aid program under the Marshall Plan (Proctor 1997: 480–81; 1999: 245–46; 2011: 44–48). During the late 1940s cigarettes served as an alternative currency in Germany, Italy, and France (Sobel 1978: 140–46). Thereafter the U.S. Agriculture Department promoted sales abroad (Wagner 1971: 118).

Few federal appointees or agencies criticized tobacco. In 1929 Surgeon General Hugh S. Cumming issued a statement criticizing the increased use of tobacco by women and children. However, his statement was low profile, led to no further statements by the Surgeon General, led to no legislation from Congress, and did not affect the industry's advertising claims or on consumer demand (Burnham 1989: 1–4 and nn. 1–2). By the 1930s, acting alone in Washington, the Federal Trade Commission occasionally forced cigarette manufacturers to kill a particular advertising campaign. In its first such foray into combating false advertising the FTC forced American Tobacco to cease advertising Lucky Strike cigarettes as a method of weight reduction (Wagner 1971: 59–60).

The federal government's few efforts to reign in the cigarette industry sometimes had exactly the opposite effect. The U.S. Supreme Court's 1911 decision to dissolve the tobacco trust re-energized sales and advertising competition and led to the first runaway market leader, Camel. Between 1910 and 1913 cigarette advertising jumped from $18 to $32 million dollars (Wagner 1971: 40). In 1910, a year before the Supreme Court's decision, Americans smoked 94 cigarettes per capita. That figure rose to 419 cigarettes per capita by 1920 and to 972 cigarettes per capita by 1930 (Rogozinski 1990: 123–28).

The federal government's tobacco-friendly stance is not surprising. Tobacco provided a steady source of tax revenue for the federal government and for the states and was a money-making export. Members of Congress from tobacco-producing states, particularly North Carolina, Kentucky, South Carolina, and Virginia, ardently defended tobacco interests (Baumgartner and Jones 1993; Sapolsky 1980; Wagner 1971). So did the Agriculture Department. Political scientists categorized the friendly ties between Congressional committees, the Agriculture Department, and the tobacco industry as an "iron triangle." Three quarters of a million American farms grew tobacco. Nearly that many wholesalers and retail stores sold tobacco products. By the early 1950s almost half of American adults smoked. By the time that Gallup Poll asked its poll questions in 1946, 1949, and 1954, described below, the federal government had given the American public no reason to believe that tobacco was a health risk. The 1929 Surgeon General's statement on smoking was long forgotten. The cautiously-worded 1957 and 1959 statements from a later U.S. Surgeon General about the health risks of "excessive" smoking were several years away.[49] The landmark 1964 Surgeon General's report was yet further into the future. A few magazines such as *Reader's Digest* printed stories about the health risks of cigarettes (Tunney 1941; Riis 1950)[50] but from the medical community and the federal government, little was heard of the matter.

CIGARETTES AND AMERICAN PUBLIC OPINION

What Americans made of the sporadic debate over cigarette smoking's health risks is a question that became possible to answer with the advent of modern public opinion polls.[51] During the 1930s George Gallup, Elmo Roper, and Archibald Crossley developed new sampling methods that required interviewing no more than a few thousand diverse people, thereby producing affordable, timely, and accurate polls that asked many questions on current political, social, and economic issues (Converse 1987: 87–121). While polling methods improved in later years,[52] for the first time polls could gauge public opinion on timely issues including smoking.

Several early poll questions asked respondents if they used tobacco and if they did, how, and if they smoked cigarettes, what brand? *Fortune* magazine tracked smoking and brand popularity throughout the 1930s, and in July 1939 reported that 41 percent of Americans smoked cigarettes. Gallup Poll put the percentage of American adults who smoked cigarettes at 43 percent in June 1939, at 41 percent in December 1944, at 48 percent in September 1946, at 44 percent in November 1949 and in March 1952, and at 47 percent in January 1954.[53] Since cigarettes were far more popular than were pipes or cigars,[54] most poll questions asked about cigarettes.

During the 1930s and 1940s pollsters asked only a few questions about smoking, perhaps because the anti-cigarette movement had by then disappeared and with it any public debate over smoking, and because of the many crises of those times such as the Great Depression, World War II, and the Cold War. As well, only a few polling firms were then in business.[55] These few poll questions offer useful insights into how Americans viewed smoking. The cigarette industry's credibility problems were apparent in a 1939 Roper Poll question that asked "*which of the following products generally have the least honest advertising? . . . Cigarettes, automobiles, insurance, liquor, drugs?*" Cigarette advertising were ranked as the least honest by 22 percent of respondents, followed by liquor and drugs (both at 21 percent).[56] When asked which products have the most honest advertising, cigarettes ranked third (at 11 percent), trailing automobiles (at 31 percent) and insurance (at 24 percent). A 1939 Gallup Poll pointed to widespread fears of cancer with 76 percent of Americans naming cancer, from a list of four diseases, as their most dreaded disease.[57] A 1947

Gallup Poll showed similar results.[58] In a 1942 Gallup Poll a quarter (25 percent) of respondents said they had seen a recent *Reader's Digest* article critical of cigarettes.[59]

A 1946 Gallup Poll asked cigarette smokers the first health-related question: *"Do you think smoking is harmful to you?"*[60] 42 percent of cigarette smokers said yes, 54 percent said no, and 4 percent offered no opinion. Unfortunately, non-smokers were not asked a similar question; nor did Gallup ask smokers exactly why they thought that smoking was harmful. Even so, these results show that anti-cigarette movement's demise did not dispel public concerns over ills of smoking.

In November 1949 Gallup asked all respondents a slightly different question on the dangers of smoking: *"Do you think cigarette smoking is harmful or not?"*[61] Nationwide 60 percent of respondents said yes, 33 percent said no, and 7 percent volunteered no opinion. The 60 percent figure seems surprisingly high since the health debate over cigarette smoking was by then virtually nonexistent. More (52 percent) cigarette smokers said yes (harmful) than no (45 percent), with 3 percent no opinion. Two-thirds (66 percent) of non-cigarette smokers said that smoking was harmful, 24 percent said no, with 10 percent no opinion. Regrettably, Gallup again did not ask respondents to explain why they thought smoking was harmful. Nor did Gallup repeat the question for another five years.

As these two poll questions show, by the late 1940s half of smokers thought smoking to be in some way harmful, as did two-thirds of non-smokers—this even before the soon-to-come outpouring of scientific evidence supporting this view. Nor had medical groups or the federal government yet publicized the dangers of smoking. The puzzling question, discussed below, is why three-fifths of Americans already believed that smoking was harmful?

Soon after the November 1949 Gallup Poll, several scientific studies were published linking smoking to cancer of the lung or of the respiratory tract. In 1950 major American and British medical journals published five studies on the dangers of smoking. All five articles were retrospective studies of hospital patients; all were based on interviews or medical records; and all used some type of a control group. Two articles in the *Journal of the American Medical Association* pointed to the high rates of cigarette smokers among lung cancer patients, and both articles hinted that the connection was causal (Wynder and Graham 1950; Levin, Goldstein, and Gerhardt 1950). A *British Medical Journal* article reported similar findings and also suggested a causal association (Doll and Hill 1950). Two articles in *Cancer Research* linked cigarette smoking to cancer of the respiratory tract (Schrek et al. 1950; Mills and Porter 1950). By the end of 1953 several other studies reported similar results based either on retrospective or prospective studies (Doll and Hill 1952; Doll 1998; Wynder, Graham, and Croninger 1953). These studies were widely reported in popular magazines and newspapers (Troyer and Markle 1983: 51–59).

THE FRANK STATEMENT

By late 1953 executives of cigarette companies and tobacco growing associations were increasingly concerned over the rising number of adverse scientific reports, negative media coverage (Norr 1952a, 1952b), slumping cigarette sales, and a drop in cigarette companies' stock prices. In mid-December 1953 executives of major cigarette manufacturers hired Hill and Knowlton, a prominent New York public relations firm with experience in managing crises for troubled industries. Hill and Knowlton quickly produced a damage-control public relations effort. On Monday, January 4, 1954 a newspaper advertisement entitled "A Frank Statement to Cigarette Smokers" kicked off a public relations campaign with large, usually full-page ads in 448 newspapers in 258 cities that reached over forty-three million readers.[62]

The Frank Statement laid out a damage-control strategy that the tobacco industry would use for many years to come (Brandt 2007; Hurt and Robertson 1998). The ad acknowledged reports linking cigarette smoking to lung cancer, while making no mention of other diseases, but denied that the results were scientifically conclusive. The ad claimed that there might be many causes of lung cancer, that there was no agreement about what "the" cause is, that there was "no proof" that cigarette smoking was a cause, that the statistical evidence was inconclusive, that the industry did not believe their products were harmful ("We believe the products we make are not injurious to health"), and that public health concerns were "paramount" to the industry. The ad then promised an independent research effort under the Tobacco Industry Research Committee (TIRC) with a prestigious scientific board. Fourteen tobacco associations and all the major cigarette companies except Liggett and Myers signed the ad. The ad did not flatly deny the smoking-to-lung cancer tie, but called into question the evidence—a strategy called "creating controversy." Nor did the ad outline any standards of proof that the tobacco industry might accept.

The Frank Statement kicked off the industry's damage control efforts, but whether the ad immediately influenced American public opinion is quite a different question. The all-print ad ran on inside pages, was usually placed among other large ads, and was visually uninteresting. Many readers may have simply skimmed the ad or only scanned the first paragraph that raised the lung cancer issue. Cigarette manufacturers were themselves already low in credibility. Apparently Hill and Knowlton did not use field tests, focus groups, or polls to test the ad's effectiveness. Even so, initial newspaper reaction was generally neutral to positive, reflecting then-current media norms to treat both sides of a controversy equally and uncritically. Many newspapers simply printed excerpts from the ad or from industry press releases in their accompanying news stories. Critics charged that TIRC never funded any significant research into the health dangers of smoking and that TIRC's greatest accomplishment was in prolonging a controversy over the health dangers of smoking by providing a stream of testimonials and rebuttals on behalf of the cigarette industry (Brandt 2007: 193–207; Cummings, Morley, and Hyland 2002).

The limited polling evidence available does not suggest that the Frank Statement favorable influenced public opinion. In a January 9–14, 1954 poll conducted a few days after the Frank Statement appeared, Gallup repeated the November 1949 *"harmful"* question[63] and reported an across-the-board 10 to 12 percent increase in the percentage of Americans who said cigarette smoking was *"harmful."* The January 1954 Gallup survey also asked respondents *"Have you heard or read anything recently that cigarette smoking may be a cause of cancer of the lung?"* Most (83 percent) respondents said that they had heard or read something recently, likely suggesting that the Frank Statement was widely seen and discussed. Yet those Americans who were then hearing or reading something about the issue were actually more, not less likely to believe that there was a tie between smoking and lung cancer. Of respondents who said that they had recently read or heard something 72 percent said that they believed cigarette smoking was harmful, compared to only 65 percent of those who said that they had not recently heard or read anything about the smoking-to-lung cancer tie. Of those who had recently heard or read something about lung cancer connection 44 percent said that smoking cigarettes was a cause of lung cancer, compared to only 25 percent of those who had not recently heard or read anything. By these figures the Frank Statement at least did not stop or reverse growing public concerns about cigarette smoking.

The percentage of American adults who believed that cigarette smoking was harmful rose from 60 percent in November 1949 to 70 percent in January 1954. Among smokers the figure rose from 52 percent to 62 percent, and among non-smokers from 66 percent to 78 percent. Among the cohort of older Americans (those born before 1900), whose generation as youth was exposed to the anti-cigarette movement, the percentage who believed cigarette smoking was harmful rose from 64 percent to 76 percent. Among the next-younger cohort of Americans—those born between 1900 and 1929 and who became teenagers and adults after the anti-cigarette movement had disappeared—the percentage saying harmful rose from 58 percent to 69 percent. Among the youngest respondents—those aged twenty-one to twenty-five who were born in 1930 or thereafter, who entered into adulthood in the early 1950s, and who were not included in the 1949 poll—65 percent said that cigarette smoking was harmful.[64]

Gallup's January 1954 poll also asked those respondents who said that smoking was harmful an "open-ended" question: *"In what way do you think cigarette smoking is harmful?"*[65] Pollsters seldom ask open-ended questions since these questions take longer to answer, elicit a wide range of answers that must be combined into categories, and are therefore expensive. Closed-ended questions that suggest the answers within the question itself (such as *"agree," "disagree,"* or *"no opinion"*) are quicker to answer, easier to code, cheaper, and far more commonly asked. Even so, open-ended questions are useful since respondents can offer their own views without having heard any suggested answers.

Those respondents who said smoking was *"harmful"* offered many different reasons as to why smoking was harmful. Gallup coded these reasons into twenty-three categories, plus a *"no opinion/don't know/no answer"* category. These reasons vary considerably. Many reasons are health-related, but some are not; some reasons are specific, some vague; some are causes of disease, others are symptoms; some are well-established health risks, others are not. Some respondents offered only one reason or none, but many respondents gave several answers, with an average of about two reasons per respondent. As a caveat, for two reasons this question, taken alone, underestimates beliefs about harmfulness. First, many respondents do not volunteer as many answers as they would agree to in a closed-ended format. For example, only 5 percent of respondents cited lung cancer as a harmful effect of cigarette smoking on the open-ended question, but on a closed-ended question within the same survey 42 percent of respondents agreed that cigarette smoking was a cause of lung cancer. Second, only those who earlier said cigarette smoking is harmful were asked the open-ended question. In this survey 4 percent of all respondents said that smoking was not harmful (or that they had no opinion), but later said that smoking was a cause of lung cancer.[66]

Reasons indicating a serious bodily health problem were classified as health-related reasons—for example, *"causes lung cancer"*; *"bad for the lungs, bronchial tubes"*; *"poison, irritant, doctors say so, dope"*; *"causes throat cancer"*; *"shortens breath, not enough air in lungs, affects breathing"*; or *"harmful to nose and throat—sinuses."* Six reasons (*"habit," "expensive, costs too much," "loosens self-discipline," "impolite socially, stinks the house,"* or *"no opinion/don't know/no answer"*) were classified as non-health-related reasons.[67] The replies were then re-combined from the original data file. Into the first group were included respondents who gave one or more serious health problems and into this group were also included those who said smoking was not harmful on the open-ended question but who later said on a closed-ended question that smoking cigarettes is a cause of lung cancer. Those who did not mention any serious health problems were combined into a second group.

When respondents are regrouped in this manner, over two thirds (71 percent) of respondents cited one or more serious health problems while 29 percent of respondents did not. That so many Americans believed there cigarette smoking had serious physical health consequences is surprising since neither medical groups nor the federal government had yet given Americans reason to believe that smoking was dangerous. The recently published Frank Statement disputed recently-published scientific studies that argued that smoking was dangerous. Yet the view that cigarette smoking was a serious health danger was held by 71 percent of men and by 72 percent of women; by 64 percent of current smokers, by 82 percent of past smokers, and by 75 percent of those who had never smoked; and by 75 percent of the "anti-cigarette movement" cohort, by 70 percent of "cigarette generation" Americans, and by 66 percent of the youngest American adults (those aged twenty-one to twenty-five).

Gallup's January 1954 survey included an important question that would often be asked in the coming years: "*What is your own opinion—do you think cigarette smoking is one of the causes of lung cancer, or not?*" 42 percent of all respondents said yes, 32 percent said no, and 28 percent offered no opinion. This particular question is widely reported but yields only a lower-bound estimate of Americans' beliefs in the dangers of smoking. For example, in January 1954 only 42 percent of respondents agreed that cigarette smoking was a cause of lung cancer, but 71 percent of respondents believed that cigarette smoking caused one or more serious health problems.[68] Many Americans described the dangers of cigarette smoking in terms other than lung cancer, often as heart disease, throat cancer, or respiratory problems. Combining answers on the open-ended "*harmful*" question better measures public opinion about the overall dangers of cigarette smoking than does the lung cancer question alone since the open-ended "*harmful*" question better captures the full range of perceived health dangers.

CONCLUSION: IN THE BEGINNING

Tobacco, public opinion, and public policy have a long and complex relationship. This chapter points to five conclusions. First, by January 1954 over two-thirds of Americans already believed that cigarette smoking was a serious health risk. This is surprising since neither the medical community nor the federal government had yet warned Americans about the dangers of smoking. Today most Americans may believe that the medical community and the federal government will quickly alert the public to important health risks but clearly this was not always so (Foreman 1994; Ward and Warren 2007).[69]

Second, early scientific reports and the accompanying media coverage (Troyer and Markle 1983: 54–58) did inform Americans about the health risks of smoking. Between November 1949 and January 1954 several scientific studies linked cigarette smoking to lung cancer or respiratory problems. As media coverage grew, the public's beliefs that smoking was harmful rose by 10 to 12 percent across cohorts and among smokers and nonsmokers alike. That these "cancer scare" reports were influential is not surprising. Americans are highly interested in scientific and health information and view scientists as credible source of information. In part, rising public knowledge may also be due to personal experiences with smoking-related illnesses[70] and even to the frequent mentions of health risks in cigarette advertising itself (Ringold and Calfee 1989, 1990). Even so, the impact of early scientific news on Americans' health beliefs was incomplete. Almost a third of Americans did not believe that cigarette smoking was harmful. On Gallup's *"harmful"* question the belief that cigarette smoking was a health danger rose at an annual rate of 2 to 3 percent between 1949 and 1954. By American standards this is a rapid rate of change but, as chapter 3 indicates, this change in attitudes then slowed until the landmark 1964 Surgeon General's report was underway and then issued.

Third, young Americans were not at this time learning much about the health risks of smoking either from schools or from popular culture. Young American adults (those aged twenty-one to twenty-five in January 1954) were by far the best educated of the three cohorts examined here but were also the least likely to describe cigarette smoking as harmful or to say that smoking was a cause of lung cancer.[71] As chapter 3 describes, this pattern changed when American schools began to focus on the health risks of smoking.

Fourth, protest movements can have a lasting impact on health beliefs. From the 1890s until World War I the anti-cigarette movement was a vigorous nationwide protest movement. Although the movement then declined and disappeared, it left behind a generation of Americans who less often smoked and who more often believed that smoking was harmful than did later generations (Ferrence 1989: 58–66; Harris 1983).[72] Being a member of the anti-cigarette cohort had almost as much impact on beliefs about the health risks of smoking as did all the scientific studies and news stories that appeared between 1949 and 1954. Several decades after the anti-cigarette movement disappeared, this older cohort remained more knowledgeable about the dangers of smoking than were younger, better educated Americans who grew up without an active anti-cigarette movement.[73] That this older cohort was already dying off by the 1950s considerably slowed for another decade rising public knowledge that smoking was a health risk.[74]

Finally, even a well-funded, professionally-managed public relations campaign does not always sway American public opinion. By the limited polling evidence available, the tobacco industry's January 1954 Frank Statement did not reduce public beliefs that smoking was a health hazard—perhaps because the Frank Statement was so tentative about the health evidence, because the ad itself raised health concerns, or because the cigarette industry already had serious credibility problems that worsened in the years ahead. As chapter 3 shows, when the U.S. Surgeon General and American schools presented a strong anti-smoking message, Americans' beliefs that cigarette smoking was a health danger rose very rapidly.

NOTES

1. Nicotiana rustica and nicotiana tabacum contain more nicotine than do other varieties of nicotiana and the tobacco used by American Indians was probably much more potent than are modern commercial blends. For reviews of early tobacco usage see Furst (1976: 25, 2005), Gately (2001), Goodman (1993: 3–6, 24–25), Goodspeed (1954), Hughes (2003), Nee (2005), Norton (2008), Robicsek (2005), Von Gernet (1995), Wilbert (1991), and Winter (2000: 320–21 and 2005).

2. Pre-contact Indians suffered from any life-threatening diseases, including botulism, yaws, endemic syphilis, tuberculosis, typhus from lice, streptococcus, staphylococcus, dental caries, pneumonia, protozoan and parasitic diseases, bacterial diseases, worms, viral disease, arthritis, iodine and iron deficiency (Alchon 2003: 43–45; Crawford 1998: 50–61 Verano and Ubelaker 1992).

3. In European medical thinking of the 1500s and 1600s tobacco was a "hot" and "dry" drug that counteracted "cold" and "wet" medical problems such as asthma, headaches, nervous disorders, congestion, and plague (Benedict 2005; Kell 1965; Norton 2008: 114–21, 137).

4. Soon thereafter France, Portugal, the Papal States, Turkey, and Austria-Hungary sought to control the manufacture, sale, or price of tobacco. During the 1900s Sweden, Japan, the Soviet Union and communist China created government-run tobacco monopolies (Baud 2005; Comin 2005: 599–602; Norton 2008: 155, 203–28; Gordillo 2005; Price 1995; Courtwright 2001: 149–65).

5. By 1671 tobacco oils were recognized as lethal (Wagner 1971: 63–65). In 1739 an account tied smoking to cancer. In 1761 John Hill, a London physician, tied snuffing to nasal cancer. In 1795 an account tied pipe smoking to lip cancer (Proctor: 1999: 179–80, 327; Wagner 1971: 65–67) In 1798 Benjamin Rush, an American physician, noted the dangers of tobacco chewing to the mouth and stomach (Barth 1997: 106, 147; Goodman 1993: 60–61, 75–78; Tate 1995: 147–48). Chinese doctors of the 1600s and 1700s recognized that tobacco damaged the lungs and internal organs (Benedict 2005).

6. Throughout this time period tobacco was expensive and well-to-do people more often used tobacco than did ordinary people. Since well-to-do people were the better fed and better housed, smokers may have lived longer than nonsmokers.

7. For an example of an early American research on the chemical composition of cigarettes and its smoke, see Bogen (1929).

8. Until the early 1900s half or more of Europeans and North Americans died before reaching age 50. Elsewhere the 50–year benchmark was seldom reached until after 1950 (Livi-Bacci 2007: 14–19, 106–07, 140–42; Flinn 1981: 17–18, 47–64).

9. Early friction matches contained harmful chemicals. Safety matches were not invented until 1855; safe-to-use matchbooks became available shortly before World War I (Sobel 1978: 64–71).

10. The *New York Times*, January 29, 1884, added that "if this pernicious practice obtains among adult Americans the ruin of the republic is close at hand."

11. This figure includes only commercially produced and taxed cigarettes. Hand-rolled cigarettes, which are not counted in this total, were also very common.

12. By 1910 the American Tobacco Company controlled over nine-tenths of cigarette output and over three quarters of the nation's output of plug, smoking, fine cut, snuff, and small cigars. The trust failed to control only the cigar industry. By 1910 the trust had an interest in nearly 250 companies and sought to expand foreign sales (Robert 1952; Tennant 1950; Winkler: 72–112).

13. The U.S. Supreme Court also upheld anti-trust convictions against major cigarette companies in *American Tobacco Company v. United States*, 328 U.S. 781 (1946), but that ruling did not lead to an increase in the number of manufacturers.

14. Annual figures from the Centers for Disease Control are slightly higher but also point to a sharp rise in cigarette sales; see http://www.cdc.gov/tobacco/data_statistics/tables/economics/consumption/.

15. The anti-cigarette movement less often opposed cigars, pipe smoking, oral snuff, and chewing tobacco, all of which were overwhelmingly used by adult men rather than by youths and women.

16. The British anti-tobacco movement of this era levied an equally wide variety of charges against smoking (Hilton and Nightingale 1998).

17. "Smoking expensive for women," *New York Times*, February 1, 1913: 12.

18. The anti-cigarette movement found its greatest support among Protestant religious groups, in the Middle West, and among middle-class women, but was less popular among immigrants, Catholics, urban dwellers, and men (Tate 1995: 166–70).

19. "Woman with tobacco heart," *Los Angeles Times*, March 7, 1907: 14.

20. Lulu Hunt Peters, "Diet and health," *Los Angeles Times*, December 29, 1926: A6.

21. "Burbank urges fight on weed," *Los Angeles Times*, July 20, 1924: B24.

22. An earlier decision by the United States Supreme Court, *Austin v. State of Tennessee*, 179 U.S. 343 (1900), allowed states to regulate cigarettes.

23. In 1892 a group of WCTU members petitioned Congress to ban the manufacture, importation, and sale of cigarettes. The Senate Committee on Epidemic Diseases answered that the federal government had no authority to do so, thus passing the problem back to state legislatures. (Segrave 2005: 42).

24. The widespread opposition to the tobacco trust itself during this period likely motivated some state legislators to support anti-cigarette legislation (Tate 1999: 46).

25. The War Industries Board estimated that servicemen used 60 to 70 percent more tobacco than in civilian life and that civilians' demand increased 15 to 20 percent during wartime (Tilley 1985: 314–18).

26. Prior to the 1920s cigarette manufacturers often marketed dozens of locally-sold and little-advertised brands; most local brands were discontinued when the tobacco trust was dissolved (Sobel 1978; Tennant 1950).

27. R. J. Reynolds, a successor company to the tobacco trust, received no cigarette brands upon the trust's dissolution. Camel was a newly-developed brand (Tennant 1950; Tilley 1985).

28. Some cigarette packs of the times contained ten, fifteen, twenty, or twenty-five cigarettes (Sobel 1978: 67). Twenty cigarettes to a pack helped keep prices low, allowed better packaging, and encouraged smokers to smoke more cigarettes daily. The first packs to include twenty cigarettes may have been Duke's Sunshine, Coupon, and Home Run brands during the 1880s.

29. Before the mid-1800s women who used tobacco typically used nasal snuff or smoked pipes. By the late 1800s cigars grew more popular and the image of tobacco grew more masculine; women's tobacco usage then apparently declined (Segrave 2005). For an estimate that fewer than 5 percent of American women smoked cigarettes prior to World War I, see "Women and Cigarettes," *Printers' Ink* 158 (February 18, 1932): 25–27, and Segrave (2005: 61).

30. "Women and cigarettes," *Printers' Ink* 158 (February 1, 1932): 25.

31. Smoking among women was more common among younger women. Of women under the age of twenty, 26 percent smoked, but only 9 percent of older women did.

32. For early ads see "Not a Cough in a Carload: Images from the Tobacco Industry Campaign to Hide the Hazards of Smoking," at http://lane.stanford.edu/tobacco/index.html.

33. In 1930 the Federal Trade Commission and American Tobacco signed a consent decree barring claims that cigarettes would keep women slender; see "Cigarette concern stops health ads," *New York Times*, January 24, 1930: 20. In 1942 the FTC barred Brown & Williamson from claiming that Kools would protect against colds. In 1950 a federal appeals court upheld an FTC order barring Lorillard from advertising that Old Gold had less nicotine and tars than did other brands, a claim that was based on a *Reader's Digest* article (Wagner 1971: 73). For a review of the Federal Trade Commission's efforts, see Kohlmeier (1969).

34. For other accounts from this time period see Knopf (1929) and Short, Johnson, and Ley (1938).

35. A brief summary of Müller's article appeared in English translation as "Abuse of Tobacco and Carcinoma of Lungs," *Journal of the American Medical Association*, September 30, 1939: 1372.

36. For a review of the American scientific evidence from this era, see the 2003 trial testimony of Jon M. Harkness at http://legacy.library.ucsf.edu/tid/oqs07a00/pdf.

37. By 1938 the Nazi regime limited tobacco sales, smoking in public places, and smoking by on-duty public employees. After December 1941 tobacco advertising was barred from making health claims, tobacco advertising was sharply restricted, and smoking was described as addictive and as a threat to nonsmokers. Even so, Nazi anti-tobacco policies remained incomplete. German troops received tobacco rations throughout World War II; on a limited basis so did German civilians (Proctor 1997, 1999: 198–206).

38. Some early studies pointed to the transmission of cigarette tars or nicotine from mother to child; see, for example, "Smoking Mothers," *Scientific American* 152 (April 1935): 217–18.

39. For a cancer specialist's statement that moderate smoking was not harmful and that cessation need not begin until lip irritation appeared, see "Denies cancer threat to women who smoke," *New York Times*, May 16, 1928: 8. For similar statements, see "The Advertising of Cigarettes," *JAMA* 136 (Oct. 30, 1948): 652–53. Schools of public health were also slow to offer tobacco-related training or courses (Rovniak, Johnson-Kozlow, and Hovell 2006).

40. Even so, *JAMA* ceased to accept cigarette advertising several years earlier than did the *British Medical Journal* and *Lancet* (Bartrip 1998).

41. Soon after publishing U.S. Surgeon General Burney's article on the health risks of smoking, *JAMA* published an editorial casting doubts on those findings ("Smoking and Lung Cancer" 1959).

42. Advances in statistics and in mainframe computers during the 1950s and 1960s also made it easier to describe the relationships between risk factors and diseases (Parascandola 20042; Susser 1985).

43. See, for example, "About smoking," *Newsweek*, June 17, 1957: 98 and "Smoking & cancer," *Time*, July 5, 1954: 37.

44. As an example of this concern, see "Tobacco Advertising Gone Mad" (1939).

45. The 1890 edition of the *U.S. Pharmacopoeia*, the federal government's official listing of drugs, included tobacco. Later editions deleted tobacco from the listing, thereby excluding tobacco from regulation under the Pure Food and Drug Act (Neuberger 1963: 49–50; Wagner 1971: 74).

46. Nearly six million American troops during the Korean War and nearly nine million troops during Vietnamese conflict received cigarettes through rations, military sales, and civilian cigarette drives. For figures on American troops, see Leland and Oboroceanu (2010: 1–5).

47. Federal policies that encourage or at least tolerate smoking by members of the military are longstanding; see Offen et al. (2011); Smith, Grundy, and Malone (2015); and Smith, Blackman, and Malone (2007).

48. The Office for Price Administration allowed the marketplace to deal with consumer shortages of cigarettes and never required ration coupons for cigarettes (Sobel 1978: 126–46).

49. In 1954 the Public Health Service staff prepared a short memo about the "statistical association" between lung cancer and cigarette smoking, expressing uncertainty on whether a cause-effect relationship existed. The memo was prepared as background for possible questions at an October 21, 1954 press conference held by Secretary of Health, Education, and Welfare, Oveta Culp Hobby. No questions were asked on the topic and the memo was archived (Harkness 2007: 174–83).

50. Occasional mentions of the smoking-to-cancer linkage appeared in popular magazines; see, for example, "Medicine—Continuing Fight," *Time*, March 7, 1949: 75–76.

51. As early as 1824 journalists used "straw polls" to report tallies of nonbinding shows-of-hand votes at local meetings held before U.S. presidential elections (Smith 1990). By the early 1900s several magazines and newspapers sponsored polls based on face-to-face interviews, drop-off ballots, or mail-out ballots. These polls used non-random sampling methods, and were often inaccurate (Robinson 1932); none apparently asked questions about smoking.

52. Until the late 1940s polls used "quota" sampling, a cost-saving but non-random method that allowed interviewers considerable discretion in selecting respondents. Only after the embarrassing miscall of the 1948 presidential election did random sampling become typical.

53. Gallup's June 1939 poll slightly underestimated cigarette smoking because of the question wording: *"What do you prefer to smoke—cigarettes, cigars, or a pipe?"* The December 1944 poll probably underestimated cigarette smoking since interviewing did not include American troops overseas.

54. In a June 1939 Gallup Poll 67 percent of smokers preferred cigarettes, 16 percent cigars, and 24 percent a pipe.

55. During the 1970s most pollsters shifted to telephone interviewing, making polling cheaper and timelier; as a result, many more polls were thereafter conducted.

56. Roper Organization for *Fortune* magazine, based on 5,244 interviews among national adults, November 1939. Unless so indicated all the surveys reported here are nationwide samples of American adults and are available through the Roper iPOLL on-line archive. The dates listed indicate the interviewing period.

57. *"Which of these diseases would you hate most to have?"*—76 percent cancer, 13 percent tuberculosis, 9 percent heart trouble, 2 percent pneumonia. Gallup Poll, 4/2–7/1939.

58. In the July 25–30, 1947 question: *"What disease or illness would you dread having most?"* 59 percent of respondents named cancer, 10 percent named tuberculosis and 7 percent named polio; some respondents named other diseases.

59. *"Did you happen to read the article on cigarettes in the July issue of the Reader's Digest?"*—25 percent yes, 74 percent no, 1 percent can't remember. Gallup Poll, 7/16–21/1942. This article reported the results of an independent study testing the advertising claims made by cigarette companies, and argued that many claims were misleading or false. Based on blind tests, smokers could identify particular cigarette brands only at random-guessing levels (Littell 1942).

60. Gallup Poll, 9/27–10/2/1946, with 1,500 adults nationwide. Because of the wording (". . . *to you*") only smokers (47 percent of all respondents) were asked this question.

61. Gallup Poll, 11/1–4/1949.

62. See http://www.tobacco.neu.edu/litigation/cases/supportdocs/frank_ad.htm or Glantz et al. (1996: 34) for the text of the Frank Statement. For discussions of the Frank Statement and of Hill and Knowlton's efforts, see Miller (1992, 1999); Courtwright (2001: 125–29); Glantz, et al. (1996: 32–46); Cummings, Morley, and Hyland (2002); and Oreskes and Conway (2010: 14–19).

63. *"Do you think cigarette smoking is harmful, or not?"* Gallup Poll, 1/9–14/1954.

64. In Gallup's January 1954 survey the older anti-cigarette movement cohort constituted 25 percent of the sample with the "cigarette generation" cohort at 66 percent and the youngest cohort (age twenty-one to twenty-five) at 9 percent.

65. Prior to asking these questions Gallup asked respondents whether they had ever smoked cigarettes regularly; whether they smoked cigarettes now; if they now smoked, how many cigarettes had they smoked in the last twenty-four hours; whether they had ever given up smoking for any length of time; and how long it had been since they smoked cigarettes regularly. Asking these questions before asking about health matters may reduce slightly the percentage of respondents who link cigarette smoking to diseases due to a question-order effect often called impression management.

66. Such seemingly inconsistent answers are not unusual. Combining poll questions yields better results than relying on only a single closed-ended question.

67. This classification is based on the health risks in *The Health Consequences of Smoking* (2004: 4–30).

68. Gallup repeated both the 1954 closed- and open-ended wording in a September 1999 poll. In several other surveys Gallup used variations on the 1954 wording, typically adding ". . . *to your health*" to the question. The percentage who agreed to the statement "*Do you think that cigarette smoking is or is not harmful to your health?*" was 90 percent in August 1977, 91 percent in June 1981, and 96 percent in July 1990. What impact the additional wording caused is unclear. In a June 1987 Gallup survey for the American Lung Association, 94 percent of respondents agreed that "*smoking (is) harmful to your health.*" During fall 1964 and spring 1966 the U.S. Department of Health, Education, and Welfare's Use of Tobacco (1969) polls asked the agree/disagree question, "*Smoking cigarettes is harmful to health*" with 81 percent of respondents strongly or mildly agreeing in both years.

69. See McCullough (1977: 421–23) for the federal government's belated attention to mosquito-borne diseases during the Panama Canal's construction.

70. In a February 1954 Gallup survey large majorities of Americans said that they personally knew someone who had cancer or heart disease (74 percent and 61 percent, respectively).

71. Gallup Poll then defined adults as twenty-one and older; this age cutoff later dropped to eighteen years old.

72. In Gallup's January 1954 poll only 28 percent of the anti-cigarette movement cohort had a high school education or more, compared to 46 percent of those in the next younger ("cigarette generation") cohort and 59 percent of those aged twenty-one to twenty-five. Within these three cohorts the percentage reporting that they had ever smoking was 38 percent, 60 percent, and 68 percent, respectively. The percentage reporting current smoking was 27 percent, 54 percent, and 57 percent. The percentage who said smoking was a cause of lung cancer was 46 percent, 38 percent, and 34 percent.

73. The evidence for cohort effects is stronger than the evidence for aging and life experiences. Within cohorts no pattern appears by age of increasing beliefs that cigarette smoking is harmful or that smoking causes lung cancer.

74. The anti-cigarette movement cohort constituted 25 percent of American adults in 1954 and thereafter fell to 21 percent in 1960 and to 6 percent by 1971. The 1971 figure is slightly depressed because Gallup included eighteen to twenty year olds in that survey and thereafter.

THREE

Public Opinion and the Health Risks of Smoking

By 1954 two-thirds of Americans believed that cigarette smoking was a health risk, but as to how great of a health risk, knowledge remained very incomplete. In a January 1954 survey 43 percent of Americans said that smoking cigarettes is a cause of lung cancer—a figure that rose to 62 percent by March 1964, to 70 percent by 1972, and to 91 percent in 2013. So, too, for heart disease, addiction, and secondhand smoking did health knowledge about the ills of cigarette smoking rise dramatically. In magnitude, these belief changes are among the largest ever reported in modern survey research—as large as the changes in Americans' attitudes on whether racial segregation is wrong, whether Americans would vote for a woman or for an African-American as president, or whether same-sex couples should be able to marry. This chapter explores how government policies, the media, interest groups, schools, generational change, and lifetime adult learning caused this remarkable transformation of American public opinion.

RISING ATTENTION TO THE HEALTH DANGERS OF SMOKING

During the 1950s mounting evidence tied cigarette smoking to lung cancer and to heart disease. A major study by the American Cancer Society released in June 1954 tracked deaths among nearly 188,000 American men and showed that smokers suffered higher death rates from lung cancer and from heart attacks (Hammond and Horn 1954).[1] A 1954 report on 40,000 British medical doctors reported that smokers, particularly heavy smokers, much more often died from lung cancer than did nonsmokers (Doll and Hill 1954, 1956; Hilton 2000).[2] Neither study identified exactly what it was in cigarettes that increased the risks of lung cancer or heart disease, but both reports received widespread media attention and helped to focus scientific, media, and public attention on smoking and health. In October 1954 the Public Health Cancer Association urged people to stop cigarette smoking. Several more scientific reports on smoking and health followed (Talley, Kushner, and Sterk 2004).

Media attention to the health risks of cigarette smoking also rose (Baumgartner and Jones 1993). Figure 3.1 depicts the *New York Times'* number of such news stories, letters to the editor, or editorials published annually. That number averaged only 8 news stories, letters, and editorials annually between 1940 and 1953, then rose to 49 in 1953 and 1954, then averaged 33 between 1955 and 1961, and rose to 91 annually from 1962 to 1993. During the 1994 to 2003 time period the average rose sharply to 240 annually and thereafter fell to an average of 125 annually from 2004 to 2014. Three major events triggered off a higher level of media attention. The first was new and troubling scientific research during the early 1950s. The second was the creation of in 1962 and then the 1964 report of the U.S. Surgeon General's advisory committee on smoking and health. The third was the rising number of high-profile lawsuits and federal actions against cigarette manufacturers beginning during the Clinton presidency in the 1990s.[3]

The growing number of scientific reports and media stories did not immediately raise public knowledge about the health risks of smoking. Beginning in January 1954 (for lung cancer) and in June 1957 (for heart disease) Gallup Poll periodically asked Americans whether they believed that smoking was a cause of these diseases.[4] Beliefs that cigarette smoking is a cause of lung cancer grew only from 42 percent to 47 percent between a January 1954 poll taken just before the American Cancer Society and the British studies were released and a May 1962 poll taken just before President Kennedy's press conference that led to the appointment of the Surgeon General's committee, described below. In July 1958 a third (33 percent) of Americans believed that cigarette smoking is a cause of heart disease and in June 1962 that figure was still only 32 percent. Only after the Surgeon General's advisory committee on smoking began its work in 1962 did Americans' health knowledge increase.

Why did Americans' health knowledge grow so little for nearly a decade despite growing scientific evidence and media attention? An often cited reason is the cigarette industry's strategy of "creating controversy" on the smoking-and-health issue (Bero 2005; Bero and Kennedy 1999; Christensen 2008; Dewhirst 2005: 473–79; Oreskes and Conway 2010; Parascandola 2004; Proctor 2008, 2011; White 1988). Beginning with the January 1954 "Frank Statement" newspaper ads, the tobacco industry carried out a long-running public relations campaign aimed at casting doubt on the link between cigarette smoking and illness, particularly lung cancer.

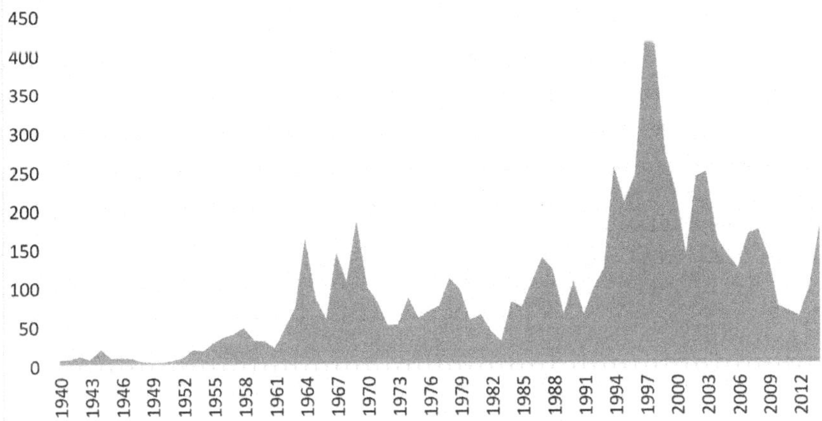

Figure 3.1. Number of *New York Times* stories, letters, and editorials on the health risks of smoking, 1940–2014.

Not until the late 1990s did the cigarette industry's top officials publicly concede that smoking was addictive and cancer-causing. By then nine-tenths of Americans believed that smoking caused lung cancer, four-fifths believed that smoking caused heart disease, two-thirds believed that smoking caused birth defects, slightly over half believed that second-hand smoke was very harmful, and three-quarters of smokers said that they were addicted to smoking.

The cigarette industry's efforts to create and to sustain controversy over the ills of smoking were far-reaching, but the polling evidence also points to two other reasons that explain the 1954 to 1962 lag in Americans' health knowledge. The first was the rising popularity of filter cigarettes. During the 1950s not only did cigarette manufacturers embark on a damage-control strategy by publishing the 1954 Frank Statement, by creating the Tobacco Industry Research Committee (TIRC), later renamed the Council for Tobacco Research (CTR), and in 1958 by organizing a new Washington-based lobbying and public relations organization, the Tobacco Institute.[5] Cigarette manufacturers also brought out dozens of new brands, including filters, king-sized, and menthol cigarettes. Between 1954 and 1975 the six major manufacturers, R. J. Reynolds, American, Philip Morris, Liggett & Myers, Lorillard, and Brown & Williamson, introduced more than seventy-two new brands. Filter cigarettes were especially popular. Between 1952 and 1962 filters rose from 1 percent to 43 percent of cigarette sales.[6] Menthols rose from 3 percent to 16 percent of sales. King-size cigarettes remained steady at 18 percent to 19 percent of sales. Regular unfiltered cigarettes fell from 78 percent to 22 percent of sales. Advertising outlays heavily promoted the new brands, especially on radio and television, until January 1971 when broadcast advertising was banned. Cigarette advertising often made implicit or explicit health claims (Ringold and Calfee 1989; Viscusi 1992: 35–43; Doron 1979: 131–34; Federal Trade Commission 1964: 2–6, 24–38; Sobel 1978: 147–209 Tursi, White, and McQuilkin 2000: 221–22).

Critics charged that Americans saw filter cigarettes as somehow safer cigarettes. In 1957 a Congressional subcommittee concluded that ". . . the connection between filter-tip cigarettes and 'protection' has become deeply embedded in the public mind" (U.S. Congress 1957: 25). The cigarette industry's polls also showed that many smokers believed that some cigarettes were safer to smoke than were others. A 1959 Gallup survey conducted for the industry asked smokers: "*Regardless of what you, yourself smoke, what one brand of cigarettes do you think is the safest to smoke from the standpoint of health?*"[7] A fifth (21 percent) of smokers said that none were the safest and 16 percent of smokers said they couldn't say, but 61 percent of smokers named a particular brand as the safest. About a third of smokers named a filter cigarette as the safest, with Kent, a filter brand, being the most often named (at 18 percent). In a March 1960 Roper survey conducted for the industry, 48 percent of smokers said that all filters give protection, 7 percent said that only high filtration filters do so, 29 percent said that no filters give protection, and 18 percent said don't know or gave no answer.[8] In a 1960 Gallup survey 74 percent of smokers said that some brands were safer than others, and 35 percent of smokers named a filter brand as the safest to smoke. Among nonsmokers these figures were much lower: 25 percent and 13 percent, respectively. Other poll questions taken both before and after the 1964 Surgeon General's report was released, show similar results and suggest how important the new and heavily-advertised filter brands were in "creating controversy."[9] The belief that filters were somehow safer to smoke was repeated when low tar and low nicotine cigarettes became popular, and when "mild," "light," and "ultra-light" cigarettes reached the market. Critics discounted the perceived benefits of low tar, low nicotine, light, mild or ultra-light cigarettes, but many smokers still saw these brands as a safer choice.[10]

A second reason that Americans' health knowledge did not rapidly increase lies in the federal government's indifferent or inconsistent actions (Marshall 2015; Yang and Novotny 2009). The "cancer scare" notwithstanding, Congress, the White House, the federal courts, and the federal agencies took little action on smoking. The federal government continued to make cigarettes easily available to the military, to protect tobacco farmers' prices, and to encourage cigarette exports, but did not mandate health warnings on cigarette packages or in print, outdoor, or broadcast advertising; did not limit advertising, vending machine sales, or giveaways of cigarettes; did not ban smoking in public places; and did not restrict smoking by minors. Neither the occasional Congressional hearings nor new consumer protection laws led to any action on smoking and health.[11] Despite his own smoking-related health problems and two statements by his Surgeon General, President Eisenhower ignored the issue. So did several later presidents.

What little action that came from Washington, DC was from the Federal Trade Commission and from the U.S. Surgeon General's office. In 1955 the FTC and the cigarette industry voluntarily agreed to ban several then-common advertising claims, including claims of medical approval for smoking in general or for any particular brand; claims that a brand was low in nicotine or tars unless so established by scientific proof, then unavailable; claims about smoking's effects on the nose, throat, larynx, respiratory track, digestive system, nerves, energy levels or other body parts; or claims about sales figures or celebrity testimonials unless accurate at the time. Nor could cigarette ads "falsely or misleadingly" disparage other brands (Calfee 1985, 1986; Friedman 1975; Ringold and Calfee 1989, 1990). Critics such as the American Cancer Society and *Reader's Digest* viewed the 1955 agreement as misguided and as removing the implicit or explicit health claims then common in cigarette ads that warned smokers that cigarettes were dangerous—yet failed to require any health warnings on cigarette packages or in print, broadcast, or outdoor advertising; failed to limit the number of ads; and failed to prohibit depictions of glamorous, sexy, young, and healthy smokers. The FTC's critics were correct. Between Gallup's June 1954 and its July 1958 polls, American's beliefs that cigarette smoking was a cause of lung cancer grew only from 42 to 44 percent, an annual increase of less than 1 percent.

The FTC later changed its policy and allowed cigarette ads to mention tar and nicotine levels, thereby setting off a three-year "tar derby" during which many cigarette ads made claims of lower tar and nicotine levels. During the tar derby Gallup's surveys between July 1958 and May 1960 show a rise from 44 percent to 50 percent in beliefs that cigarette smoking was a cause of lung cancer, an annual increase of about 3 percent. In 1960 the FTC again switched course and banned tar and nicotine claims. Between Gallup's May 1960 and May 1962 polls, beliefs that cigarette smoking was a cause of lung cancer dropped from 50 percent to 47 percent. By the polling evidence the FTC's erratic regulations were counterproductive. The health claims made by cigarette ads better alerted the public to the health dangers of smoking than did the FTC's blackout policy. In 1967 the FTC switched policy again and allowed tar and nicotine claims in cigarette advertising, and after 1970 required that tar and nicotine yields be published (Friedman 1975: 37–49), but by then public knowledge about the health risks of smoking had already increased dramatically and the new policy had no apparent impact.

That the FTC's actions were ineffective or even counterproductive is part of a familiar story. Decades earlier the U.S. Supreme Court's decision to break up the tobacco trust triggered off a rapid rise in cigarette advertising and led to rising smoking rates. Congress' 1965 package warning label requirement, discussed below, banned the states and the FTC from imposing even tougher regulations. The 1971 ban on radio and television cigarette advertising eliminated most of the widely-viewed anti-smoking ads. Federal policies sometimes increase health awareness, but they do not always do so.

Nor did the U.S. Surgeon General any more successfully alert Americans to the health risks of smoking. In 1957 and 1959 then-Surgeon General Leroy Burney issued statements tying "excessive" cigarette smoking to lung cancer, but neither statement positively impacted American public opinion (Burney 1957, 1959). Following Burney's 1957 and 1959 statements beliefs that cigarette smoking is a cause of lung cancer actually dropped by 3 percent and by 5 percent, respectively, in Gallup's polling. For heart disease, beliefs dropped 2 percent in 1957 and were unchanged in 1959. Government actions can sometimes inform public opinion but by early 1962 no such actions (except, ironically, the brief "tar derby" period) had actually done so.[12]

Although health knowledge among all Americans did not increase until 1962 and thereafter, a few as-yet-small signs of change did appear. Doctors and scientists were among the first to recognize the health risks of smoking ("Doctors Have Changed Their Smoking Habits" 1957; Simon 1969; Burnham 1989: 27, n. 89; Lawton and Goldman 1961; Garfinkel and Stellman 1986; Cortas and Talley 2006: 329–34; Snegireff and Lombard 1959). Doctors and scientists are important opinion leaders but their numbers are far too small to affect nationwide poll results. Attitude change also appeared among teenagers and young adults well before changes appeared among older adults, but these changes did not immediately affect nationwide poll results since polls then defined adults as twenty-one years or older and since there were relatively few young adults due to low birth rates during the 1930s and 1940s.

Changing beliefs among teens and young adults show that interest groups and schools can influence health beliefs, albeit gradually so. During the late 1950s, alarmed at the mounting evidence on the dangers of cigarette smoking and frustrated by Washington's continuing inaction, health activists turned to the schools to warn young people about the risks of smoking. The American Cancer Society, a well-known and popular group, sent materials to over half of American schools (Talley, Kushner, and Sterk 2004: 370–71; Cortas and Talley 2006: 332–34; Neuberger 1963: 79–80). By 1968 over two-thirds of teens reported that their schools offered anti-cigarette presentations ("Teenage Smoking" 1968: 5). These efforts reflect a uniquely American tradition that health education is more decentralized and open to grass-roots advocacy than in other democracies (Courtwright 2005; Nathanson 1999, 2007).

In actually reducing teen smoking rates these efforts reported only modest success, but these efforts did at least raise students' health knowledge (Krosnick et al. 2006). In a 1959 survey in Newton, Massachusetts, 90 percent of junior high school students and 95 percent of senior high school students said that they had heard that lung cancer may be caused by smoking, and 82 percent said that cigarette smoking was bad for health (Salber et al. 1963). In a 1960 nationwide survey for *Senior Scholastic* magazine, two-thirds of American teenagers said that smoking was a risk factor for lung cancer. In a 1961 survey three-quarters of high school sophomores, two-thirds of high school seniors and college juniors and seniors, and slightly over half of non-school young adults said that cigarette smoking is a cause of lung cancer.[13] All these figures are higher than those found among all adults. Several other surveys conducted prior to the 1964 Surgeon General's report also show that most high school and college students believed that smoking was a health risk and linked to cancer (Arnett 1962; Horn 1960; Monk, Tayback, and Gordon 1965).

Student surveys conducted after the 1964 Surgeon General's report was issued show even higher levels of knowledge that smoking is a health risk. A nationwide survey conducted in 1967 and 1968 showed that 91 percent of youth aged twelve to eighteen said that smoking was harmful to health (Horn 1968). In a 1969 survey for the American Cancer Society, three-quarters of teenagers said that cigarette smoking is a proven cause of lung cancer, and three-fifths said that it is probably or definitely true that smoking triples the chances of a heart attack (American Cancer Society 1969). Other nationwide and local surveys show similar results ("Teenage Smoking" 1972; Streit 1967; Harlin 1972; Kelson, Pullela, and Otterland 1975; "Smoking and Health" 1967; Steel 1965; Kenkel 1991). Over time young Americans' growing health knowledge began to affect nationwide poll results. In Gallup's January 1954 survey, the youngest adults (those aged twenty-one to twenty-five) were the least well-informed age cohort on the health risks of smoking, with only 36 percent saying that cigarette smoking is a cause of lung cancer. By 1960 60 percent of young adults age twenty-one to twenty-five said that cigarette smoking is a cause of lung cancer. Stated otherwise, in 1954 young adults were 5 percent *less* likely to link cigarette smoking to lung cancer than were older adults, but by 1960 young adults were 10 percent *more* likely to link cigarette smoking to lung cancer than were older adults.

THE 1964 SURGEON GENERAL'S REPORT

Much like President Eisenhower, John Kennedy ignored the smoking and health issue—at least until a May 23, 1962 press conference when a reporter asked him a pointed question about whether he agreed with reports linking cigarette smoking to cancer and heart disease. President Kennedy did not immediately answer the question but promised an answer soon.[14] Two weeks later, the U.S. Surgeon General's office announced that an advisory committee would review the evidence. Surgeon General Luther Terry allowed both health groups and tobacco interests to propose, review, and veto names from a list of over 150 scientists and physicians.[15] Terry then named ten prominent scientists and physicians to produce a report. The committee spent one-and-a-half-years reviewing several thousand articles, making site visits to examine the records of important research, and producing its final report. All this was done with a level of secrecy rare in federal investigations. On Saturday morning, January 11, 1964, the committee presented its final report to well over a hundred reporters, thereby ensuring that the report would not immediately unsettle the stock market, which was closed on Saturdays, but would receive prominent coverage in Sunday newspapers (Whelan 1984; Brandt 1990; Parascandola 1998).

In three ways the 1964 report was a landmark. First, the report was a pioneering expose and the first in what became a series of Surgeon General's reports on smoking. Second, the report accepted a major shift then underway in scientific thinking about chronic diseases. The report abandoned for the study of chronic diseases both the "germ theory" view and the necessity for controlled experiments. Instead, the report endorsed five criteria for examining the smoking-to-health relationship: the strength, consistency, specificity, temporal relationship, and coherence of the evidence. Third and most immediately important, the report tied cigarette smoking to several diseases and unequivocally so to lung cancer: "Cigarette smoking is causally related to lung cancer in men; the magnitude of the effect of cigarette smoking far outweighs all other factors. The data for women, though less extensive, points in the same direction." The report linked smoking to nine-tenths of the rapidly rising number of lung cancer deaths, and called smoking causative of chronic bronchitis, cancer of the larynx, and (for pipe smoking) lip cancer. For coronary artery disease, the link to smoking was not called causal but as likely to be proven so. The report described, but did not term causal an association between smoking and cancer of the esophagus, the urinary bladder (in men), and the stomach; peptic ulcers; tobacco amblyopia; liver cirrhosis; and low birth weight in newborns. Several carcinogens in cigarette tars were described. Cigarette smoking was tied to a 70 percent increase in men's age-specific death rates. The report discounted nicotine as a health hazard except for its addictive qualities; downplayed as "comparatively inconsequential" the alleged benefits of smoking such as mental health, combatting obesity, and contentment; described smoking as a habit rather than an addiction; and called for "appropriate remedial action," albeit only in general terms.

Although it carried no policy-making authority, the 1964 report was what President Theodore Roosevelt once called a "bully good pulpit." So were several of the Surgeon General's later reports (Brandt 2007: 239; Kagan and Vogel 1993). The 1964 report received prominent, in-depth, and sustained news coverage.[16] Nearly all the nation's Sunday newspapers gave the report front-page coverage (98 percent did) as the largest front-page story (63 percent did), with a bigger headline than for any other story (48 percent did), and placed the story "above the fold" where readers were most likely to see it (94 percent did). Half of Sunday newspapers carried a front-page picture along with the story (48 percent did). Nearly all newspapers continued the story on one or more inside pages (96 percent did). Newspapers covered the lung cancer danger (98 percent did) as well as other risks such as heart disease, bronchitis, and emphysema (94 percent did). Nearly all Sunday papers described the call for appropriate remedial action (94 percent did), attributed the findings to prominent scientists (96 percent did), and all cited the U.S. Surgeon General. Most newspapers described the tobacco industry's response calling for more research, but usually only briefly so. Headlines were often simple and dramatic. The *Los Angeles Times* headlined "Report Calls Smoking Definite Health Peril—U.S. Surgeon General's Panel Links Tobacco to Cancer, Other Diseases." The *Chicago Tribune*'s full-page-wide headline read "Tie Cancer To Cigarettes." The *Washington Post* headlined "Cigarette Smoking Cited as Main Cause of Deadly Lung Cancer." The *Cincinnati Enquirer* headlined the story in courtroom terms: "Change Vs. Cigarettes: Menace . . . Verdict Guilty." Almost all papers carried follow-up stories on Monday (98 percent did) and mostly on the front page (66 percent did). On Tuesday 96 percent of newspapers wrote one or more further stories, many (40 percent) on the front page. Television news and popular magazines such as *Time*, *Life*, and *Newsweek* also extensively covered the story. Media coverage of smoking grew steadily more negative after the 1964 report as coverage of health-related issues and government regulations increasingly crowded out news stories on the economic and financial aspects of tobacco (Baumgartner and Jones 2009: 264–71).

Americans' beliefs about the ills of cigarette smoking had not greatly changed before the report got underway in 1962, but thereafter changes came more rapidly. Between Gallup's May 1962 and February 1964 polls, the percentage of Americans who said that cigarette smoking was a cause of lung cancer rose by 15 percent (from 47 percent to 62 percent) and for heart disease rose by 18 percent (from 32 percent to 50 percent)—annual rates of change of 8 percent and 10 percent, respectively. About half of this change occurred before the report's release in January 1964 and about half occurred soon thereafter. Among smokers, lung cancer beliefs rose from 38 percent to 53 percent and beliefs on heart disease rose from 26 percent to 44 percent. Even so, awareness remained incomplete (Proctor 2011: 309–15). A third of Americans still did not believe that smoking caused lung cancer. Half of Americans still did not believe smoking caused heart disease.

By American standards these are large and rapid poll changes.[17] Americans' beliefs and preferences on familiar issues rarely change at such rapid rates (Baumgartner, DeBoef, and Boydstun 2008: 5, 166–98; see also Page and Shapiro 1982). Public knowledge of smoking-related health risks often rises at 1 or 2 percent a year, occasionally at 3 percent a year if high profile events occur, but seldom more rapidly. Sometimes, as from 1954 to 1962 or after the early 1990s, public knowledge may not rise at all. Generational replacement cannot explain large and rapid short-term rises in health knowledge but a powerful event such as the 1964 report can. Short-term poll changes of 3 percent or more provide evidence that a real change in attitudes occurred beyond what might be due solely to random sampling, thus setting a threshold for identifying especially important events.

By another comparison the 1962 to 1964 increases in health knowledge about smoking were more rapid than increases in public knowledge about AIDS during the 1980s and 1990s.[18] This two-year rise in Americans' knowledge about smoking and lung cancer or heart disease also exceeded the rate of change in Americans' preferences on several racial and religious issues where little or no well-organized opposition to social change existed.[19] During the mid-1960s the cigarette industry's success at "creating controversy" began to wane. A 1970 Roper report warned its client, the Tobacco Institute, that "there is little in this study that can be termed encouraging to the tobacco industry in terms of public opinion on the smoking and health controversy. . . . Reports on the ill effects of smoking appear to be fairly widely accepted as authoritative—which is perhaps not surprising in view of the fact that there has been little to refute them." The industry's "creating controversy" strategy became even more of a failure as Americans' knowledge of the link between smoking and lung cancer and heart disease continued to rise by 1 or 2 percent annually until the mid-1990s.

The tobacco industry closely followed these belief changes but kept their poll results private. Hill and Knowlton, the industry's public relations firm, commissioned three polls to track the impact of the Surgeon General reports, the first conducted on Friday, January 10, 1964 (the day before the Saturday press conference); the second on Monday, January 13 (two days after the press conference); and the third on February 24 and 25 (about six weeks later). These polls showed that the report won a large audience. In Monday's polling 78 percent of Americans said that they knew of a recent report, typically so through newspaper or television reports. Only a sixth of Americans reported hearing or reading anything about the tobacco industry's low-key and equivocal response.[20] The percentage of Americans who agreed that smoking is "*a major cause*" of lung cancer jumped from 34 percent on the Friday before the report was issued to 52 percent the next Monday and was 48 percent six weeks later. The 14 percent six-week increase for lung cancer was greater than the equivalent 4 percent increase (from 22 percent to 25 percent to 26 percent, respectively) for heart disease. More Americans expressed interest in hearing the views of the medical profession than those of the government or the tobacco industry (72 percent, 44 percent, and 46 percent, respectively).

If these poll results were troubling for Hill and Knowlton's clients, several other poll results were not. The percentage of Americans who supported "*drastic government action*" against cigarettes rose slightly but then fell back to earlier levels (37 percent, 42 percent, and 36 percent, respectively). Support for warning labels on cigarettes showed the same pattern—65 percent, 72 percent, and 64 percent, respectively. Two-thirds or more of Americans pinned the primary responsibility for dealing with smoking on the individual himself or herself rather than on the tobacco industry, the medical profession, or the government. A Roper poll conducted for Philip Morris two weeks after the report's release reported similar results. Nearly all (95 percent) of respondents had heard about the Surgeon General's report. Although 5 percent of smokers said that they had stopped smoking since the report and 23 percent had cut down on smoking, the Roper survey hinted that the drop in smoking might be short-lived. Of those who stopped smoking, half had already resumed; of those who had cut down, a fifth said that it was only temporary. These trends were also reported in other studies.[21] In short the industry's polls showed an increase in beliefs tying smoking to lung cancer and heart disease, but no changes in attitudes about what actions the government should take and probably only a small, temporary drop in smoking.

Two nationwide surveys conducted for the federal government during fall 1964 and spring 1966 showed that the rise in health knowledge did not disappear but neither did it continue to grow so rapidly. The percentage of Americans who said that smokers were more likely than nonsmokers to get lung cancer was almost unchanged—68 percent in fall 1964 and 69 percent in spring 1966. For coronary heart disease, the figures were 42 percent and 44 percent, respectively, and for emphysema and chronic bronchitis, 51 percent and 52 percent.

Large and rapid gains in health knowledge can occur after a major report or expose, but more typically gains occur slowly. The 1964 Surgeon General's report had an unusually large impact on Americans' health beliefs for several reasons. In 1964 the federal government enjoyed high levels of popular trust and confidence, but soon thereafter trust in the federal government began to fall, never fully to recover.[22] The 1964 report was authored by prestigious doctors and scientists—opinion leaders who rank high in public esteem and credibility. The report was clear, unanimous, and widely publicized in pointing to the health risks of smoking. When the report was the most clear, as it was on lung cancer, the polls shifted the most. When the report was vague, as in its call for unspecified "appropriate remedial action," attitude shifts were far smaller. Further, in 1964 the percentage of Americans who believed that smoking was a cause of lung cancer or heart disease was much lower than in later years, leaving more room for attitude changes. As a caveat, generally-worded poll questions on health beliefs are more easily affected by new information than are beliefs about one's own personal risk, support for particular government policies, or actual smoking behavior.[23]

PACKAGE WARNINGS, THE FAIRNESS DOCTRINE, AND THE BROADCAST BAN

The 1964 Surgeon General's report urged "appropriate remedial action" but did not endorse any particular changes. Demands for action nonetheless followed. The Federal Trade Commission soon proposed mandatory warning labels for cigarette packages and for both print and broadcast ads.[24] Several states appeared likely to take action.[25] Prodded by cigarette lobbyists and the industry's supporters to limit the potential damage, Congress in 1965 mandated instead a weakly-worded warning only on cigarette packages ("Caution: Cigarette Smoking May Be Hazardous To Your Health") to take effect in 1966. The industry's strategic concession was a shrewd one. The tobacco industry could claim publicly that it did not oppose a widely-popular health warning. Broadcast advertising was exempted from the required warning and the FTC and the states were barred for four years from requiring any other wording.[26] The newly-required warnings could be placed on the little-noticed side panel of cigarette packages, not on the front panel (Fritschler 1983: 107–29). As a side benefit for the industry the new warning served as a legal defense to bolster its claims that the health risks of smoking were common knowledge among the public and that sick or dying smokers, but not the industry, should be held responsible for their illnesses. Critics blasted the new warning as timid and weakly-worded but their complaints had little effect (Brandt 2007; Drew 1965; Kohlmeirer 1969: 55–56; Tursi, White, and McQuilkin 2000: 85–97).[27]

Warnings of some sort had long been popular with the public and even with smokers. In a 1957 Gallup Poll a 53 to 35 percent majority of Americans favored a warning by government health department. In Hill and Knowlton's polling conducted a day before the 1964 Surgeon General's report was released, 65 percent of Americans favored a warning. In the federal government's fall 1964 Use of Tobacco survey, 60 percent favored package warnings and 77 percent said that cigarette packages should list the amount of tar and nicotine. Most Americans supported more far-reaching measures than Congress' mildly-worded warning. In an April 1968 Roper poll 83 percent of respondents agreed that "*all cigar-*

ette advertising should be required to warn people that smoking may be hazardous to health"; most (74 percent) said that cigarette advertising "*should not be allowed to make smoking look glamorous*"; and 73 percent said that "*cigarette advertising should not show young people smoking.*" Over half (57 percent) said that "*the present warning statements on cigarettes should be made stronger.*" Later Roper surveys showed large majorities in favor of much stiffer warnings.[28] Perhaps not surprisingly, the weakly-worded 1965 package warnings did not immediately increase health knowledge. In the fall 1964 Use of Tobacco survey 81 percent of Americans agreed with the statement "*Smoking cigarettes is harmful to health*"—a figure unchanged in a spring 1966 survey conducted soon after the warnings appeared.[29] The warnings did become increasingly popular, once required. Between March 1965 and 1969 Harris Poll showed that the percentage of Americans in favor of the package warning rose from 68 percent to 89 percent, an increase of about 5 percent annually (Page and Shapiro 1992: 155).

Federal policy-making is often a decentralized process and one that is open to activists and interest groups. In 1967 the Federal Communications Commission, prodded by a young attorney, John F. Banzhaf, III, required television stations that aired paid cigarette advertisements also to air unpaid anti-smoking commercials. Since cigarette commercials were then common, this led to a stream of anti-smoking ads at a frequency of one anti-smoking ad for every three to six paid cigarette ads.[30] The FCC's "fairness doctrine" lasted about three years. Congress then banned all broadcast advertising for cigarettes as of January 2, 1971, a move that also eliminated the requirement for anti-smoking ads.

The fairness doctrine's required anti-smoking ads were widely seen. In a fall 1967 Roper survey 67 percent of smokers and 64 percent of nonsmokers said that they had recently seen commercials or advertising about the health hazards of cigarette smoking. In a July 1968 Roper survey 85 percent of smokers and 80 percent of non-smokers had seen some anti-cigarette advertising in the media. The ads and related news coverage more greatly affected public opinion than did the tobacco industry's reassurances. Forty percent of respondents said that they had read or heard something during the past year that made them either more worried or less worried about smoking; among these respondents the "*more worried*" responses outnumbered the "*less worried*" responses twelve-to-one. The anti-smoking ads also modestly reduced per-capita smoking (2014 Surgeon General: 18, 25; O'Keefe 1971; Lewit, Coate, and Grossman 1981; cf. McAuliffe 1988). In the 1968 Roper survey 16 percent of smokers who had seen the ads said that they cut down on their number of cigarettes, another 6 percent switched to another brand perceived as less harmful, and 19 percent did nothing but worried more. Among nonsmokers who had seen the ads, 3 percent reported that they had stopped smoking, 1 percent decided not to smoke, 12 percent were glad to have stopped smoking, and 55 percent were glad that they were not a smoker.

Taken together, the package warning labels and the fairness doctrine only modestly raised health knowledge. In a Gallup Poll taken just after the 1964 Surgeon General's report was issued, 62 percent of Americans believed that cigarette smoking is a cause of lung cancer. That figure was 70 percent in July 1969, then 71 percent in a May 1971 survey about four months after the fairness doctrine's anti-smoking ad requirement ended—an average annual increase of only about 1.3 percent between 1964 and 1971 and far less than the average annual rise of 7.6 percent during the 1962 to 1964 period.

On January 2, 1971 the "broadcast ban" ended both paid cigarette advertisements on radio and television and the required anti-cigarette ads.[31] The broadcast ban was by no means an anti-smoking gesture. The ban allowed cigarette manufacturers at least temporarily to reduce their advertising costs, virtually ensured that no new major brands would appear, eliminated nearly all the anti-smoking ads, and led to an uptick in smoking (Warner 1979: 441–42). The broadcast ban won only mixed public opinion support. In a 1967 C. E. Hooper survey conducted for the industry, Americans were closely divided on the proposed broadcast ban with 45 percent in favor and 42 percent opposed.[32] In an April 1968 Roper survey only 25 percent said that "*cigarette advertising should not be allowed on TV*" but 49 percent said that "*cigarette advertising should be allowed on TV late in the evening when young people under 18 are not likely to be watching*." The broadcast ban slightly reduced health knowledge. Prior to the ban, beliefs that smoking is a cause of lung cancer were rising at a rate of slightly over 1 percent a year, but between May 1971 and April 1972 that belief dropped very slightly from 71 percent to 70 percent.

RISING AWARENESS ABOUT LUNG CANCER AND HEART DISEASE

Government policies and exposes sometimes increase health knowledge but do not always do so. The 1964 Surgeon General's report increased Americans' health knowledge much more than did the 1965 package warning labels, the fairness doctrine, or the broadcast ban. Figure 3.2 shows that after 1964 Americans' belief that cigarette smoking was tied to lung cancer or heart disease rose slowly and steadily for about thirty more years before stabilizing. In 1992 Gallup pegged these beliefs at 92 percent and 80 percent for lung cancer and heart disease and in 2013 at 91 percent and 81 percent, respectively. No single event caused another large and sudden increase in this knowledge. Instead, these beliefs rose fairly steadily at about 1 percent annually until the early 1990s, but thereafter did not increase. Although gradual and long-term poll changes are more difficult to explain than are large and short-term changes, two important explanations for these gains in health knowledge merit attention: generational replacement and adult learning.

Figures 3.3 and 3.4 depict the percentages by age cohort, tracked over time, who believed that cigarette smoking is a cause of lung cancer. Figure 3.3 depicts the Gallup trends for the three oldest cohorts: the "anti-cigarette generation" (those born before 1900), the "cigarette generation" (those born from 1900 to 1929), and those who were only twenty-one to twenty-five years old in 1954. Each cohort's beliefs are tracked from 1954 until 1999 or until the cohort grows so old that its numbers dwindle and the poll figures become unreliable. Figure 3.4 depicts the smoking-to-lung-cancer awareness among four younger age groups (those aged twenty-one to twenty-five in 1960, in 1969, in 1977, and in 1990), again tracked through 1999.

Three important patterns appear in Figures 3.3 and 3.4. First, each successive cohort of young adults was better informed about the smoking-to-lung-cancer risk than had been young adults a few years earlier. In 1954 only 36 percent of the youngest adults (those aged twenty-one to twenty-five) said that smoking was a cause of lung cancer. That figure was 60 percent for the later cohorts of youngest adults in 1960, 81 percent in 1969, 82 percent in 1977, and 98 percent in 1990. The changes among young adults' beliefs best capture health advocates' successful efforts in American schools.

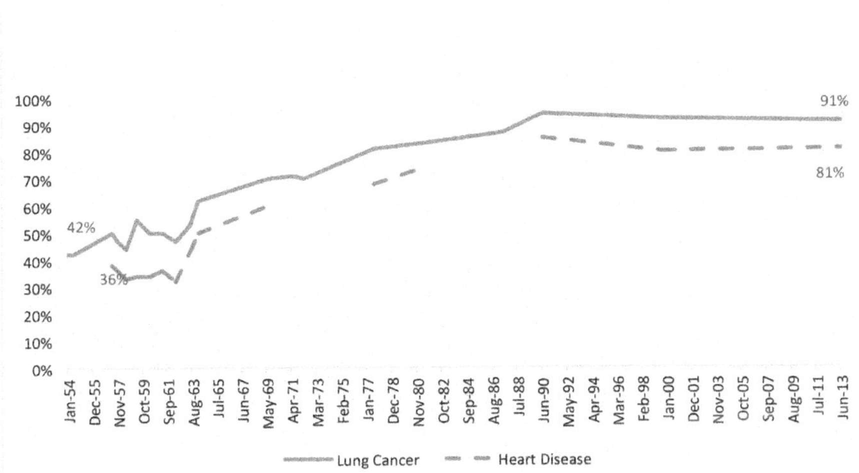

Figure 3.2. Americans' beliefs that cigarette smoking is a cause of lung cancer or heart disease, 1954–2013.

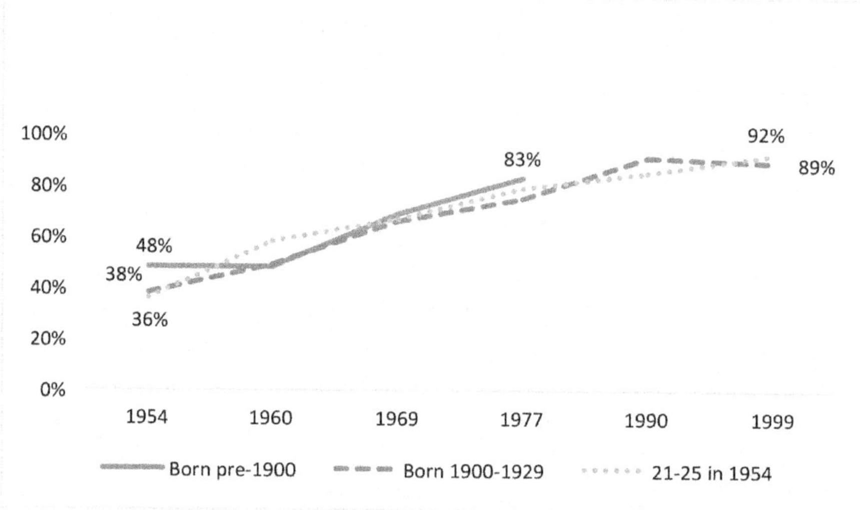

Figure 3.3. Rising beliefs that cigarette smoking is a cause of lung cancer, three oldest cohorts.

Second, each new cohort of young adults was better informed about smoking and lung cancer than were older adults at the time. With one notable exception, the 1962 to 1964 time period around the original Surgeon General's report, rising knowledge that cigarette smoking is a lung cancer risk is partly due to generational replacement. The steady addition of better-informed young adults after the mid-1950s, together with the death of older and less well-informed generations, helps to explain rising knowledge about the lung cancer risks of smoking.

Third, each cohort's health knowledge grew slowly and gradually throughout adult life. For example, in 1954 only a third (36 percent) of young adults aged twenty-one to twenty-five believed that smoking cigarettes is a cause of lung cancer. Among this particular group that 36 percent figure rose to 58 percent in 1960 (when this group was twenty-seven to thirty-one years old), and then to 67 percent in 1969, to 79 percent in 1977, to 85 percent in 1990, and to 92 percent in 1999. Learning about the health risks of smoking did not cease after high school and college but increased throughout adult life. Gains in adult learning were largest during a person's twenties. Not until a person's thirties and thereafter did the rate of learning about the lung cancer risks of smoking drop off. By decade, the largest adult learning gains occurred during the 1960s when the first Surgeon General's report was issued.

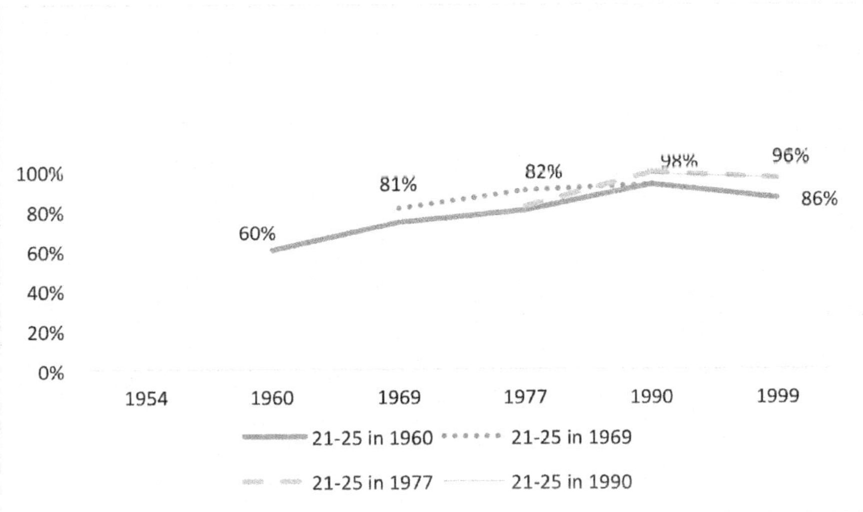

Figure 3.4. Rising beliefs that cigarette smoking is a cause of lung cancer, four younger cohorts.

SECONDHAND SMOKE, ADDICTION, BIRTH DEFECTS, AND THROAT CANCER

The charge that cigarette smoking causes many illnesses other than lung cancer and heart disease is not a new one.[33] During the early 1900s the anti-cigarette movement so accused cigarettes. In Gallup's January 1954 open-ended poll question, those Americans who said smoking was a serious health risk named a wide variety of diseases. By 2014 thirty-three Surgeon General's reports had linked smoking to many different diseases with the 2014 report adding diabetes, rheumatoid arthritis, tuberculosis, colorectal cancer, age-related macular degeneration, immune functions, ectopic pregnancy, men's erectile dysfunction, and liver cancer to the list (U.S. Surgeon General 2014). Only a few poll questions, if any at all, measure Americans' beliefs on many of these illnesses, but for secondhand smoke, addiction, birth defects, and throat cancer, enough poll questions exist to track over-time belief changes and to examine the impact of key events.[34]

Secondhand Smoking

Secondhand smoke, sometimes also called environmental tobacco smoke (or ETS), side stream smoke, involuntary smoking, or passive smoking, became a high-profile issue during the 1970s. This presented cigarette manufacturers with a serious problem since smoking could harm nonsmoking adults and children, not just smokers themselves (Glantz 1996: 391–435; Proctor 2011: 303–04; Trichopoulos et al. 1981). High-profile reports on secondhand smoke include a 1981 Japanese study showing higher lung cancer rates among the nonsmoking wives of husbands who smoked compared to nonsmoking wives of husbands who did not smoke; U.S. Surgeon General reports in 1972, 1975, 1979, 1982, 1986, and 2006; a 1986 National Academy of Science report; a 1992 Environmental Protection Agency report that labeled secondhand smoke as a human carcinogen; a 1997 California study linking secondhand smoke to cardiovascular problems; a 1998 British report; and a 2002 World Health Organization report. Early restrictions on public smoking included federal rules for airlines in 1973 and for buses in 1974; statewide laws in Arizona (in 1973), Connecticut (1974), and Minnesota (1975); and local ordinances in Madison, Wisconsin (1976), Berkeley, California (1977) and San Francisco (1983). Vigorous, if loosely-organized grass-roots efforts sprung up to press for restrictions on smoking in public places. A growing number of states, localities, federal agencies, and businesses restricted smoking in workplaces, bars, restaurants, and hotels (Bayer and Colgrove 2002). The "nonsmokers' rights" movement did not always succeed in restricting smoking in public places, but succeeded often enough to worry the tobacco industry and its pollsters (Hanauer, Barr, and Glantz 1996; Kloepfer 1985; Nathanson 1999; Roper 1978: 8–10). Several pollsters queried the issue, including the cigarette industry's pollsters.[35] The cigarette industry disputed the evidence on secondhand smoking, tried to frame the issue as one of personal freedom and common courtesy, and worked to slow the growing number of public smoking restrictions (Barnes and Bero 1998; Brandt 2007: 279–315; Landman, Cortese, and Glantz 2008; Oreskes and Conway 2010: 136–62; Ong and Glantz 2000; Pacheco 2013; Proctor 2008, 2011; U.S. Surgeon General 2014: 26–29).[36]

Figure 3.5 depicts three poll series, each based on different question wording including six Roper poll questions for the Tobacco Institute between 1974 and 1984; two Cambridge Reports poll questions, one each in 1985 and 1987; and eighteen Gallup Poll questions between 1994 and 2015.[37] The Roper results show a large increase in beliefs that secondhand smoking *"probably is hazardous"*—from 46 percent in 1974 to 58 percent in 1980, a 3 percent annual rate of change. This rapid increase apparently resulted from early grass-roots efforts, from the Surgeon General's 1972 and 1975 statements, and from rising media attention. Another sharp increase from 58 percent to 68 percent occurred between 1980 and 1984, well before the 1986 studies cited above. Early reports and grass-roots activism effectively raised public awareness even if the scientific evidence was less complete and the activism less extensive than it would become in later years (Bayer and Colgrove 2002; Pacheco 2013). As a 1978 Roper report cautioned its client, the Tobacco Institute: "The issue, as we see it, is no longer what the smoker does to himself, but what he does to others. . . . (T)he battle to convince the public of the dangers of passive smoking is in the process of being lost, if indeed it is not already over" (Roper 1978: 8, 10).

By comparison, the 1986 National Academy of Science report and the landmark 1986 Surgeon General report had less immediate impact on Americans' beliefs. In an October 1985 Cambridge poll, 31 percent of Americans said that inhaling secondhand smoke is a *"very serious"* health threat; in June 1987 that figure was 32 percent. Nor had the 1997 California study an immediate effect. In 1994 61 percent of Americans called secondhand smoke *"a serious health risk"* and in 1998 62 percent did.[38]

In Gallup Polls beliefs that secondhand smoke is *"very harmful"* to adults show a large, albeit irregular increase of about 6 percent annually (from 36 percent in 1994 to 55 percent in 1997 and perhaps attributable to Congressional hearings and state lawsuits) well after the two 1986 reports and the 1992 EPA report.[39] However, no increases appear thereafter or from before until after a 2006 Surgeon General's report. Also notable is a large gap in beliefs between smokers and nonsmokers, averaging a little over 30 percent, with smokers more skeptical about secondhand smoke. By the early 2010s half to two-thirds of nonsmokers considered secondhand smoke to be *"very harmful"* but only a quarter to a third of smokers did so. To summarize: Americans have grown much more knowledgeable about the health risks of secondhand smoke since the early 1970.[40]

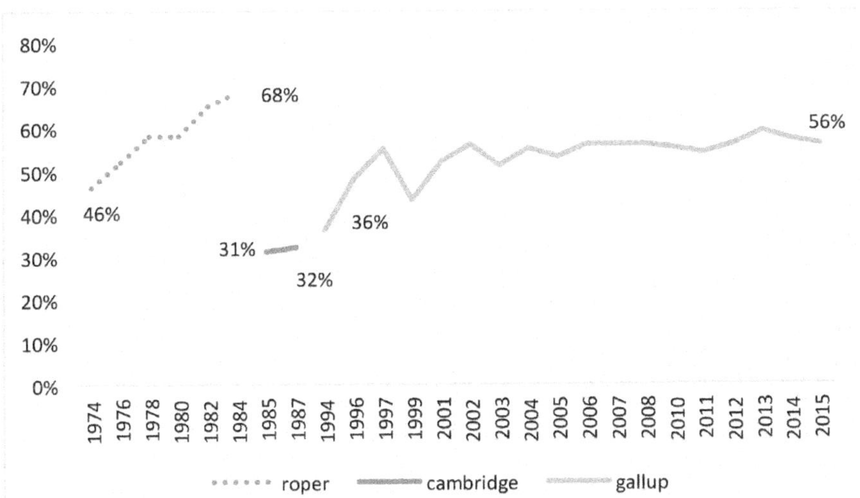

Figure 3.5. Rising beliefs that secondhand smoke is harmful, 3 poll series 1974–2015.

These gains were chiefly due to grass-roots activism, Congressional hearings, lawsuits, lifetime adult learning, and generational replacement.[41]

Addiction

Before the 1970s cigarette smoking was typically described as a habit rather than as an addiction. The 1964 Surgeon General's report so described cigarette smoking on the grounds that few smokers had obvious personality disorders, that withdrawal symptoms were ordinarily mild, that many smokers intermittently stopped and started smoking, and that smokers typically did not continually increase the number of cigarettes smoked daily. During the 1970s and 1980s most researchers abandoned the "habit" description and focused on nicotine's addictive qualities and on how cigarettes so efficiently delivered nicotine (Proctor 2011: 376–81; Schelling 1992). A landmark 1988 U.S. Surgeon General's report, summarizing these findings, pointed to nicotine as the addictive agent in cigarettes, a view that office had described more cautiously in 1979 and that cigarette manufacturers themselves had long studied (Glantz et al. 1996; Hurt and Robertson 1998; Hilts 1996; Lewan 1998; Proctor 2011). Many substitutes for cigarette smoking came onto the market including chewing gums, skin patches, lozenges, and nasal sprays. High-profile events on addiction include the 1988 Surgeon General's report; two spring 1994 ABC *Day One* news programs charging that manufacturers "spiked," that is, added nicotine to cigarettes; and 1994 Congressional hearings at which cigarette industry executives, televised and under oath, said that they did not believe nicotine was addictive, a claim later abandoned in 1997 when cigarette executives publicly conceded the addiction issue.[42]

Poll questions on addiction can be difficult to interpret since the word "addiction" is widely and colloquially used, and since many people (and some pollsters) seemingly use the words "addiction" and "habit" interchangeably.[43] Soon after the 1964 Surgeon General's report was released, pollsters asked several questions about the perceived difficulty of quitting smoking without using the word "addiction." The results were mixed. In the federal government's spring 1966 Use of Tobacco survey 62 percent of all respondents (and 56 percent of current smokers) agreed that "*most cigarette smokers can stop if they want to,*" but large majorities (66 percent of all respondents and 60 percent of smokers) also disagreed that "*a cigarette smoker can always quit later in life in plenty of time to avoid any bad effects.*" A 1978 to 1982 Roper poll series asked whether smoking was "*only a habit*" or whether it was "*an addiction.*" The percentage saying a habit fell from 50 percent to 45 percent; those saying an addiction rose from 29 percent to 33 percent; those saying "*both*" rose from 15 percent to 19 percent. By 1982 the responses for nonsmokers were 41 percent for "*habit,*" 37 percent for "*addiction,*" and 19 percent for "*both,*" and for smokers the results were 52 percent, 25 percent, and 19 percent, respectively. In a 1984 Roper question 54 percent of smokers and nonsmokers alike said that tobacco was *"a substance a person could be addicted to,"* with *"habit forming but not addictive"* at 44 percent, and with *"neither habit forming nor addictive"* or *"don't know"* at only 3 percent. In short, beliefs that cigarettes were addictive were still incomplete but rising well before the 1979 or 1988 Surgeon General's report, the 1994 ABC news program, or the 1994 Congressional hearings, and due to early scientific news, and related media coverage.

Since 1990 Gallup has queried cigarette smokers (only): *"Do you consider yourself addicted to cigarettes or not?"* As Figure 3.6 shows, between 1990 and 1991 the percentage of smokers who said *"yes, addicted"* rose sharply from 61 percent to 70 percent. However, no short-term changes occurred from before until after the high-profile 1994 events (70 percent in 1991, then 69 percent in 1996) and only a small increase (69 percent in 1996, then 72 percent in 1999) from before until after the 1997 cigarette companies' admissions about addiction and lung cancer. As with secondhand smoke, smokers' beliefs that cigarettes were addictive grew from the 1970s until the early 1990s, but thereafter remained largely flat: 70 percent in 1991 and 72 percent in 2013. The rise in beliefs that cigarettes are addictive is not closely tied to major government reports or exposes. On both issues beliefs have now remained essentially flat for two decades. By Gallup's 2013 polling figures, tens of millions of Americans are not yet convinced either that secondhand smoke is very harmful or that smoking is addictive.

Birth Defects

The 1964 Surgeon General's report described the problem of low birth weights among the newborns of women who smoked. The 1969, 1971, 1973, 1979, 2004, and 2006 Surgeon General reports reported mounting scientific evidence about the risks of smoking for stillbirths, neonatal death, preterm births, restricted fetal growth, and other perinatal or neonatal problems (2014 Surgeon General: 459–89). Regrettably, pollsters have asked few consistently-worded such questions. In a series of Gallup Poll questions ("*. . . do you think that cigarette smoking is or is not one of the causes of birth defects?*") the percentage of Americans saying "yes" rose from 41 percent in 1977 to 54 percent in 1981, 68 percent in 1990, and 67 percent in 1999.[44] The rapid rise in awareness between 1977 and 1981, exceeding an annual rate of 3 percent, suggests that the 1979 Surgeon General's report successfully informed public opinion. Knowledge about birth defects thereafter rose by 1.6 percent annually until 1990, but thereafter not at all.

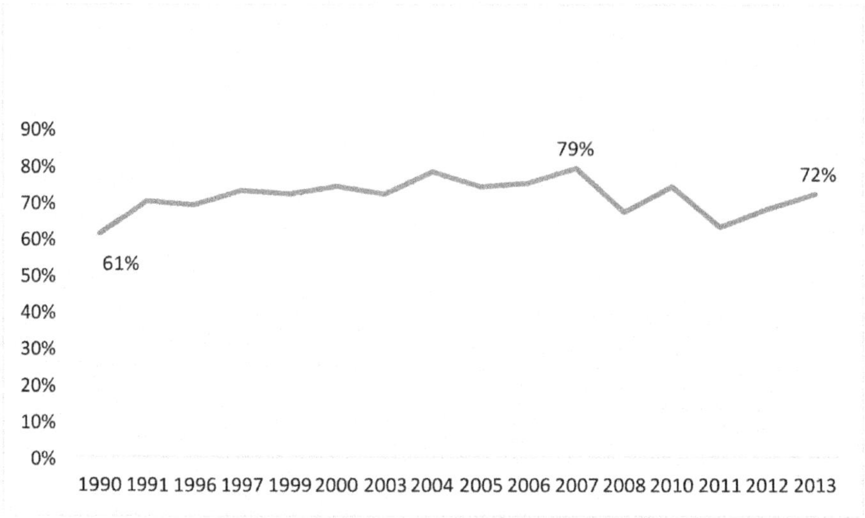

Figure 3.6. Percent of smokers who consider themselves addicted to cigarettes.

Throat Cancer

The 1964 Surgeon General's report causally linked cigarette smoking to laryngeal cancer among men. That report also suggested that tobacco use might cause oral cavity and pharyngeal cancer, relationships that were termed causal in 1979, 1980, and 1982. Pollsters did not ask questions on these issues until the 1970s. In a 1977 Gallup survey 79 percent of adults said that cigarette smoking was a cause of throat cancer. That figure rose to 81 percent in 1981 and to 90 percent in 1999. Four-fifths of Americans already tied smoking to throat cancer even before 1979 Surgeon General's report. After 1977 the slow and steady rise in beliefs—at an annual rate of less than 1 percent—suggest that the Surgeon General's 1979, 1980, and 1982 reports did not greatly affect these beliefs. As in several other areas, a pattern of better-informed younger generations and steady adult learning appears in Gallup's 1977 to 1999 results.[45]

CONCLUSION: UNDERSTANDING THE HEALTH RISKS OF SMOKING

Since the early 1950s Americans clearly have become much more aware of the health risks of cigarette smoking. By the 1990s the belief that that smoking is a cause of lung cancer was Americans' most widely-accepted scientific fact.[46] The belief among smokers that cigarette smoking is addictive is now nearly as widespread. Beliefs on heart disease and secondhand smoke lag not far behind, with beliefs on birth defects further behind. Until the mid-1990s Americans grew steadily better informed about the health risks of smoking although the rate of that progress was often only about 1 percent annually, sometimes less than 1 percent annually, and seldom as much or more than 3 percent annually.

The cigarette industry's record of creating and sustaining controversy on the ills of smoking should be cautiously evaluated. When confronted only by a few well-publicized scientific studies but aided by indifferent, inconsistent, or even tobacco-friendly government policies, the industry successfully sustained a controversy about the ills of smoking for nearly a decade—until 1962 when the original U.S. Surgeon General's advisory committee began its work and 1964 when that committee issued its report. When confronted by that high-profile report, by a vigorous grassroots tobacco control movement, by growing scientific evidence and media coverage on the issue, and by the efforts of American schools, the tobacco industry was far less successful in sustaining that controversy. This pattern was repeated on several other health risks of smoking. Chapter 4 returns to the industry's polling and public relations efforts.

This chapter points to the importance of health-oriented activists and interest groups, American schools, media coverage, scientific research, and the growing number of state and local restrictions of smoking. Except for a few time periods of rapid change due to high-publicity events, Americans' beliefs about the health risks of smoking typically change only slowly and through a gradual process of generational change and lifetime adult learning. Health-oriented activists and interest groups, American schools, new scientific evidence, and media coverage can sometimes speed up this slow progress.

Government policies, reports, and exposes can increase health knowledge but the record is very mixed. The rapid increases in health knowledge resulting from the 1964 Surgeon General's advisory committee report and from the struggles over secondhand smoking during the early to mid-1970s are exceptions to the norm. Many reports or policies did not immediately increase health knowledge, among these the 1965 package warnings, the 1967 fairness doctrine, and several later scientific and most Surgeon General reports. Some federal policies probably slowed the rise in health knowledge, among these the Federal Trade Commission's on-and-off-again policy-making during the 1950s and the 1971 broadcast ban. The limited polling evidence does not allow a clear conclusion, but other policies likely slowed the rise in Americans' health knowledge—such as the federal government's long-standing policies allowing cigarette sales on military bases (Smith, Blackman, and Malone 2007) and on Indian reservations; the federal courts' several cigarette-friendlier decisions; and the U.S. Food and Drug Administration's slow-moving regulatory process. Chapter 5 returns to federal-level policy issues.

Two issues deserve more attention. Americans' growing knowledge about the ills of smoking, including lung cancer, heart disease, secondhand smoking, birth defects, and (for smokers) addiction stalled during and after the mid-1990s. Admittedly, public knowledge of the lung cancer risk may have reached a practical ceiling, but knowledge about heart disease, secondhand smoke, birth defects, and addiction all stagnated at a lower level. The reasons for this are unclear since at the time state and local anti-smoking ballot initiatives fared relatively well, since there were several government reports and news reports critical of smoking, and since several anti-smoking publicity campaigns were then being funded (Davis 1995). Arguably, recent reports by the U.S. Surgeon General and other scientific research have not produced any high-profile breakthroughs. New tobacco products, including e-cigarettes and light, mild, slim, or ultra-slim cigarettes, may have led some Americans to believe that the cigarette smoking is now less of a serious health problem.[47] The declining percentage of smokers coupled with limits on public smoking may for some nonsmokers reduce awareness of the problem. The long-stalled progress on requiring graphic warnings on cigarette package and the Food and Drug Administration's slow-moving, low-visibility rule-making process may also reduce public concerns. The schools' educational efforts may have weakened, as witness the fading patterns of better-informed young adults on some issues such as birth defects.

Many Americans still do not accept that cigarette smoking can lead to some major illnesses and many smokers yet do not fully recognize their own health risks. Since the late 1940s most Americans have known that cigarette smoking is harmful and since the mid-1960s most Americans have known that smoking can cause lung cancer. On many other illnesses public knowledge remains much lower. Many Americans underestimate the risks to their own health or believe that they can quit smoking in time to avoid ill health (Slovic 2001; cf., Viscusi 1992, 1994). Nor do most smokers know very many specific facts about cigarette construction or its additives (Kozlowski et al., 1996). Depending on the poll question and the illness, this lack of knowledge may include only a third, a fifth, or a tenth of all Americans, but, even so, this is tens of millions of Americans. Gaps in health awareness between smokers and nonsmokers remain stubbornly large—depending upon the illness in question, a gap of 10 percent and sometimes up to 30 percent. Six decades of scientific and government reports, media coverage, and educational efforts have yet not closed the knowledge gap between smokers and nonsmokers and seem unlikely soon to do so.

NOTES

1. "Cigarette-Cancer Question Is Left Open in Report," *New York Times*, June 27, 1954: 53 and "Tobacco Tied to Rising Death Toll in British Doctors' Lung Cancer," *New York Times*, June 25, 1954: 3. For a review, see Talley, Kushner, and Sterk (2004) and Whelan (1984): 81–96. For a later American Cancer Society study see Stellman and Garfinkel (1986, 1989).

2. Half a century later continued cigarette smokers among this cohort of British doctors (born 1900 to 1930) had died an average of ten years before lifelong non-smokers. Cessation at age sixty, fifty, forty, or thirty regained three, six, nine, or ten years of life expectancy, respectively (Doll et al. 2004).

3. The *New York Times* coverage is similar to that of the *Reader's Guide to Periodical Literature* (Troyer and Markle 1983: 57–59; Baumgartner and Jones 2009: 90–93, 114–17, 257–59; Ford, Ringold, and Rogers 1990) although the *Times* typically prints more stories on tobacco-related issues than do other major newspapers (Nelson et al. 2015). For evidence that media coverage generally favors the tobacco control movement, see Smith, Wakefield, and Edsall (2006).

4. Gallup polled the cigarette smoking and lung cancer issue twenty times between 1954 and 2013 either in publicly-available polls or in polls conducted for the tobacco industry. The former may be found in iPOLL; the latter are available in the Legacy Tobacco Documents on-line library at http://legacy.library.ucsf. Gallup results herein are based on the question, "*Do you think that cigarette smoking is one of the causes of lung cancer, or not?*" or close wording variations thereof. These questions may slightly under-count the percentage of Americans who link smoking to lung cancer since some Americans confuse symptoms with causes or else report higher smoking-to-cancer beliefs with other question wording (Toch, Allen, and Lazer 1961a, 1961b). The phrasing "*a cause*" yields higher estimates of health risk than does the phrasing "*a major cause*" used by several other pollsters.

5. The Tobacco Institute, the Council for Tobacco Research, and the later-created Center for Indoor Air Research were dissolved under the 1998 Master Settlement Agreement.

6. By 1972 filters won 84 percent of sales and 99 percent of advertising expenditures (Friedman 1975: 30). The "Big Six" cigarette manufacturers also increased their sales overseas, diversified by purchasing nontobacco companies, and in three cases were acquired by another conglomerate (Cullman 1998; Friedman 1975: 33–37; Jones 1997).

7. The 1959, 1960, 1961, 1962, 1963, and 1964 Gallup reports entitled "Trends in Public Attitudes on the Possibility of a Health Hazard in Cigarette Smoking" and related documents are available through the on-line legacy archive.

8. Elmo Roper and Associates, "A Study of Cigarette Smokers' Habits and Attitudes in 1960," Vol. 1: "*As compared to non-filters, do you think that all filters give you more protection than non-filters, or that only the high filtration filters give you any added protection but other filters don't, or that none of the filter brands give you any added protection?*"

9. See, for example, Gallup Poll, "A Study of Cigarette Smokers' Attitudes toward Smoking and Related Issues," April 1969: "*Do you think there are some cigarettes or types of cigarettes that are less hazardous than others, or not?*" in which 49 percent of smokers said that some cigarettes are less hazardous than others, 31 percent disagreed, with 21 percent don't know. In a 1967 Roper survey 45 percent of smokers said that some cigarettes were more harmful than others and 44 percent said that all cigarettes are about the same. Filter cigarettes' popularity did not rest solely on lower perceived health risks. In a March 1960 Roper survey, for example, the most common reason smokers gave for smoking filters was that "*they keep tobacco out of your mouth*" (at 61 percent), with 38 percent saying that "*they are easier on the throat*" and 28 percent apiece saying that "*they are safer*" or that "*they are better tasting*"; see Elmo Roper and Associates, "A Study of Cigarette Smokers' Habits and Attitudes in 1960," Vol. 1, April 1960.

10. For an early review of low tar and nicotine cigarettes, see Federal Trade Commission (1981: 1–57). Any benefit from lower tar content was often offset by smokers' covering the ventilation holes, drawing in more heavily, smoking more cigarettes, or smoking more of each cigarette (Proctor 2011: 357–76). Nor did low tar and nicotine cigarettes, lights, or ultralight cigarettes reduce the effects of harmful gasses and additives (Proctor 2011: 381–417).

11. Neither a 1957 House subcommittee report critical of filter cigarettes nor Oregon Senator Maurine Neuberger's frequent criticisms of the cigarette industry led to further action (Brandt 2007: 246–47). The Food and Drug Administration declined to require warning labels on cigarette packages under the 1960 Hazardous Substance Labeling Act's provision covering illnesses produced through inhalation (Neuberger 1963: 49–50, 129). Neither did any U.S. Cabinet secretaries nor the American Medical Association at the time pursue the issue (Whelan 1984: 97–98; Harkness 2007; Talley, Kushner, and Sterk 2004: 354–56; Cortas and Talley 2006).

12. A 1962 British report, *Smoking and Health* (1962), linked cigarette smoking to lung cancer, bronchitis, coronary heart disease, ulcers, and tuberculosis, but the British report received little attention from the American media and did not increase Americans' health knowledge (Berridge 2007; Marshall 2015: 23).

13. The survey, conducted by Public Opinion Surveys, appears in *Saturday Evening Post*, August 1961: 6.

14. *Smoking and Health* (1964: 7); Brandt (2007: 219); "Kennedy Promises Reply On Smoking," *New York Times*, May 24, 1962: 26.

15. For the tobacco industry's review of proposed names, see a Hill and Knowlton memo entitled "Nominees to committee," available at http://legacy.library.ucsf.edu/tid/ege66b00/pdf.

16. These results are based on a stratified (by region and circulation) sample of 49 of the 100 largest American newspapers. About a third of newspapers published stories on Friday or Saturday, January 10 or 11 describing the upcoming report and often speculating as to what the report might include. Only minor differences in coverage exist by region, circulation size, or if the newspaper was from a tobacco-growing region. The *Atlanta Constitution*, the *Los Angeles Times*, the *Chicago Tribune*, and the *New York Times* printed an average of twelve further smoking-related news stories and two front-page stories, per paper, during the remainder of January 1954. Transcripts of television coverage for CBS and ABC may be found in the Legacy Tobacco Documents Library. Newspaper coverage and the Hill and Knowlton polls indicate that several television news reports or special programs aired after the Surgeon General's report was issued.

17. Pollsters asked many other questions on health beliefs during this time period but except as reported herein, none both before and after the release of the 1964 Surgeon General's report. Widespread public uncertainty existed about exactly how great a lung cancer risk cigarette smoking was. For other diseases the level of health knowledge was much lower than for lung cancer. In the federal government's fall 1964 and spring 1966 Use of Tobacco surveys, 65 percent and 66 percent, respectively, said that cigarette smoking is definitely or probably a major cause of lung cancer; the figures among current smokers were 53 percent and 59 percent, respectively. On whether a smoker's chances of getting lung cancer were greater than for a nonsmoker, 68 percent in 1964 and 69 percent in 1966 said yes; for coronary heart disease, the figures were 41 percent and 44 percent, and for emphysema and chronic bronchitis, 51 percent and 51 percent. In a 1968 Roper survey (1970) 20 percent of respondents said that cigarettes were the major cause of smokers having more of "certain (unspecified) illnesses" than nonsmokers; 50 percent said smoking was only one of many causes; 3 percent said don't know; and 27 percent disagreed that smokers had more illnesses. A 1981 Federal Trade Commission report and a 1989 U.S. Surgeon General's report review many of these polls.

18. Average annual rates of belief change averaged 3.5 percent for poll questions on whether AIDS can be transmitted from a toilet seat (a CBS/*New York Times* poll series

from 1985 to 1993), by working near someone with AIDS, by attending school with a child who has AIDS, or by eating in a restaurant where the cook has AIDS (a National Center for Health Statistics poll series from 1987 to 1992); see also Singer, Rogers, and Corcoran (1987) and Singer, Rogers, and Glassman (1991).

19. Public opinion changed at an annual rate of about 1 percent on whether children of different races should attend the same school (a 1954 to 1994 Gallup Poll series); whether a respondent would vote for a well-qualified woman, Jew, Catholic, or black for president (a Gallup series, 1945–2003, 1958–1987, 1940–2003, and 1958–2003, respectively); whether white people have a right to keep blacks out of their neighborhoods (a 1964 to 1996 NORC series); and whether there should be laws against racial intermarriage (a 1963 to 2002 NORC series).

20. The tobacco industry's low-key response calling for further research, reflected disagreements within the industry on how best to react to the report (Kluger 1997: 260–61; Brandt 2007: 230–37).

21. The CDC reported a 3.5 percent drop in per-capita cigarette consumption for 1964, compared to an 8.9 percent two-year per-capita drop during the 1953–1954 "cancer scare." Gallup surveys showed a small drop (from 51 percent to 47 percent) in adults' smoking rates between June 1963 and February/March 1964, but no drop in the average daily number of cigarettes smoked by current smokers. Among men smoking prevalence began a long-term decline in 1965, but for women not until the mid-1970s (Warner 2006: 22–23). For a discussion of the effects of health warnings and cigarette advertising on cigarette consumption during this time period, see Seldon and Doroodian (1989)

22. In the 1964 American National Election Study 78 percent of Americans said that "*you can trust the government in Washington to do what's right*" either "*just about always*" or "*most of the time*." That figure fell to 25 percent by 1980, then rose and fell again and was 30 percent in 2008. The 1964 Surgeon General's report occurred at a time when the federal government was enacting many new programs including the Peace Corps, anti-poverty programs, Medicare, Medicaid, federal aid to education, mass transit, mental health, civil rights, public broadcasting, endowments for the arts and humanities, consumer protection, and environmental programs (Cross 2001: 291–93).

23. Research in health cognition, psychology, and risk analysis now views continued cigarette smoking as influenced by a smoker's level of addiction and smoking history; education, social, family, and peer situation; restrictions on advertising and public smoking; and taxes, and not solely a smoker's beliefs in the smoking-to-disease link (Bogart and Delahanty 2004: 214–28; Fisher et al, 2002; Kenkel 1991; Weinstein 1998, 1999, 2001, 2004, 2005; Weinstein and Waters 2004). Typically smokers, particularly adolescents underestimate their risks and overestimate their own ability to quit smoking in the future (Slovic 1998; Weinstein, Slovic, and Gibson 2004a).

24. The FTC proposed one of two warnings: "CAUTION—CIGARETTE SMOKING IS A HEALTH HAZARD. The Surgeon General's Advisory committee has found that cigarette smoking contributes to mortality from specific diseases and to the overall death rate." or "CAUTION: Cigarette smoking is dangerous to health. It may cause death from cancer and other diseases."

25. At the time few federal requirements for consumer products existed (Viscusi 2002: 136–39).

26. In 1969 the warning became "The Surgeon General Has Determined That Cigarette Smoking Is Dangerous to Your Health."

27. In 1964 cigarette manufacturers adopted a voluntary code of advertising; for a critique see Richards, Tye, and Fischer (1996) and Pollay (1994a, 1994b)

28. In a 1978 Roper survey conducted for the Tobacco Institute, a 61 to 34 percent majority favored a new warning label ("Warning: Cigarette smoking is dangerous to health, and may cause death from cancer, coronary heart disease, chronic bronchitis, pulmonary emphysema and other diseases") instead of the then-current "Warning: The Surgeon General has determined that cigarette smoking is dangerous to your

health." By a 69 to 26 percent majority nonsmokers favored the stronger wording; smokers were evenly split, 47 to 47 percent.

29. Current research suggests that an effective package warning should be large; rotate periodically; appear on otherwise "plain" packages; include pictures; appear on the front and back (not the side) of a cigarette package; and emphasize losses and the immediate, not distant health or social risks; current U.S. package warning labels achieve none of these goals (Hammond et al. 2006, 2007; Hammond 2011, 2012; Bansal-Travers et al. 2011; O'Hegarty et al. 2006; Thrasher et al. 2011).

30. Lewit, Coate, and Grossman (1981: 546) put the number of anti-smoking ads that aired at 1,300 in 1968 and at 1,560 in 1970, representing a market value of $75 million, about one-third of the value of cigarette commercials.

31. The 1971 broadcast ban did not prohibit cigarette manufacturers from sponsoring widely-viewed sports events nor prohibit the paid placement of cigarettes on television programs or in movies, for none of which was counter-advertising required (Pollay 1994a, 1994b).

32. The C. E. Hooper survey "Smoking Attitude Survey" and accompanying documents may be found in the on-line legacy tobacco documents archive.

33. For a review of other illnesses associated with cigarette smoking see Samet (2001).

34. Both a 1981 Federal Trade Commission report and a 1989 report from the U.S. Surgeon General review these polls.

35. A 1978 Roper report suggested that restaurants, cabs, and other public places post signs describing their own smoking policies as *"a short term tactic that might prove helpful in situations where widespread smoking restrictions are being proposed."*

36. Restricting smoking in public places also reduces cigarette consumption (Glantz and Jamieson 2000; Pierce, Gilpin, and Farkas 1998). For an argument that the American overestimate the risks of secondhand smoking, see Viscusi (2002: 101–32).

37. The Roper question is: *"Well, as you probably know, some people have said it's bad even to be around people who smoke because of the smoke you inhale even if you're not smoking yourself. How do you feel about that—do you think it probably is hazardous to your health to be around people who are smoking, even when you're not smoking yourself, or that is probably doesn't have any real effect on your health?"* The Cambridge Reports question is: *"Recently there has been a lot of discussion about the potential health threats to non-smokers from tobacco smoke in public buildings, restaurants and business offices. How serious a health threat to you personally is the inhaling of this secondhand smoke, often called passive smoking? Is it a very serious health threat, somewhat serious, not too serious, or not serious at all?"* The Gallup question is: *"In general, how harmful do you feel secondhand smoke is to adults?"* For a comparison of Americans' beliefs about the harm of secondhand versus third-hand smoke in 2005 see Winickoff et al. (2009).

38. The March 1994 ABC/*Washington Post* poll question is *"Do you feel that secondhand cigarette smoke is a health risk or not"* and if yes: *"Would you call it a serious health risk or not serious?"* The October 1998 Marist poll question is: *"Do you feel that secondhand smoke is a serious health risk, a minor health risk, or not a health risk at all?"* Gallup's figures show a decline in beliefs that secondhand smoke is *"very harmful"* from 55 percent in June 1997 to 43 percent in September 1999; the latter figure may be an anomaly.

39. Indirect evidence on the 1986 Surgeon General report's impact is by comparing the 1986 Adult Use of Tobacco survey, conducted prior to the issuance of the 1986 report, to a 1987 NHIS survey or to a 1987 Gallup survey for the American Cancer Society. Eighty-one percent of adults said that secondhand smoke was harmful to nonsmokers in all three surveys, suggesting that the 1986 Surgeon General's report had no short-term impact on public opinion. As a caveat, the three questions are slightly differently worded.

40. Support for smoke-free bars, restaurants, indoor workplaces, malls, sporting events, and hospitals increased through the early 2000s and across a wide variety of demographic groups (Osypuk and Acevedo-Garcia 2010).

41. Until 1999 beliefs that secondhand smoke is *"very harmful"* rose by roughly 1 percent a year for most adult age groups; each new group of young adults (age eighteen to twenty-four) was also better informed than were older adults. For reasons that are not clear, after 1999 both patterns ceased among younger adults.

42. Cummings, Brown, and Douglas (2006) and Waxman (2003) argue that the industry's admissions were incomplete and inconsistent, particularly so in lawsuits.

43. See, for example, Harris Poll (2000, 2001).

44. In a differently worded (*"the mother smoking during pregnancy"*) 2006 Gallup question 88 percent said yes.

45. Among the youngest adults, those eighteen to twenty-five years old, beliefs that smoking caused throat cancer were 82 percent in 1977 and 92 percent in 1999. Between 1977 and 1999 adult learning also clearly occurred; among specific age cohorts beliefs about throat cancer rose from 76 percent to 90 percent for the "cigarette generation" (those born 1900 to 1929), from 82 percent to 86 percent for those born between 1930 and 1951, and from 82 percent to 92 percent for those born between 1952 and 1959.

46. In the National Science Foundation's 1985 to 2001 "game show" questions, available through iPOLL, Americans' beliefs that *"cigarette smoking causes lung cancer"* ranged from 91 percent to 96 percent—a higher level of beliefs than on any other question including whether the sun goes around the earth, whether the center of the earth is very hot, whether the earliest humans lived at the same time as dinosaurs, and whether electrons are smaller than atoms (Miller 1998). For evidence that smoking was viewed as a relatively high-risk behavior, at least by well-educated Americans, see Slovic (1987). For the impact of question wording, see Slovic (1998).

47. For evidence that cigarette packages could convey the same impression see Kotnowski and Hammond (2013)

FOUR

Polls and the Battle over Smoking

The tobacco industry first began to use polling during the early 1950s when Philip Morris commissioned several large-scale surveys as part of its efforts better to market their new filter-tip brands, to target consumer groups such as college students or African-Americans, and to sharpen their advertising messages.[1] By the early 1960s other cigarette manufacturers, Hill and Knowlton, and the Tobacco Institute hired top polling firms including Roper, Gallup, and Opinion Research Corporation. In later years many other nationally- or regionally-known pollsters, focus group, advertising, and marketing firms also conducted surveys for the industry, among them Gallup & Robinson; Response Analysis Corporation; C. E. Hooper; Foote, Cone & Belding; Audits & Surveys; Mason-Dixon Opinion Research; Zogby International; the Wirthlin Group; Tarrance & Associates; Charlton Research Company; Louis Harris and Associates; Roper Starch Worldwide; Peter D. Hart Research Associates; Frederick Polls, Penn and Schoen; Fabrizio, McLaughlin & Associates; Yankelovich Skelly & White; Yankelovich Clancy Shulman; National Analysts; Political Surveys and Analyses; Nowland; The Public Sector; and Voter/Consumer Research.[2] The industry steadily expanded its polling efforts to track concerns about the health risks of smoking; to explore the industry's deteriorating image; to track the growing stigma of smoking; to test new and more effective public relations messages; and to fight off anti-smoking efforts at the federal, state, and local level. The industry's many efforts show that it viewed public opinion as of considerable importance. That the tobacco industry compiled only a mixed record of successes and failures, despite all its efforts, tells an important story about how difficult it is effectively to manage American public opinion.

TRACKING EARLY CONCERNS ABOUT SMOKING

The tobacco industry's polling efforts began during the 1953–1954 "cancer scare" period and just as filter cigarettes were becoming popular. A growing number of scientific reports and Gallup's publicly-reported poll questions had focused public attention on the smoking-and-health issue. Beginning in the early 1950s polls conducted for Philip Morris included a few health-oriented questions in its otherwise marketing and advertising-focused polling.[3] Hill and Knowlton, the Tobacco Institute, and several cigarette manufacturers working jointly commissioned polls on the public's beliefs about smoking and health and on attitudes toward possible government policies. These early polls include a 1959 to 1964 Gallup series of poll questions, a 1960 to 1976 Roper Poll series for Philip Morris, and a 1967 to 1984 series of Roper polls.[4] By the late 1960s the industry's regularly-commissioned Roper reports acknowledged that most Americans believed that cigarette smoking was a cause of lung cancer and heart disease. Confirming that result were several Gallup surveys; the federal government's Use of Tobacco surveys in 1964, 1966, 1970, 1976, and 1986; and surveys conducted by the American Cancer Society and the American Lung Association.

Within a decade the industry's pollsters acknowledged the same result for secondhand smoking. A 1978 Roper report warned the industry that its efforts had not persuaded Americans that secondhand smoke was harmless. For several more years industry-sponsored Roper polls continued to track the issue, but Americans' beliefs that secondhand smoke was a serious health threat steadily rose. Occasionally one of the industry's pollsters suggested a new approach. For example, a 1972 Roper proposal to the Tobacco Institute proposed a large-scale study that might tie smokers' ill health to a wide range of "excessive behaviors" rather than solely to smoking.[5] Yet even high quality polling could not "fix" the industry's increasingly serious public opinion problems. The industry's polling later turned its attention to other issues including public perceptions of new cigarette brands with lower tar and lower nicotine, the so-called "light" cigarettes.[6]

However dated these early polls seem, the industry's early surveys remain important in two ways. In debates over enacting stricter warning labels and advertising restrictions the cigarette industry often argued that further regulations were not needed since there had long been widespread public awareness of the health issue and a high level of public belief that smoking was harmful.[7] Tobacco control advocates argued the opposite. The tobacco industry also used polling evidence of public knowledge about the health risks of smoking as a defense in lawsuits brought by smokers who suffer from smoking-related illnesses. In its legal defenses the industry's expert witnesses often argued that by the 1960s a typical smoker would almost certainly have heard a great deal about the health-and-smoking issue and might well have known that cigarette smoking could cause lung cancer and other diseases—thus absolving cigarette companies from liability. Many expert witnesses, mostly historians, debated whether or when Americans had a "common knowledge" about the health hazards of smoking and whether or how much the industry's advertising practices and concealment of research documents reduced the public's knowledge of these health risks (Kyriakoudes 2006; Proctor 2011: 305–16, 459–81).[8]

TRACKING THE TOBACCO INDUSTRY'S IMAGE

The industry's pollsters closely followed the tobacco industry's increasingly negative image and declining credibility. After the mid-1960s the cigarette industry's unfavorable image became one of its most serious and steadily-worsening problems, notwithstanding the industry's best public relations efforts (Glantz et al. 1996: 354–63). In Roper polls conducted between 1968 and 1986 the percent of Americans who held a favorable view on "*the way they (the tobacco industry) have reacted to the controversy on smoking and health*" dropped from 51 percent to 37 percent. The percentage of respondents who said that the tobacco industry "*knows it's true*" ("*about the case against cigarettes*") rose from 36 percent to 57 percent, a rate of change of about 1 percent annually. In 1970 when asked to choose which of six different kinds of organizations were the most reliable sources of information on smoking and health, most (62 percent) respondents picked "*organizations like the American Cancer Society,*" half (47 percent) picked "*organizations like the American Medical Association,*" but only 11 percent picked government agencies and only 3 percent picked the tobacco companies. During the 1960s, 1970s, and 1980s surveys by Roper, Opinion Research Corporation, Gallup, and Cambridge Reports all reported that the tobacco industry ranked as one of the less favorably rated and sometimes even as the least favorably rated of large American industries, companies, or interest groups. Depending upon the poll question's timing and wording, only a fifth to a third of respondents typically reported favorable opinions of the tobacco industry or of its leading companies such as Philip Morris. In a 1975 Roper survey, for example, respondents ranked a tobacco company in last place (at only 2 percent from a list of thirteen types of companies) as a company that they would like to work for, but in first place (at 30 percent) as a company they would not like to work for.

The industry's image did not improve in later years (McDaniel and Malone 2009: 452). In a 1998 Time/CNN/Yankelovich survey two-thirds (65 percent) of Americans said that the tobacco companies "*purposely target young people to get them to start smoking*" and only 32 percent disagreed. In a 1998 NBC/*Wall Street Journal* poll only 9 percent of

Americans said that *"the cigarette industry (is) doing all it can to produce that cigarettes that are not harmful to health"* while 83 percent said that *"they could do more."*[9] In a 1997 Harris Poll 80 percent of Americans said that *"some tobacco companies' marketing campaigns are aimed at children and teenagers."* In Harris Polls conducted between 1998 and 2009 only a quarter to a third of respondents said that the *"tobacco companies generally do a good job of serving their consumers,"* the lowest ratings given to any large industry. In a 1999 Harris Poll only 21 percent of Americans said that they would trust a tobacco company to do the right thing if it had *"a serious safety problem with one of their products or services"*—by far the worst rating of any major industry queried. In a 1997 NBC/*Wall Street Journal* survey Philip Morris Tobacco Company received the lowest positive ratings (only 15 percent) of any person or entity queried. Other polls show similar results. In short, the tobacco industry was already unpopular by the 1960s and in later years stood out as a pariah.

A few poll questions directly compare the credibility of the tobacco industry with that of tobacco control groups. Once again, tobacco companies and their allies fared very poorly. In a 1959 Roper survey conducted for the industry 39 percent of respondents reported that they would be *"most apt to believe"* the American Cancer Society if it *"said that there was no connection whatsoever between lung cancer and cigarette smoking"* but only 3 percent named the Tobacco Industry Research Committee (from a list of seven organizations). Nor did the industry's credibility improve. In a 1992 Wirthlin survey conducted for Philip Morris, Americans rated Philip Morris and RJR Nabisco as the least credible (from a list of seven large corporations) to speak out about scientific and regulatory issues.[10] In a 2000 I.C.R. survey on who could be trusted *"to recommend the right thing to do about underage smoking,"* the American Cancer Society (at 88 percent yes), organizations of children's doctors (at 95 percent yes), and the U.S. Surgeon General (at 71 percent yes) ranked highly but tobacco companies ranked as the lowest (at only 14 percent yes) of all organizations queried. Despite its efforts, individual cigarette companies and the Tobacco Institute never found any effective way to reverse the industry's poor public image and its low credibility. The industry's credibility and image ratings began to drop well before tobacco control advocates regularly began to win local and statewide tobacco control elections, before any successful lawsuits were mounted against the tobacco companies, before any American president openly criticized the industry, before federal actions to restrict smoking in public places, and before tobacco critics opened their the drive to "denormalize" the tobacco industry. The industry's steady drop in public approval can best be attributed to early scientific exposes, grass-roots anti-smoking efforts, and continued media criticism.

In later years, mostly beginning during the 1990s, tobacco control advocates broadened their efforts to "denormalize" and "delegitimize" the tobacco industry. Denormalization describes efforts to weaken the tobacco industry's standing and to worsen its image both in the public's view and among policy-makers. Such efforts include conducting publicity campaigns against tobacco products and against cigarette manufacturers, banning tobacco industry-sponsored research from being published in academic journals or from being conducted at universities, exposing tobacco industry-allied "front" groups, publicizing the industry's internal documents, and encouraging investors to divest from tobacco stocks (Smith and Malone 2003a, 2003b; McDaniel and Malone 2005; McDaniel, Smith, and Malone 2006). Denormalization may reduce smoking rates, particularly among teens and young adults (Malone, Grundy, and Bero 2012). Cigarette manufacturers responded to denormalization efforts in different ways. Most companies did very little but Philip Morris, by then the largest American cigarette manufacturer, sought to reposition itself as a more socially responsible corporation, for example, by conceding the smoking-to-lung cancer connection and in 2003 by changing its corporate name to Altria. That company's thoroughly poll-tested efforts did not go so far as to exit from the cigarette market (McDaniel and Malone 2005, 2012; Yang and Malone 2008).

THE STIGMA OF SMOKING

Just as the tobacco industry's image deteriorated, so did the image of individual smokers—a process often called the creation of stigma or of deviant behavior (Bleda and Sandman 1977; Markle and Troyer 1979; Nuehring and Markle 1974; Troyer and Markle 1983). The earliest such poll questions focused on the annoyance of being near a smoker. In the federal government's 1964, 1966, 1970 and 1975 Use of Tobacco surveys the percentage of Americans who agreed that it is "*annoying to be near a person who is smoking*" steadily rose from 66 percent to 79 percent among those who had never smoked, and rose from 20 percent to 35 percent even among current smokers. In a 1986 survey conducted for the federal government 83 percent of those who had never smoked and 73 percent of current smokers said that "*the smoke from someone else's cigarette*" was very or somewhat annoying.

As the non-smokers' rights movement got underway during the mid-1970s, the industry's polls showed that these trends continued. Between 1974 and 1984 Roper polls showed that the percentage who agreed that it "*probably is hazardous to your health to be around people who are smoking, even when you're not smoking yourself*" rose from 57 percent to 77 percent among nonsmokers. Even among smokers the percentage agreeing rose from 30 percent to 51 percent. Between 1976 and 1984 the percentage of smokers who said that they "*frequently*" or" *occasionally*" feel uncomfortable about smoking around others rose from 48 percent to 58 percent. Even so, nonsmokers seldom reported confrontations with smokers. In

Roper surveys conducted between 1974 and 1984 only about a sixth of nonsmokers said that they had asked a nonsmoker to stop smoking or that they had indicated disapproval without saying so; two-fifths to half of nonsmokers said that they tried to move away. These surveys may have encouraged the tobacco industry's "common courtesy" campaigns against a ban on smoking in public places, discussed below.

By 1976 Roper's polling showed that majorities of Americans favored separate smoking sections in trains, airplanes, buses, eating places, theaters, indoor sporting events, workplaces or offices, and public meetings.[11] By 1984 nearly all (91 percent) Americans favored bans on smoking in elevators, 76 percent did in doctors' or dentists' waiting rooms, 62 percent did in retail stores, and 50 percent did in theaters. Between a fifth and a third of Americans favored bans in several other public places. In 1984 two-fifths of Americans agreed that insurance companies should charge higher life insurance premium to a smoker.[12] In Gallup polls conducted between 2003 and 2014 majorities of Americans ranging from 65 percent to 58 percent agreed that it would be justified to set higher health insurance rates for smokers.[13]

During the 1970s and 1980s Americans' beliefs that smoking was a stigma steadily increased at a rate of 1 or 2 or 3 percent a year—evidence that the stigma of smoking was already well-established and increasing. In later years pollsters used differently-worded questions but also reported that the stigma of smoking was widespread and growing. In Gallup surveys, for example, the percentage of respondents agreeing they would respect less a person who smoked rose from 17 percent in 1990 to 25 percent in 2011. Between a fifth and a quarter of Americans said that they would be less likely to hire a smoker for a job.

Although its pollsters closely tracked the growing stigma of smoking, the tobacco industry never could reverse these trends. Many smokers themselves shared the view that smoking was a social stigma. A 1974 Foote, Cone & Belding survey reported that 61 percent of smokers agreed that "*cigarette smoking today is less acceptable than it used to be.*" In a 1997 ABC News poll 25 percent of smokers agreed that "*many people feel you lack strength of character because you smoke*" and 37 percent of smokers felt "*ashamed sometimes because you smoke.*" In Gallup polls conducted between 1994 and 2014 a third to a half of smokers said that they felt "*unjustly discriminated against as a result of increased restrictions on smoking in public places,*" but half to two-thirds of smokers said that these restrictions were justified. When asked about "*increased taxes on cigarettes*" most smokers (68 percent in 2002 and 58 percent in 2014) said that they felt unjustly discriminated against, but 29 percent and 39 percent of smokers, respectively, said that the tax increases were justified. These widely shared attitudes by smokers and nonsmokers alike help to explain why many smokers accepted without protest the increasing number of tax hikes and bans on smoking in public (Kagan and Skolnick 1993).

Some tobacco control advocates saw the growing stigma attached to cigarette smoking as a useful way to discourage smoking. One study described stigma as equally effective to a large tax increase on cigarettes in reducing smoking rates (Alamar and Glantz 2006; see also Kim and Shanahan 2003). Nationwide surveys reached the same conclusion. In a 2014 Gallup survey 25 percent of smokers said that they smoked less because of restrictions on smoking in public places and 26 percent of smokers said that they smoked less because of tax increases on cigarettes. A few critics of the tobacco industry saw stigmatizing individual smokers as a misdirected approach. Douglas (1993) argued that a focus on stigmatizing individual smokers turns attention away from more effective ways to reduce smoking rates, such as tax hikes, laws on cigarette sales to minors, or limits on the advertising and marketing of cigarettes.[14]

REFRAMING SMOKING

Negative media attention, rising public beliefs that smoking was a health risk and constituted deviant behavior, and the tobacco industry's deteriorating image led the industry and its pollsters to search for more favorable ways to present cigarette smoking. This approach is sometimes described as "reframing" the issue.[15] The tobacco industry poll-tested at least six frames for cigarette smoking, some of which proved to be more useful than others. During the early 1960s the industry poll-tested the limited government frame—that smoking may be a serious health problem of widespread public concern but, even so, not a government responsibility. For the industry the results were encouraging. In a 1962 Gallup survey conducted for the industry only 36 percent of Americans favored "*the government taking any action at this time,*" about half of whom favored more research and education. In 1963 and 1964 the percentage favoring government action rose to 44 percent and 41 percent, respectively, but research and education remained the most popular suggestions.[16] These Gallup figures were well below the percentage of Americans who believed that smoking was a cause of lung cancer (47 percent in 1962, 53 percent in 1963, and 62 percent in 1964). In a 1968 Roper survey only 7 percent of Americans thought the federal government was spending too little time and money on the problem of smoking cigarettes. Only 22 percent thought that the government should "*take* more *steps to protect the public*" against "*the advertising and sale of cigarettes and tobacco,*" a lower level of public support than for many other public-safety issues.[17] Majorities of Americans supported package warning labels, educational programs, and more research but far fewer Americans at the time favored stronger measures such as additional taxes or outright bans.

The limited-government frame continued to poll well for the tobacco industry as public trust and confidence in government declined after the early 1960s. The industry often used this frame in its campaign advertising during state and local issue elections on raising cigarette taxes or on banning smoking in public places. In these elections, discussed below, the industry's pollsters often polled beliefs on whether the government would mismanage or divert the funds raised from higher cigarette taxes, whether excise taxes are unfair, whether someone else other than smokers should pay for programs that would receive funding from higher cigarette taxes, whether taxes are already high enough or too high, and whether regulating smoking is only a low-priority government concern. The industry's pollsters and campaign consultants called this the "big brother" strategy and it was a potent campaign message in many state and local issue elections.

The industry's pollsters also began very early to test a second frame—that smoking was a personal responsibility and an individual choice or even a right (Haltom and McCann 2004: 227–35, 253; Sweda and Daynard 1996). In surveys conducted for Hill & Knowlton just before and after the 1964 Surgeon General's report was released, two-thirds to three-quarters of respondents said that the major responsibility for doing something about the smoking and health problem was that of the individual himself.[18] Only one in seven respondents said the major responsibility was that of the tobacco industry, and only one in twelve said the major responsibility was that of the government.[19] The Tobacco Institute's polling during the 1970s and 1980s further explored this argument.[20] During the 1990s in a Penn and Schoen poll for Philip Morris only 24 percent of Americans believed that government should decide whether employees could smoke in offices; 17 percent believed that individuals should decide, and 58 percent believed that businesses should decide.[21] The freedom-of-choice frame became a reliable mainstay for the tobacco industry's efforts to forestall unfavorable actions from state legislatures (Jacobson, Wasserman, and Raube 1993); to contest lawsuits brought by ill, dying, or dead smokers; and to defeat anti-smoking initiatives and referendums.

A third poll-tested frame held that cigarette smoking brought personal benefits that offset its harm and the tobacco industry provided significant economic benefits such as providing jobs and paying taxes. In a 1968 Roper survey conducted for the industry respondents were asked to evaluate five statements in favor of smoking. Four-fifths (79 percent) of respondents agreed that "*smoking is pleasurable for most smokers.*" Two-thirds (65 percent) agreed that "*smoking cigarettes reduces nervous tension for most smokers.*" Half (55 percent) agreed that "*smoking cigarettes helps control appetite and therefore keeps weight down.*"[22] The Tobacco Institute field-tested this argument with magazine inserts and follow-up recall polls but the argument's impact proved to be limited. Exposure to a magazine ad on the tobacco industry's tax-paying and job-providing benefits produced less favorable attitudes toward the industry than did exposure to an ad on smokers' rights (among smokers) or to an ad on the importance of smoking courteously (among non-smokers).[23]

A fourth poll-tested frame held that smoking was not particularly harmful, at least compared to other health risks.[24] The industry tested several versions of this argument. In a 1959 Roper survey only 11 percent of respondents said that "*smoking a pack or more of cigarettes a day*" was the "*most dangerous to life*"—a lower figure than for several other risks listed on a card.[25] Many industry-sponsored poll questions probed beliefs about whether smoking was only slightly harmful, that only heavy smoking was harmful, that the harm that resulted from cigarette smoking was exaggerated, or that safer cigarettes were or would soon become available. In the same 1959 Roper survey 69 percent of smokers agreed that "*as long as you are careful not to smoke too much, cigarettes won't do you any real harm.*"[26] In a 1968 Roper survey only 6 percent of respondents said that smoking isn't hazardous and 42 percent said that smoking any amount is hazardous, but 47 percent said that only heavy smoking is hazardous.[27] In a 1969 survey 49 percent of smokers agreed that some cigarettes were less hazardous than others, 31 percent disagreed, and 21 percent said don't know.[28] Although the industry's polling often tested this argument, it was seldom used in state and local anti-smoking elections since the industry's pollsters and campaign consultants advised that the health issue was one to avoid.[29]

A fifth frame tested the so-called "constitutional theory" that smoking itself does not cause illness but that those who are prone to illness are also more likely to smoke; thus, the smoking-to-illness link is only a spurious correlation.[30] A 1968 Roper survey for the first time asked respondents whether or not smokers lived as long as non-smokers. Those who said that smokers did not were then asked: "*It could be that smokers don't live as long as non-smokers because they smoke. On the other hand, it could be that the kind of people who die younger are also the kind of people who are likely to smoke. What do you think—that smokers die younger because of the cigarettes they smoke, or that the kind of people who are likely to die younger are also the kind who are likely to smoke?*" Forty percent of respondents denied that smokers don't live as long as do non-smokers, 27 percent supported the constitutional theory, 21 percent attributed earlier death to cigarettes, and 13 percent said smokers don't live as long but did not choose between the two reasons. Among smokers, the percentages were 50 percent, 27 percent, 12 percent, and 11 percent; among non-smokers the figures were 33 percent, 26 percent, 27 percent, and 13 percent, respectively.[31] The Roper report conceded that the constitutional theory was probably difficult for many respondents to grasp and that the poll question was difficult to write, but viewed the results as "surprising" and "encouraging," while adding the caveat "if the question is fully understood." Roper polled this question several more times through 1984 but the constitutional theory steadily lost support among both smokers and nonsmokers.

The tobacco industry sometimes used the constitutional theory in its public relations efforts but less often so over time, perhaps because the theory is hard to explain, seems to disparage smokers, had little scientific support, and suffered from declining public support.

As the stigma of smoking increased, as tobacco taxes rose, and as bans on smoking in public places grew more common, the industry poll-tested a sixth frame—that smokers were unfairly treated and that smokers and nonsmokers should deal with each other on an informal basis. This frame was often used in targeted appeals to smokers in state and local anti-smoking elections and led to the industry's "common courtesy" and "smoketiquette" public relations campaigns.[32] In field tests using magazine inserts and recall tests, for example, smokers and nonsmokers were asked about their feelings toward each other and toward the tobacco industry. A quarter of smokers felt that non-smokers were more acceptable than were smokers. Four-fifths of smokers felt that smokers and non-smokers should work out their own relations "*on the basis of common sense*." A third of smokers felt that most non-smokers were intolerant of smokers. Only a third of smokers favored physically segregating smokers and non-smokers in all public places.[33] Many other surveys tested similar questions.[34] During the 1990s this frame was often used in the industry's efforts to "accommodate" smokers in restaurants and bars (Samuels et al. 1992). During the 1990s Penn and Schoen surveys for Philip Morris expanded this approach in trying to reframe smoking as a privacy right.

PUBLIC OPINION IN STATE AND LOCAL ELECTIONS

The tobacco industry faced new challenges when a growing number of states and localities enacted limits on smoking in public places, tax hikes on cigarettes, and restrictions on the sale of tobacco products to minors (Jacobson, Wasserman, and Anderson 1997; Jacobson, Wasserman, and Raube 1993; Wolfson 2001). Sometimes antismoking activists chose these new forums carefully and strategically but often the choice of a new forum was due to limited resources and limited options (Pralle 2006). Sometimes these changes came through the actions of state legislatures or city councils and sometimes through statewide and local issue elections. In these contests the tobacco industry was not without considerable influence of its own. The industry often managed to pass non-discrimination employment laws for smokers, to pass statewide laws preempting anti-smoking local ordinances,[35] and to limit state-funded anti-smoking publicity campaigns (Givel and Glantz 2000a; Givel 2006; Begay, Traynor, and Glantz 1993; Bialous and Glantz 1999; Bialous, Fox, and Glantz 2001; Ibrahim, Tsoukalas, and Glantz 2004).

Beginning during the mid-1970s anti-smoking advocates increasingly often sought to convince voters to raise taxes on tobacco products, to limit smoking in public places, or to fund anti-smoking publicity campaigns.[36] Nearly half of the states and most American cities allow such issue elections, commonly called referendums (if the election is to uphold or reject a state law or local ordinance already passed) or initiatives (if the election is to enact a new law and ordinance). These elections can occur if elected officials place the issue on the ballot or alternatively if a sufficient number of voters sign a petition, typically a number ranging from 2 to 10 percent of the number of registered voters or of votes cast in a recent election.[37] Anti-smoking activists who chose the election route enjoyed several advantages: fairly easy ballot access in many states and localities; frequent media attention to and rising public awareness about the ills of smoking; local networks of dedicated health advocates; and widespread public annoyance toward smokers. Further, the tobacco industry was less well organized locally than at the state level (Glantz and Begay 1994; Monardi and Glantz 1998). Even so, the tobacco industry, a well-funded, well-organized oligopoly, could quickly and easily raise large amounts of cash and outspend its typically poorly-financed opponents; hire skillful pollsters, focus group consultants, and campaign managers; rally its business, media, and political allies; and rely on support from the many voters who were smokers.

Smoking-related issue elections were not new to the mid-1970s. Between 1920 and 1972 pro-cigarette forces won ten of thirteen tobacco-related statewide elections, most of which involved proposed tax increases. The total number of statewide and local initiatives and referendums declined during the 1950s, 1960s, and early 1970s before rising again after the mid-1970s just as anti-smoking public sentiment was also rising. Two early and important anti-smoking initiatives to restrict smoking in public places came in November 1978 in California and in May 1979 in Dade County, Florida. In both elections the tobacco industry's early ("benchmark" or "baseline") polls found that the proposed anti-smoking ballot measures led by large margins: by a 68 percent to 24 percent margin in California in a December 1977 and January 1978 poll and by a 65 percent to 24 percent margin in Dade County in a January 1979 poll. Yet the industry's early polling also showed voter attitudes changed after being asked several poll questions on possible campaign messages, mostly against the initiatives. After voters were exposed to possible campaign arguments, support for the California measure dropped to 61 percent to 34 percent in favor[38] and support for the Dade County measure dropped to just 47 percent to 45 percent in favor.[39] Several weeks of industry-sponsored campaign ads closed the poll margin to just 50 percent to 40 percent in favor in California by August 1978 and to just 47 percent to 45 percent in favor in Dade County by March 1979. Following a well-funded media, endorsement, mail, telephone, and get-out-the-vote campaign, the industry defeated both initiatives by 54 to 46 percent in California and by a narrower 50.2 percent to 49.8 percent in

Dade County (Givel and Glantz 2000b). As the California and Dade County results showed, the tobacco industry could win issue elections even if most voters believed that smoking caused deadly illnesses, disliked the tobacco industry, favored restrictions on smoking in public, and were annoyed by smokers.

The tobacco industry's back-to-back wins established a six-point game plan that it used in many other statewide and local elections. First, the industry hired skillful pollsters, focus group experts, and campaign consultants as soon as an election seemed likely and often used the same consultants in different elections around the country.[40] Second, early polls and focus groups identified the most persuasive arguments (or frames) to shift public opinion and to cut into the anti-smoking measure's large initial lead. The industry's best poll-tested argument was often an anti-government ("big brother") frame that included hostility to increased taxes; beliefs that new taxes would be misspent; opposition to any new costs for taxpayers or businesses to comply with the proposed anti-smoking restrictions; resistance to banning smoking in some public places but not in others; or even fears that smokers might be arrested, that police would be diverted from serious crimes, that the enforcement of public smoking bans would be unequally applied, or that higher taxes might lead to increased cigarette smuggling. The industry's early polling sometimes identified other useful campaign frames, among them hostility to new taxes that benefitted large hospital chains, complaints that excise taxes fell hardest on low-income smokers, or, ironically, unease that too little of a tax hike would go to anti-smoking prevention programs (Bjornson and Sahr 1997; Smith, Savell, and Gilmore 2013). The tobacco industry often used several different frames during a single campaign but sought to avoid debating the health issue; to avoid focusing attention on the unpopular cigarette companies; and, except in targeted messages to smokers, to avoid defending smokers' rights. Third, the industry formed a newly-named campaign organization seemingly unconnected to the tobacco industry (such as Californians For Common Sense or Dade Voters for Free Choice) and sought out prominent business, sports, media, or civic leaders to oppose the anti-smoking measure (Fallin, Grana, and Glantz 2014; Mandel and Glantz 2004).[41] Fourth, the industry began its campaign advertising several weeks earlier than did the anti-smoking campaign. If actively opposing a ballot measure, the industry heavily outspent its opponents, on the average by a five to one margin (Lum, Barnes, and Glantz 2009). Early and one-sided spending allowed the industry to frame the early campaign debate around its best campaign messages and to reinforce these messages late in the campaign.[42] Fifth, the industry used several rounds of polls and focus groups to keep its campaign well-informed and on-message, typically including an early benchmark poll, periodic "brushfire" polls during the campaign, daily tracking polls during the campaign's last few weeks, and sometimes even election-day exit polls or post-election polls.[43] Sixth, eligible voters were carefully segmented into groups and targeted with appropriate poll-tested messages. Voter groups such as smokers who were the most likely to vote against an anti-smoking ballot initiative received frequent mail, telephone, and personal contacts to encourage voter turnout—an important task since voter turnout in issue elections is often low.

Between 1972 and 1990 the tobacco industry successfully defeated five of seven statewide anti-smoking initiatives.[44] In time anti-smoking advocates learned from their failures and improved their campaign tactics in two important ways. First, anti-smoking advocates increasingly often lobbied city councils and county commissioners to enact local tobacco control ordinances or, failing at that, gathered enough signatures to put onto the local ballot tobacco control measures to restrict public smoking, to reduce youth access to cigarettes, or to raise cigarette taxes. At the city or county level anti-smoking advocates often succeeded since the tobacco industry was poorly organized locally (Givel and Glantz 2001; Goldstein and Bearman 1996; Monardi and Glantz 1998; Morley et al. 2002). Passing a local anti-smoking ordinance or winning a local election often led to a similar success in a nearby city or county and sometimes to a new statewide anti-smoking law (Shipan and Volden 2006).[45] Even before anti-smoking advocates began to enjoy much success statewide, by 1990 their local efforts had succeeded in passing over 400 local anti-smoking ordinances (Glantz and Balbach 2000; Samuels and Glantz 1991; Traynor, Begay, and Glantz 1993). By the early 2000s nearly every state and many cities and counties had enacted limits on smoking in public, some through popular votes and many others through legislation (Jacobson, Wasserman, and Anderson 1997: 82–86; Pacheco 2011; Warner 2006; Wolfson 2001).

In a second important change anti-smoking advocates began to run more professionally-managed and better-funded ballot campaigns, often forming coalitions with wealthier allies such as hospital corporations, medical groups, pro-health interest groups, or charitable foundations.[46] Anti-smoking advocates also often ran campaign attack ads against the highly-unpopular tobacco companies themselves. Endorsements and financial support from popular interest groups such as the American Cancer Society, coupled with more frequent attack ads against cigarette manufacturers, helped many anti-smoking voters to make more fully informed voting decisions, increasingly so against the tobacco industry.[47] Although typically outspent,[48] anti-smoking ballot campaigns often raised sufficient funds to convey their campaign message earlier, more frequently, and more effectively; to hire professional pollsters, campaign consultants, and attorneys; and to win favorable media coverage and newspaper endorsements.

Improved campaigns by tobacco control advocates and steadily less favorable public opinion toward the tobacco industry took its toll on the industry's win-loss ratio in these elections. From 1991 through 1999 the industry won only two of six statewide issue elections.[49] During the late 1990s the tobacco industry, well aware of its growing number of expensive losses, turned to its pollsters in an attempt to find better voter segmentation models by which to identify from baseline polling which anti-smoking ballot measures could likely be defeated and which ballot measures were so unlikely to be defeated that the industry would not fund an opposition campaign.[50] From 2000 through 2012 the industry defeated only seven of twenty-seven statewide ballot campaigns, and left unopposed several others (Lum, Barnes, and Glantz 2009). Equally bad for the tobacco industry, in seven statewide elections during the 1990s and 2000s the industry itself sponsored and heavily funded a tobacco-friendly ballot measure that proposed a small tax increase or modest restrictions on public smoking but with a statewide preemption (or ban) on locally-passed restrictions. The tobacco industry's sponsorship and funding allowed anti-smoking advocates to tie the pro-industry ballot measures to the highly unpopular tobacco industry, leading to the defeat of six of these seven initiatives. The industry's only successful ballot measure (in California in 2004) was later limited in scope by state court rulings (MacDonald, Aguinaga, and Glantz 1997).[51]

These ballot measures are an important part of the tobacco control story. If only state legislatures or the U.S. Congress had made the policy decisions on smoking, far fewer restrictions on smoking in public places would have been imposed, cigarette taxes would have remained much lower (Chaloupka, Wakefield, and Czart 2001: 42–45), and fewer anti-smoking publicity campaigns would have been funded. The success of antismoking ballot measures in part reflected a growing public disapproval of cigarette smoking. Yet these elections also helped to sustain a vigorous public debate on smoking at a time when most state legislatures would not act (Givel and Glantz 2001) and when little federal-level action was forthcoming. Ballot measures that raised taxes, that restricted smoking in public places, and that funded antismoking publicity campaigns increased public antipathy toward smokers and increased public knowledge that secondhand smoke was harmful (Pacheco 2013). These elections made cigarette smoking more expensive and less widely acceptable; increased the chances that nearby cities or neighboring states would pass anti-smoking restrictions (Pacheco 2013; Pacheco and Boushey 2014; Shipan and Volden 2006); and modestly reduced smoking prevalence and, for continued smokers, the number of cigarettes smoked (Peterson et al. 1992; Albers et al. 2007). Sometimes, as in California, Massachusetts, and Oregon, successful ballot initiatives reduced smoking prevalence significantly (Al-Delaimy et al. 2007; Apollonio and Malone 2009; Farrelly, Pechacek, and Chaloupka 2003; Farrelly et al. 2008; Fichtenberg and Glantz 2000; Friend and Levy 2002; Ibrahim and Glantz 2007; Levy,

Mumford, and Gerlowski 2007; Licari and Meier 2000; Roeseler and Burns 2010; Terry-McElrath et al. 2013).[52]

The tobacco control elections repeated an important limit on the tobacco industry's influence. During the 1950s the tobacco industry successfully sustained for about a decade public doubts about the health risks of smoking. The industry's success declined during the mid-to-late 1950s when a vigorous grass-roots anti-smoking movement arose and when the U.S. Surgeon General advisory committee issued its bold and unequivocal report in 1964. Thereafter the industry was far less successful at sustaining a controversy about the ills of smoking. So, too, was the tobacco industry for a time able to defeat higher taxes on cigarettes, bans on public smoking, and publicly-financed anti-smoking publicity campaigns when the industry could operate within state legislatures, Congress, and the White House. During the 1970s and the 1980s when confronted with grass-roots anti-smoking ballot campaigns, the industry continued to successfully employ its strengths for about a decade. Thereafter anti-smoking advocates learned from their mistakes, refashioned their campaign strategies, and began to succeed. In short, the tobacco industry's well-funded and well-organized efforts to manage public opinion successfully "bought time" but were eventually undone.

CONCLUSION: SHIFTING PUBLIC OPINION ON SMOKING

Successfully managing American public opinion is not a simple task. Despite its financial and organizational advantages and despite its efforts to reframe smoking, the tobacco industry enjoyed only mixed and passing success at managing American public opinion. Beginning in the early 1950s the industry hired many well-regarded pollsters, focus group analysts, and campaign managers to track and to remedy its mounting problems. Yet American public opinion steadily if slowly became better informed about the health risks of smoking, then more negative toward the tobacco industry and toward smokers, and still later increasingly supportive of state and local anti-smoking ballot measures. The industry delayed but could not reverse these changes.

As each new problem arose the industry "bought time" and for about a decade until antismoking advocates grew more skillful. Thereafter the industry was much less often successful. Growing public beliefs that cigarette smoking was a serious health risk, the tobacco industry's worsening image, and the growing stigma of smoking had real-world consequences. Higher taxes were imposed on cigarettes, more limits were placed on public smoking, and several highly-visible anti-smoking publicity campaigns were funded. The industry's problems did not stop here. Chapter 5 turns to American public opinion and the federal-level tobacco control policies.

NOTES

1. Philip Morris, an early leader in market research, commissioned its first large-scale Roper poll in 1953 and then several more during the 1950s. Most of this polling focused on advertising and marketing but a few poll questions asked about health fears. Hill & Knowlton and the Tobacco Institute coordinated the industry's joint efforts. Other cigarette companies also commissioned polls, chiefly on marketing and advertising strategies, but with a few questions on health fears, current issues, state and local elections, and the industry's image.

2. Since the 1950s many national and regional polling companies surveyed attitudes on smoking. Some pollsters worked only for the tobacco industry and not for "antismoking" government agencies such as the Public Health Service or for anti-smoking groups such as the American Cancer Society or the American Lung Association. A few pollsters worked for both the tobacco industry and for its opponents, occasionally during the same time period. Some pollsters worked for the tobacco industry at one time but later ceased to do so. Some pollsters only conducted surveys for government agencies or for anti-smoking groups, but not for the tobacco industry. Still other pollsters asked tobacco-related poll questions but were employed for neither tobacco firms nor anti-smoking organizations. Several marketing and advertising firms conducted surveys, typically for individual tobacco companies. Copies of these polls and related correspondence number well over twenty thousand documents and may be searched through the legacy library's on-line collection of tobacco documents, using dates, report titles, key words, or polling organizations' names. As a caveat, several polling organizations changed their names.

3. The 1959 Roper report, "A Study of Attitudes Toward Cigarette Smoking and Different Types of Cigarettes" and the 1960-to-1967 Roper reports, "A Study of Cigarette Smokers' Habits and Attitudes," and accompanying documents are available through the on-line Legacy Tobacco Documents Library.

4. The 1959-to-1964 Gallup series, "Trends in public attitudes on the possibility of a health hazard in cigarette smoking" and the 1967-to-1984 Roper series, "A Study of Public Attitudes Toward Cigarette Smoking and the Tobacco Industry" and related documents are available through the on-line Legacy archive.

5. The proposal for a large-scale test of the constitutional theory, was never carried out; see a 1986 deposition of Burns Roper in *Cipollone v. Liggett Group*, available at the on-line Legacy archive.

6. See Philip Morris's report "Marlboro Lights: lowered Tar Vs. "Numbers," April 18, 1974, and "Executive Summary: A Qualitative Study for Merit Ultima," April 1996, at the on-line Legacy archive.

7. See a 1962 statement of Professor Yoram Wind and the 1988 and 1990 statements of Professor Gerald M. Goldhaber given at U.S. congressional committee hearings, available at the on-line Legacy archive.

8. Some historians view the level of media coverage or of public awareness about the smoking-and-health issue, rather than beliefs about the harmfulness of cigarette smoking, as defining "common knowledge." For examples see the depositions or trial testimony of Dr. Luis Martinez-Fernandez in 2010 and Dr. Lacy K. Ford in 1997, 2000, and 2002. For a view that many smokers believed that low nicotine, low tar "light" cigarettes were less harmful to smoke, see Dr. Joel B. Cohen's 2002 and 2010 reports; for an opposing view of the survey evidence see Dr. Charles R. Taylor's 2010 report. For experimental evidence of the impact of a tobacco company's admission of the harmfulness and addictiveness of smoking on public opinion, see Dr. Jon A. Krosnick's 2001 deposition. All these sources are available through the on-line Legacy archive.

9. The 1998 NBC/*Wall Street Journal* results are much more negative toward the cigarette industry than are the results in a March 1960 Gallup question using the same wording. In the Gallup survey 37 percent said the cigarette industry was "*doing all it can*," 34 percent said "*can do more*," and 28 percent said "*don't know*."

10. In the Wirthlin survey anti-smoking groups such as the American Lung Association, the American Cancer Society and the U.S. Surgeon General were all ranked as more truthful and credible when speaking on smoking-related issues than were the Tobacco Institute or the Tobacco Merchants Association. Favorable ratings for individual cigarette companies were uniformly low and ranged from 34 percent for R. J. Reynolds to 24 percent for Lorillard.

11. During the 1970s tobacco control advocates often sought separate sections for smokers and nonsmokers, a move resisted by the tobacco industry. By the 1980s tobacco control advocates demanded a total ban on public smoking, and poll question wording also often changed. Beginning in 1987 Gallup Poll differentiated between separate smoking sections and a total ban in hotels and motels, restaurants, and workplaces.

12. Sugarman (1993) and Schauffler (1993) review early smoking regulations in employment and insurance.

13. In a 2014 Gallup Poll 66 percent of nonsmokers, but only 26 percent of smokers agreed that higher health insurance rates for smokers were justified. Only 16 percent of nonsmokers and 3 percent of smokers agreed that companies should be allowed to refuse to hire smokers.

14. The growing stigma of cigarette smoking troubled some ethicists since in other areas such as drug addiction or HIV status stigma is commonly seen as a barrier to effective treatment and as discrimination against low-status and marginalized groups (Bayer 2008, 2010; Bell et al. 2010).

15. Framing refers to the way in which a complex argument is presented, or to a "story line" that suggests what in essence the controversy is about (Gamson and Modigliani 1987: 143). The choice of a frame can significantly affect opinion formation by determining what past information is recalled from memory, what new information is best understood, and what information is retained (Berinsky and Kinder 2006; Chong and Druckman 2010; Jacoby 2000; Nelson, Oxley, and Clawson 1997). In an even earlier frame cigarette manufacturers presented cigarette smoking as a harmless and pleasurable activity. After 1954 "creating controversy" was the industry's first attempt to reframe smoking (Courtwright 2005: 425–27). The industry's reframing strategies did not end with the time period discussed in this chapter. Several cigarette manufacturers, particularly Philip Morris/Altria, later sought to frame themselves as responsible corporate citizens.

16. The Gallup Organization, "Trends In Public Attitudes on the Possibility of a Health Hazard in Cigarette Smoking," 1962, 1963, and 1964 reports, are available at the on-line Legacy archive.

17. Protecting the public against crime in the streets, named by 78 percent of respondents, was the top public concern; see Roper Research Associates, "A Study of Public Attitudes Toward Cigarette Smoking and the Tobacco Industry in 1968," July 1970: 14, available at the on-line Legacy archive.

18. See Brandt (2007: 230–37) on the origins of this strategy.

19. Opinion Research Corporation, "The Impact On Public Attitudes Of The Surgeon General's Report," January and February 1964, available at the on-line Legacy archive.

20. The Tobacco Institute continued to develop this argument in later years; see, for example, Gallup & Robinson, "The Impact of an Ad for the Tobacco Institute—Common Knowledge," August 18, 1980, available at the on-line Legacy archive.

21. The Penn and Schoen report, "The Right to Privacy," August 16, 1995, available at the on-line Legacy archive.

22. Roper Research Associates, "A Study of Public Attitudes Toward Cigarette Smoking and the Tobacco Industry in 1968," July 1970: 29–30. Only 35 percent said that "*smoking cigarettes help people cope with their psychological problems and illnesses.*" Only 27 percent said that "*smoking cigarettes is no more harmful to health than eating butter or other foods with a high cholesterol content.*"

23. See Gallup & Robinson, "A Special Magazine Advertising Impact Analysis for the Tobacco Institute," August 26, 1975, and related documents, available through the on-line Legacy archive. For an example of this frame in specialized publications see Wilbur (1996).

24. Sometimes the industry used print media or films to test whether attitudes about health risks could be changed (Proctor 2011: 315–16).

25. Elmo Roper and Associates, "A Study of Attitudes Toward Cigarette Smoking and Different Types of Cigarettes," January 1959, vol. 2. The question was "*In a sense everyone is a gambler—every time we cross the street there is a chance that we will get hit by a car. Assuming a person does all of the following things, which one of these activities do you think is most dangerous to life?*" "*Going for a long swim in a large lake*" (at 26 percent) and "*taking a trip in a car*" (at 24 percent) were rated as the most hazardous of seven activities.

26. Elmo Roper and Associates, "A Study of Attitudes Toward Cigarette Smoking and Different Types of Cigarettes," January 1959, vol. 2, page 232, available at the on-line Legacy archive.

27. Seventy-four percent of those who said "*only heavy smoking is hazardous*" said one and a half packs a day or more was "*heavy*" smoking. Roper Research Associates, "A Study of Public Attitudes Toward Cigarette Smoking and the Tobacco Industry in 1968," July 1970, p. 23, available at the on-line Legacy archive.

28. Political Surveys and Analyses, April 1969, "A Study of Cigarette Smokers' Attitudes Toward Smoking and Related Issues," vol. 2, page 122, available at the on-line Legacy archive.

29. For examples of these questions, see the 1984 Roper report at 31–32, available at the on-line Legacy archive.

30. For views on the constitutional theory, see Hirshbein (2011); Lilienfeld (1959); Matarazzo and Saslow (1960); Thomas (1960); Tursi, White, and McQuilkin (2000: 137–38); and Williams (1971).

31. Roper Research Associates, "A Study of Public Attitudes Toward Cigarette Smoking and the Tobacco Industry in 1968," July 1970 includes the earliest question testing the constitutional theory's popularity; the question was later repeated several times.

32. Roper polls for the tobacco industry and a 1987 National Health Interview Survey showed that the "common courtesy" campaign was ineffective at curbing unwanted smoking. About half of smokers lit cigarettes without asking permission from nonsmokers, and few nonsmokers were willing to object (Davis, Boyd, and Schoenborn 1990).

33. Gallup & Robinson, "The Impact of An Ad for The Tobacco Institute "Common Knowledge," August 18, 1980; "A Special Magazine Advertising Impact Analysis for The Tobacco Institute," August 26, 1975; and "Media Advertising—A Review," July 1977, available at the on-line Legacy archive.

34. In a May 1976 Roper survey conducted for Philip Morris, half (56 percent) of smokers said that they "*at least occasionally feel uncomfortable about smoking around others.*" See also the Roper Organization 1976 report, "A Study of Smokers' Habits and Attitudes With Special Emphasis on Low Tar Cigarettes," page 10, available at the on-line Legacy archive.

35. Preemption can occur at either the state or the federal level. For a review see "Preemption: The Biggest Challenge to Tobacco Control" (Tobacco Control Legal Consortium, October 2014 at www.publichealthlawcenter.org).

36. Tobacco-related ballot measures were compiled from Ballotpedia; Nicholl (1998); and Lum, Barnes, and Glantz (2009). The tobacco industry was also involved in several local and statewide ballot measures on general sales tax increases, state spending limits, and product liability. Most tax increases on tobacco products and restrictions on public smoking were passed by state legislatures or by locally elected officials (Kagan and Nelson 2001; Warner 1981), not by initiatives or referendums. This section

does not include several ballot measures that allocated tobacco taxes held soon after the 1998 Master Settlement Agreement.

37. Procedures for placing an initiative on the ballot vary widely from state to state (Bowler, Donovan, and Tolbert 1998: 3–9; Bowler and Donovan 2004; Lupia and Matsusaka 2004; Magleby 1995; Matsusaka 2004: 1–9, 149–52, 160–61; and Schmidt 1989: 3–20, 296–97).

38. The January 1978 California poll then asked the 61 percent of respondents who still favored the anti-smoking position several additional anti-initiative questions, after which these respondents were polled again; at that point 57 percent of prior supporters still favored the initiative and 40 percent switched to opposing it with 3 percent no opinion.

39. The first question was asked early in the survey before respondent typically knew much about the upcoming ballot measure. Respondents were then asked several questions on the pros and cons of the ballot measure, and then were again asked their voting preference. The earlier question is commonly called the "uninformed heads-up" question and measures public opinion at the time of the survey. The latter question is the "informed heads-up" question and estimates how greatly public opinion might change during the campaign. Poll questions on the pros and cons of the ballot measure also suggest which arguments might be the most persuasive during the campaign.

40. For a discussion of the importance of professional campaign consultants, see Magleby and Patterson (1998) and Hanauer (1985).

41. The tobacco industry often used seemingly unaffiliated "front groups" organizations in its political efforts; for examples see Apollonio and Bero (2007a, 2007b); Ong and Glantz (2001); White and Bero (2004).

42. Research on framing effects suggests that early, frequent, and late campaign messages have different effects on attitude formation. Early advertising can shape the public debate, persuade early-deciding voters, and provide arguments that voters use to evaluate later and conflicting messages. Mid- and late-campaign messages help voters recall earlier messages and persuade late-deciding voters (Chong and Druckman 2010).

43. Exit polls and polling conducted after election day cannot influence voters in that particular election, but allow a better understanding of why and when voters made decisions, and how different advertising messages affected voter choices. This information may prove helpful in future elections.

44. For case studies see Lum, Barnes, and Glantz (2009); Hanauer (1985); Harris et al. (2010); Moon, Males, and Nelson (1993); and Nicholl (1998).

45. The tobacco industry often successfully lobbied state legislatures to pass statewide laws preempting locally-imposed taxes on tobacco products, bans on vending machines, or restrictions on public smoking in restaurants, bars, or workplaces (Siegel et al. 1997). By 1998 at least twenty-five states had enacted some form of preemption against locally-imposed tobacco controls (Gorovitz, Mosher, and Pertschuk 1998: 40). By the early 1990s thirty-three state legislatures had passed "smokers' rights" nondiscrimination legislation (Kagan and Nelson 2001: 17).

46. Anti-smoking advocates sometimes persuaded national organizations such as the American Cancer Society or the American Lung Association to donate significant funds and to take an active role in these campaigns. In a few campaigns anti-smoking advocates turned to hospital groups, to medical associations, or to foundations for campaign funding (MacDonald, Aguinaga, and Glantz 1997).

47. Even a less-well-informed voter can rely on interest group positions as an effective "short cut" to decide on ballot measures, thereby producing votes that as often agree with his or her underlying attitudes as occurs among well-informed voters (Lupia 1994; Bowler and Donovan 1994).

48. Some studies report that campaign spending by anti-smoking groups is more important than spending by pro-smoking groups (Lum, Barnes, and Glantz 2009). Internal campaign documents from the tobacco industry suggest the same conclusion.

The political science literature on campaign spending is mixed as to whether anti- or pro-ballot measure spending is the more effective (Stratmann 2006).

49. During the 1990s the tobacco industry successfully disqualified proposed statewide ballot measures in Arkansas and Nebraska by challenging enough signatures to prevent the measures from qualifying for the ballot.

50. A 1997 report by Voter Consumer Research guided the industry's efforts to improve the forecasting abilities of its baseline polling by including a better voter segmentation model, available at the on-line Legacy archive.

51. Even after losing an anti-smoking ballot election, the tobacco industry often successfully turned to elected officials to limit the funding or the content of anti-smoking publicity programs (Balbach, Traynor, and Glantz 2000; Begay, Traynor, and Glantz 1993; Bialous and Glantz 1999; Goldman and Glantz 1999; Ibrahim and Glantz 2006; Tsoukalas and Glantz 2003). For the industry's efforts to limit the use of initiatives and referendums see Laposata, Kennedy, and Glantz (2014).

52. In the CDC's Behavioral Risk Factor Surveillance System's 2012 state-by-state estimates, the estimated percentage of adults who smoked was 12.6 percent in California, the second-lowest state rate after Utah (at 10.6 percent) with the nationwide U.S. estimate at 19.6 percent. California's tobacco control program combines high taxes, public smoking bans, and anti-smoking advertising and education programs.

FIVE

Public Opinion, Federal Policies, and Smoking

The federal government has long made policy decisions about cigarettes. During the mid to late 1800s Congress several times raised or lowered taxes on imported cigarettes. During the heyday of the early anti-cigarette movement Congress ignored reformers' urgings to ban cigarette shipments sent through the mail to states that restricted the sale of cigarettes. In 1911 the U.S. Supreme Court ordered the breakup of the then-powerful tobacco trust. Beginning during World War I the federal government generously supplied cigarettes to American troops. Federal policy grew even tobacco-friendlier during the 1930s and 1940s. The Federal Trade Commission did occasionally force a cigarette company to cancel a particular advertising campaign. During the 1950s and the 1960s the FTC reached voluntary agreements with the tobacco industry on the industry's advertising practices. Regrettably, no public opinion poll questions exist on these issues making it impossible to know whether or not most Americans supported these early policies. As the health risks of smoking became better understood, pollsters began to ask many more questions on smoking-related disputes, thereby making it possible to compare American public opinion with federal policies on smoking.

MODERN TOBACCO CONTROL POLICIES

After the U.S. Surgeon General's advisory committee issued its landmark 1964 report, federal policies on cigarettes began to change although at first only modestly so.[1] The policy change was not dramatic at first (Worsham 1998, 2006). In 1964 the Federal Trade Commission threatened to require warning labels on cigarette packages, but, under political pressure, deferred to Congress which in 1965 enacted a watered-down package warning. In fall 1964 the U.S. Department of Health, Education, and Welfare funded the first in what became a series of nationwide surveys measuring Americans' beliefs about smoking and health and gauging preferences for anti-smoking policies. In 1967 the Federal Communication Commission required television and radio stations that aired paid cigarette advertising also to air unpaid anti-smoking ads. In 1970 Congress banned cigarette ads from television and radio, beginning on January 2, 1971, a move that ended the required anti-smoking ads. In 1971, under pressure from the FTC, manufacturer agreed to disclose cigarettes' tar and nicotine levels in their advertising. In 1972 the FTC and the cigarette companies reached an agreement to include a health warning in all cigarette advertising. These policies notwithstanding, the federal government continued its price support program for tobacco growers, did not raise taxes on cigarettes, did not restrict or ban cigarette sales, did not completely ban cigarette advertising, did not ban vending machine sales, and did not require any evidence that cigarettes were safe to smoke before allowing their sale (Fritschler 1983: 149–61).

As public opinion grew more negative toward cigarette smoking, anti-smoking interest groups, grass-roots advocates, and some members of Congress and federal bureaucrats pushed for more effective controls on smoking. At first their efforts aimed at cigarette advertising. The earliest such policy that could be matched with nationwide poll questions was the 1965 cigarette package warning. As chapter 3 described, most Americans favored a package warning. According to the polls large majorities of Americans favored a requirement that all cigarette advertising carry a health warning and that cigarette packages disclose tar and nicotine levels. The polls were more mixed on the 1971 broadcast ban. The debate over cigarette advertising did not end in the 1970s, and poll majorities typically if not quite always favored new restrictions on advertising. In a 1993 Gallup survey large majorities of Americans favored adding package warnings on high blood pressure, addiction, environmental tobacco smoke, and heart and lung problems, although these particular warnings were not at the time mandated. In 1997 a 55 to 41 percent Harris poll majority favored banning the then-popular cartoon character "Joe Camel."[2] In 1997 a poll majority supported a ban on outdoor advertising of cigarettes, but a 52 to 45 percent majority opposed banning cigarette companies from sponsoring sporting events. Large poll majorities supported several advertising restrictions that were included in the 2009 tobacco control bill. As these examples show, public opinion usually supported limits on cigarette advertising particularly those involving stronger health warnings or limits on advertising that reached youth.[3]

Restricting one type of cigarette advertising, however, is of limited effectiveness since cigarette manufacturers can easily shift their efforts to other outlets (Loomis et al. 2006). When cigarette ads on television and radio were banned in 1971, cigarette companies turned to magazines, billboards, point-of-sale advertising, discounts, coupons, and company-sponsored and often televised sports and music events.[4] Not surprisingly, tobacco control advocates also sought limits on cigarette sales. Banning cigarette sales by vending machines was a favorite strategy, particularly since the ban prevented minors from so easily purchasing cigarettes. The federal government's polls in 1964 and 1966, however, showed that pluralities (of 49 percent to 42 percent and of 50 percent to 39 percent, respectively) opposed a ban on vending machine sales and no federal-level ban was at the time enacted. Over time public opinion changed. By 1997 a 66 percent to 31 percent poll majority favored a ban on cigarette sales by vending machines. Even so, federal law did not enact a near-complete ban on vending machine sales until 2009.[5] By 2007 a 94 percent to 5 percent majority of Americans favored identification checks and fines for retailers who sell tobacco to minors. Admittedly, little support ever existed for a complete ban on cigarette sales or for a complete and immediate ban on smoking. In a 1964 survey only 22 percent of Americans favored completely banning the sale of cigarettes. In a 1990 Gallup survey only 14 percent favored making smoking totally illegal; in 2015 that figure was 24 percent. Perhaps predictably, the federal government never took such action nor seriously considered doing so.

Beginning in the mid-1970s and the 1980s tobacco control advocates increasingly often sought to limit smoking in public places such as offices, restaurants, or hotels, at first through separate smoking sections and later by complete bans. Banning cigarette smoking in public places has several apparent benefits. A complete ban protects nonsmoking employees and patrons from exposure to secondhand smoke. Bans also encourage smokers to quit or at least to smoke fewer cigarettes (Chapman et al. 1999; Fichtenberg and Glantz 2002; Warner 2006: 47–52). Levy and Friend (2003) reported that comprehensive public clean air laws reduced smoking prevalence and consumption rates by about 10 percent; private workplace regulations reduced prevalence rates by about 6 percent and reduced the quantity of cigarettes smoked by continuing smokers by 2 to 8 percent. By a different account, a workplace ban reduces by nearly 5 percent employees' smoking prevalence and reduces a smoker's daily cigarette consumption by one or two cigarettes (Evans, Farrelly, and Montgomery 1999; Fichtenberg and Glantz 2002). In a 2014 Gallup Poll nine of the ten states with the lowest smoking rates ban smoking in workplaces, restaurants and bars, but the three states with the highest smoking rates (Kentucky, West Virginia, and Mississippi) had no such bans.[6] As chapter 4 described, many of these bans were first imposed by businesses or by local governments. Over time most states enacted some restrictions on smoking in public places with a few specific bans occurring at the federal level.[7]

Federal-level smoking bans have often agreed with public opinion, and when policy and the polls disagree, federal policy typically lags behind the polls. In a 1978 Gallup Poll American opinion was about evenly split (43 percent for, 47 percent against) on a complete ban on cigarette smoking on commercial airlines; no ban then occurred. A decade later by two or three to one majorities Americans favored the 1988 and 1990 smoking bans on airline flights. In 2000 a 57 percent to 40 percent Gallup/CNN/*USA Today* poll majority favored automatic fines for violating the no-smoking airline rules, consistent with federal policy. Federal policy on cigarette smoking in the workplace lagged well behind changing American attitudes. In 1994 a 62 percent to 34 percent *Los Angeles Times* poll majority favored a Clinton-era proposed regulation to ban smoking in virtually all indoor workplaces, but the proposed Labor Department regulation stalled and only a limited ban on smoking within federal office spaces was in 1997 imposed by executive order. On making it completely illegal to smoke in public places, federal policy now lags behind shifting attitudes. In Gallup's polling from 2001 through 2007 only 30 to 40 percent of Americans favored making totally illegal smoking in all public places, but in 2011, 2013, and 214 poll majorities (of 59 percent, 55 percent, and 56 percent, respectively) did. This lag reflects a common pattern: large and rapid poll shifts do not quickly translate into new federal policies.

Tobacco control advocates regularly sought to raise cigarette taxes (Chaloupka, Wakefield, and Czart 2001; Grossman et al. 1993; Sloan et al. 2004; Warner 2006: 35–43), a strategy with several perceived advantages. Unless the costs are absorbed by cigarette manufacturers, higher taxes raise the per-pack price of cigarettes and keep the inflation-adjusted prices of cigarettes from falling.[8] As added political advantages nonsmokers do not pay the tax and federal, state, and local governments that raise these taxes gain added revenue. Unlike tax hikes imposed by state or local governments, federally-imposed tax hikes on cigarettes cannot easily be thwarted by cross-border shopping or by the illegally smuggling cigarettes from low-tax states to high-tax states.

Tax increases effectively reduce smoking prevalence and the number of cigarettes that smokers consume daily (DeCicca, Kenkel, and Mathios 2008; Levy, Chaloupka, and Gitchell 2004), particularly so as cigarette smoking has become a practice more common among low-income adults and teens than among wealthier and better educated adults. In 1965 smoking rates varied little by education; by 2008 only 11 percent of college graduates smoked but 28 percent of those without a high school diploma did (Warner and Mendez 2010: 880; see also Viscusi 1990, 2002: 64). The admittedly highly-regressive tax hikes on cigarettes reduced the number of smokers and reduced the number of cigarettes smoked per smoker—thereby also reducing health care costs and the number of smoking-related deaths.[9] Steep price hikes are especially effective in reducing smoking rates.[10] For example, by 2002 the large per-pack price increases imposed by the 1998 Master Settlement Agreement, discussed below, caused smoking rates to drop by 13 percent among those aged eighteen to twenty and among those older than sixty-five, and to drop by 5 percent for those aged twenty-one to sixty-four (Sloan and Trogdon 2004).[11] Not surprisingly, steep tax hikes are an important part of international efforts to reduce smoking, discussed in chapter 7 (Chaloupka, Yurekli, and Fong 2012).

Pollsters have often queried Americans on proposed tax hikes on cigarettes. In a 1964 federal survey most Americans opposed a proposed tax hike, but thereafter poll majorities favored proposed tax hikes in 1982, 1994, 1997 and 2009 surveys. All these poll-queried tax hike proposals passed except those in 1964 and 1994. As with many other areas, public policy and the polls often agree, but when the two disagree, a status quo, pro-tobacco policy bias typically appears. The last part of this chapter reexamines this status quo bias.

Tobacco control advocates also challenged the federal government's quota and price support program for tobacco farmers.[12] Over time, public opinion shifted decidedly against this program. In the federal government's 1964 and 1966 surveys, small pluralities (42 percent to 33 percent and 40 percent to 34 percent, respectively) favored continuing tobacco price supports. By 1970 a 43 percent to 39 percent plurality opposed continuing the program. In 1985, 1991, and 2004 poll majorities opposed tobacco price supports. After the tobacco price support program was eliminated in 2004, public opinion and public policy became consistent, but with a long lag time before that happened.

Reducing smoking rates among minors has long been an important goal for tobacco control advocate, beginning with the anti-cigarette movement of the early 1900s (DiFranza and Dussault 2005; Warner 2006: 52–59; Studlar 2002: 148–52). Since few smokers initiate cigarette smoking after their teenage years, preventing minors from experimenting with cigarettes and from becoming habitual smokers effectively reduces adult smoking rates and smoking-related health problems. During the 1950s and 1960s most such efforts focused on anti-smoking educational programs in the schools, but these programs had only mixed success. Later efforts to reduce youth smoking included anti-smoking media campaigns aimed at minors; stronger enforcement of laws against stores' selling cigarettes to minors; penalties against minors who purchase, possess, or smoke cigarettes; limits on outdoor cigarette advertising near schools; and improved in-school programs. Most of these programs were carried out at the state and local level; a few were federally funded. Some programs at least modestly reduced teen smoking rates. The most aggressive, far-reaching, and well-funded programs, as in California or Florida, had much more impact. Bans on cigarette sales through vending machines; bans on free samples or single cigarette sales; limits on outdoor advertising for tobacco products; bans on cigarette-sponsored sports and music event; bans on give-away items, brand-name clothing, or caps; tax hikes; and criticism of smoking depicted in movies also aim to reduce youth smoking. Even so, the alarming rise in youth smoking rates during the 1990s, at a time when adult smoking prevalence was declining, showed that reducing youth smoking was very difficult.

Poll majorities typically, if not quite always supported federal-level efforts to reduce youth smoking rates. In 1995 a 74 percent to 24 percent Associated Press poll majority favored requiring the tobacco industry to spend $150 million a year on a campaign to discourage teenage smoking. In 1998 an 87 percent to 12 percent Gallup/CNN/*USA Today* poll majority favored putting "*severe restrictions on the advertising and sale of cigarettes to minors*." In 2007 a 77 percent to 22 percent majority of Americans favored giving the FDA authority to impose "*restrictions on sales and marketing to children*." Nearly all (94 percent) Americans favored ID checks for younger buyers and fines for retailers who sell tobacco to minors. An 84 percent to 15 percent majority favored tobacco marketing restrictions "*such as limiting advertising in magazines with lots of readers under age eighteen*."

At times the polls did not so strongly support youth-oriented tobacco control policies. In 1998 the polls were split (47 percent in favor, 50 percent opposed) on imposing penalties on the tobacco companies if teen smoking was not reduced by a certain date. Occasionally support for youth-oriented tobacco control provisions was even lower. In a 1995 survey only 38 percent favored, but 54 percent opposed "*allowing only black and white text, without color or pictures, on tobacco billboards and in cigarette advertisements in magazines read by many young people*"—the so-called "tombstone ad" requirement omitted from the final 1998 Master Settlement Agreement. In 2000 a 55 percent to 42 percent majority of Americans favored "*allowing the tobacco companies to run their own anti-smoking ads on television aimed at young people under 18*"—ad campaigns that tobacco control advocates viewed as ineffective or even as counterproductive.

Federal regulations such as occasional tax hikes or limited smoking bans did not seriously threaten the cigarette industry's financial health or its survival until the 1990s when the industry faced much more serious challenges from the Clinton White House, Congress, the federal agencies, and from an unusual lawsuit (Baumgartner and Jones 2009: 264–81). The Clinton administration's first proposal was to raise the federal tax on cigarettes to fund in part a national health care plan. The proposed 75–cents-a-pack tax hike won support from about three-quarters of Americans, but failed when the Clinton health care plan died in Congress in 1994. The Clinton administration then proposed that the FDA regulate the nicotine content of cigarettes—a move that would have subjected cigarettes to unprecedented federal regulations but not banned their sale (Derthick 2002: 50–70; Kessler 1996, 2001). In several poll questions, each differently worded, majorities of Americans ranging from 58 percent to 75 percent favored the action. Cigarette manufacturers defeated that effort in a 5 to 4 U.S. Supreme Court decision, *FDA v. Brown & Williamson Tobacco Corp.* (2000). In September 1999 Congress rejected the Clinton Administration effort to win a share of the states' payout of $246 billion under the Master Settlement Agreement, discussed just below. The Clinton Administration then filed a federal lawsuit against cigarette manufacturers to recover many billions of dollars for tobacco-caused, federally-paid health care costs (Derthick 2002: 189–95). When described as an effort *"to recover billions of dollars in federal health care costs for smoking-related illnesses"* a bare 51 percent to 42 percent majority of Americans in September 1999 said that they agreed more with the Justice Department than with the tobacco companies. Although its cost-recovery ambitions failed, that lawsuit did succeed on a few minor issues. The Clinton Administration's repeated failures show that tobacco control proposals may not succeed despite the tobacco industry's unpopularity, despite poll majorities that support the specific policy in question, and despite Americans' overwhelmingly viewing cigarette smoking as a serious health risk.

Beginning in 1994 tobacco control efforts took a decidedly new twist when several state attorneys general joined with prominent plaintiff attorneys to try to recover the enormous costs that the states paid to cover tobacco-caused illnesses under the Medicaid program.[13] The argument that tobacco companies had been "unjustly enriched" by evading the health care costs resulting from cigarette smoking was at first widely dismissed as a legal long-shot. Yet as more and more state attorneys general joined the lawsuit (Spill, Licari, and Ray 2001), uncertainty grew that the cigarette companies would win in court. In 1997 the tobacco industry and the states signed off on a far-reaching out-of-court consent agreement, the Global Settlement Agreement.[14] The proposed Global Settlement included a well-publicized $369 billion payout to the states over the next twenty-five years. That payment would have raised the per-pack price of cigarettes by about 62 cents. Other concessions by the industry included several limits on marketing and lobbying and a new set of package warnings (Viscusi 2002: 15–25; Givel and Glantz 2004).

Although negotiations had not included federal agencies or members of Congress, among the Global Settlement's many provisions were limits on class action lawsuits and on punitive damage awards, an annual cap on payouts in individuals' lawsuits, and a measure of regulation by the Food and Drug Administration. All this required Congressional approval.[15] In the spring of 1998 the action moved to Congress where U.S. Senators at length debated and amended the proposed agreement and in so doing made the agreement more costly and less attractive to the industry. By April cigarette manufacturers announced their opposition to the amended Senate bill and mounted a heavy lobbying effort and a $40 million dollar media blitz (Derthick 2002, 2005; Viscusi 2002: 20–30). In June the heavily-amended Senate agreement died by failing to win the sixty votes required to allow a final Senate vote.

The proposal's failure in Congress and its mixed support in the polls is not surprising. Complicated, multipart, frequently-amended legislation is hard to explain to the public, easy to criticize, and often fails to win majority poll support even if some parts of the package are popular. That experience was shared by the failed 1993–1994 Clinton health care bill and by the 2010 Affordable Care Act ("Obamacare") health care bill (Marshall 2012). Anti-smoking advocates themselves favored some parts of the agreement, but many advocates opposed some provisions (Derthick 2002: 130–31). Public opinion was also divided (Blendon and Young 1998; Derthick 2005: 132–37; Ladd 1998; Pertschuk 2001; Saad 1998). More than two-thirds of Americans favored requiring the industry to disclose its health research findings, favored a ban on cigarette vending machines, favored severe restrictions on cigarette advertising and sales to minors, and favored requiring the industry to fund a major media campaign about the risks of smoking. Three-fifths of Americans favored a ban on outdoor advertising of cigarettes. Other parts of the MSA were less popular. Fewer than half of Americans favored barring cigarette companies from sponsoring sports events, banning class-action lawsuits against tobacco companies, or setting an annual cap on payouts in lawsuits.

Further, only a third of Americans thought that increasing the cigarette tax by $1.10 a pack would discourage young people from starting to smoke. Only a fifth of Americans thought that the U.S. Senate bill would significantly reduce teenage smoking. Two-thirds of Americans saw the Senate bill as primarily a tax hike. Only a tenth of Americans believed that advertising, low prices, and easy access to cigarettes were the most important reason why teenagers begin to smoke. Fewer than half of Americans favored imposing penalties against the tobacco companies if teen smoking were not reduced by a certain date. By a 54 to 41 percent margin Americans opposed requiring tobacco companies to refund to the states the tobacco-related health care costs for poor people. Nor did passing a tobacco control bill rank as a *"most important problem"* for more than a handful of Americans. Public trust in the federal government was at the time very low. Only a third of Americans said that they *"trusted the government in Washington to do the right thing"* either *"just about always"* or *"most of the time."*

Poll support for the Congressional tobacco agreement as a whole ranged only from 37 percent to 49 percent in polls conducted soon after the 1997 consent agreement was announced and thereafter poll support never greatly increased (Blendon and Young 1998). Between 38 percent and 55 percent of Americans favored the agreement in polls conducted just before or just after the U.S. Senate bill died. Both publicly-available polls and the industry's private but widely circulated polling showed that members of Congress who opposed the bill would not suffer major vote losses in the upcoming November 1998 election. In a June 1998 ABC News Poll, for example, 20 percent of respondents nationwide said that they would be "*more likely to oppose*" their Senator if he or she voted to kill the tobacco bill, but 15 percent said that they would be "*more likely to support*" reelection, and 60 percent said that the vote would not make much difference.

Failing Congressional approval, the states and the industry renegotiated the proposal. In November 1998 the cigarette companies and the state attorneys general signed off on a modified package of regulations, the Master Settlement Agreement, that provided a $246 billion dollar payout to the states over twenty-five years with further payments continuing in perpetuity, and with some limits on the industry's advertising and marketing lobbying efforts, including a ban on outdoor billboards. The 1998 agreement did not ban individual, class action lawsuits, or punitive damages, and did not include the annual liability caps that the cigarette manufacturers had sought.[16] The MSA did not regulate the growing international market (Fritschler and Rudder 2007: 146–51); did not give the FDA any jurisdiction; nor required stronger package warnings; and did not contain any penalties if teenage smoking rates did not decline (Rabin 2001). The MSA did abolish the Tobacco Institute, the Council for Tobacco Research, and the Center for Indoor Air Research, but allowed individual companies to lobby on most other matters. Many critics viewed the 1998 agreement as modestly advancing tobacco control efforts (Givel 2006; Wood 2006). Other critics argued that the 1998 agreement effectively protected the largest cigarette manufacturers by virtually ensuring that no major new brands would emerge (Derthick 2005; Viscusi 2002: 37–41). To still other critics the 1998 agreement was at least a little better for tobacco control efforts than was the proposed 1997 agreement (Givel and Glantz 2004; Daynard 1988). After 1998 the states' spending on tobacco prevention programs increased modestly, but, even so, amounted to only about 6 percent of the states' total payouts with the tobacco-growing states spending even less (Gross et al. 2002; Loomis et al. 2006; Sloan et al. 2005; Studlar 2002: 154–55; Wolfson 2001: 213–14; Viscusi 2002: 56).

The 1998 agreement with the states notwithstanding, the industry's image problems did not improve. Philip Morris, by far the largest American cigarette manufacturer and in 2003 renamed Altria, reconsidered and reversed its long-standing opposition to federal oversight (Derthick 2005: 229–30). A decade then ensued with protracted negotiations, sharp divisions among cigarette manufacturers and among tobacco control advocates, and between Congress and the White House. After a Democratic Party takeover at Congress in the 2006 election and at the White House in the 2008 election, in June 2009 Congress passed and President Obama signed a bill, the Family Smoking Prevention and Tobacco Control Act, finally establishing the FDA's authority to regulate cigarettes.

Among its many provisions the 2009 act established FDA oversight of tobacco products; banned the sale of fewer than twenty cigarettes per pack; banned flavors except for menthol; set a minimum age at eighteen to buy cigarettes and required face to face sales; banned cigarette companies from sponsoring sporting events; banned vending machine sales or free samples except in adults-only facilities; required graphic warning labels on half of the front and back panels of cigarette packages (a provision still delayed by court challenge as of 2015); required manufacturers and importers to reveal all the product ingredients; required pre-approval from the FDA before the marketing of any new tobacco products; limited marketing and advertising that would reach youth and teens; allowed the FDA to reduce but not to eliminate nicotine levels in cigarettes; and banned descriptions such as "light" or "mild" that implied a less dangerous cigarette.

The 2009 tobacco control bill was controversial. Most cigarette manufacturers, all except Altria, opposed the bill as overly friendly to Altria's strong market share.[17] Some tobacco control advocates viewed the bill as too weak significantly to reduce cigarette smoking and as tacitly accepting the cigarette manufacturers' freedom-of-choice logic (McDaniel and Malone 2005). The 2009 bill pre-empted some state and local regulations and grandfathered in and exempted from regulation existing tobacco products. The 2009 bill also set out legal standards for regulations on tobacco products and their marketing and advertising that seemed likely to (and, in fact, did) result in several important controls on cigarettes being struck down in federal court. Among these standards are pre-regulation evidence of the likelihood of encouraging more contraband and the likelihood of increased cessation of smoking among smokers or decreases in smoking initiation (Glantz, Barnes, and Eubanks 2009; Barker 2009). The 2009 bill allowed, at least in theory, the marketing of reduced-risk cigarettes, itself highly controversial within tobacco control advocates, and with the FDA relying primarily on company-produced scientific claims. The 2009 bill banned most flavorings but allowed menthol. To some tobacco control critics the bill might allow the tobacco industry to "capture" a regulatory agency or at least to limit the FDA's regulatory reach through lawsuits (Barker 2009: n. 46). As an overburdened and underfunded agency, the FDA is poorly positioned to challenge cigarette manufacturers (Brandt 2007: nn. 158–86). All these limits, now enshrined in federal law, pose a serious problem for the end-of-smoking tobacco control efforts discussed in chapter 7. The passage of the 2009 bill also effectively kept the United States out of international efforts on tobacco control, discussed in chapter 7.

Public opinion toward the 2009 tobacco control bill was mixed. In a June 2009 Gallup survey only 46 percent approved and 52 percent disapproved *"of a new law that gives the federal government power to regulate the manufacturing and marketing of cigarettes and other tobacco products?"* Even so, parts of the 2009 bill enjoyed broad popular support. Ninety-four percent of Americans favored provisions to prevent cigarette sales to minors; 84 percent favored limits on tobacco marketing that reached minors; and 84 percent favored barring advertising claims that some tobacco products are less harmful than others without FDA approval for those claims.

Tobacco control policy has clearly come a long way since 1964 but the issue is far from being finally settled. The 2010 Affordable Care Act, among its many provisions, imposed financial penalties against smokers who enrolled and received subsidies under that program. After Congress passed the 2009 tobacco control act federal courts struck down at least temporarily an FDA requirement that cigarette packages must carry large and graphic visual health warnings on cigarette packages, struck down the FDA's proposed regulations of e-cigarettes under the strict standard of drugs and devices, and struck down a "plain packaging" requirement that cigarette packages not use colors and pictures. During the early 2000s the U.S. Supreme Court, upon appeal, declined to review cigarette manufacturers' legal appeals from lower court rulings allowing multi-million-dollar damage awards in lawsuits brought by ill or dying smokers or on behalf of dead smokers. Increasing numbers of employers now do not hire smokers. Chapter 6 returns to public opinion on tobacco-related lawsuits. Chapter 7 discusses public opinion on so-called "end of smoking" proposals.

STUDYING PUBLIC OPINION AND FEDERAL DECISIONS ON SMOKING

As this discussion suggests, tobacco control advocates sometimes successfully changed federal policy toward smoking but at other times the tobacco industry has prevailed, at least for a time, and a pro-tobacco status quo continued. Some policy decisions are made by the elective branches, Congress and the White House, and others by the federal agencies or by the federal courts. Some, but not all these policy decisions receive widespread attention from the media, from the American public, and from pollsters. Some decisions are far-reaching, others narrowly-focused. The tobacco industry, its lobbyists, and its lawyers fought long, hard, and expensively against some of these policy decisions, but were divided on or even acquiesced to others.

This chapter now asks two simple but important questions. First, how often do tobacco-related policies agreed with American public opinion? Second, does American public opinion influence tobacco policy-making?

American pollsters often ask poll questions on tobacco-related issues, especially when an issue is currently being debated or soon after a policy decision occurs. On low-profile controversies pollsters may ask only a single poll question, if any at all, but on high-profile controversies such as the Master Settlement Agreement, pollsters ask dozens of questions. Comparing carefully-measured poll questions with a final policy decision makes it possible to judge whether or not a decision is consistent with public opinion. Herein fifty-nine federal-level tobacco control policy decisions are compared (or "matched") with timely nationwide polls; each poll to policy match is classified as either "consistent" or as "inconsistent" with public or in a few cases as "unclear."[18] A consistent policy decision is one that agrees, in substance, with a timely nationwide poll majority (or occasionally with a plurality). An inconsistent policy decision is one that disagrees with a current poll majority or plurality. In a few cases of evenly-divided or inconsistent poll results, the poll to policy match is classified as unclear.

As an example of a consistent decision, consider the 1965 requirement that a warning label (at that time: "Caution: Cigarette Smoking May Be Hazardous to Your Health") appear on cigarette packages. Several poll questions showed that most Americans favored a package warning. In an industry-sponsored poll conducted a day before the 1964 Surgeon General advisory committee's report was released, a 65 percent to 22 percent majority favored a warning. That figure jumped to 72 percent to 21 percent in favor a few days later and was 64 percent to 25 percent in favor six weeks later (Marshall 2015). Other polls show the same result. In the federal government's fall 1964 Use of Tobacco survey 60 percent of Americans favored a package warning, and in spring 1966 75 percent of Americans did. In a December 1966 Harris poll a 76 percent to 10 percent majority favored the warning; a 57 percent to 32 percent majority said that it was not necessary to place the warning where it could be more easily seen. Accordingly, the 1965 package warning requirement is classified as "consistent" with public opinion.

Some tobacco control policies are inconsistent with American public opinion. As an example of an "inconsistent" poll to policy match consider the U.S. Supreme Court's 5 to 4 ruling in *Food and Drug Administration v. Brown & Williamson (2000)* that the FDA lacked authority to regulate tobacco products. That ruling that conflicted with a 69 percent to 25 percent majority in favor of FDA regulation in an October 1999 nationwide poll.[19] In a few cases the polls were either evenly divided (within the .05–level margin of error) or else different poll questions yielded conflicting results; if so, the poll to policy match was classified as "unclear."

Matching a large and diverse number of polls and policies requires several protocols. Following earlier studies (Monroe 1979, 1998; Marshall 1989, 2008) only publicly-available polls using representative national samples of all American adults are used to match poll questions with policies.[20] Poll questions are not used if based on subsamples of adults, such as smokers only or likely voters only. A policy outcome was counted when, after a tobacco control policy was actively considered, a "final" outcome was reached.[21] If a poll majority favored a more expansive policy but a similar although somewhat less expansive policy decision occurred, the match is still classified as consistent.[22] In classifying the poll results, the 95 percent confidence level for the margin of error is used—typically a 3 percent or 4 percent margin of error for the polls used here. Appropriate poll questions could be used whether the poll was taken before or after the final policy decision, although most poll questions were taken before the final policy decision occurred. Poll questions were used if the poll was taken within five years of a policy decision; nearly all poll questions were taken within two years of a policy outcome.[23] A poll to policy match on a specific issue was counted only once unless a substantially different decision occurred at least five years later; for example, several different proposed federal tax increases on cigarettes were each counted as separate matches. A poll question's wording must clearly refer to the specific policy being considered. Poll questions were not used if the wording included an end to means wording—that is, not if the wording was on whether a policy should be enacted in order to achieve a more general purpose unless the ends to means relationship was clearly a part of the policy debate itself. Nor were "push-style" questions used—that is, no questions were used that followed prior "push" questions designed to determine how many respondents would change their position if given additional information and typically using wording such as "What if you knew . . ." When several poll questions could be matched with a final policy decision, the most timely question is used as the poll match. Ordinal-level responses are dichotomized into favorable/unfavorable responses—for example, "strongly agree" and "somewhat agree" are combined into "agree." If one policy-maker's decision was soon overturned by another policy-maker's decision (typically a federal court ruling that overturned an agency decision), then the last decision was counted as the final decision.[24]

HOW CONSISTENT WITH THE POLLS ARE FEDERAL TOBACCO POLICIES?

Past research shows that American public policies are more often consistent than inconsistent with public opinion. Nonetheless, wide variations occur across policy areas and across time periods. Monroe (1979, 1998) reported that 63 percent of federal policies were consistent with the polls during the 1960 to 1979 time period and that 58 percent of federal policies were consistent with the polls during the 1980 to 1993 time period. In a few policy areas, such as constitutional amendments and basic political reforms, most policies are inconsistent with the polls. If polls and policies disagree a status-quo bias toward inaction typically appears. Little evidence is available on how often tobacco-related policies agree with public opinion. In the only prior report (Monroe 1998: 26) about half (55 percent) of tobacco and alcohol-related policies (combined) were consistent with the polls during the 1980 to 1993 time period.

Using these methods fifty-nine tobacco-related policies could be matched with nationwide polls. By time period, these fifty-nine matches range over almost half a century. The earliest matches occurred shortly after the U.S. Surgeon General's advisory committee issued its landmark 1964 report and prompted a round of poll questions and policy initiatives. The two most recent matches include a provision under the 2010 Affordable Care Act that cigarette smokers pay a surcharge on the subsidized price for health insurance received under that program, and a requirement that Medicare and Medicaid cover tobacco addiction.[25] These fifty-nine matches more often date from the 1960s, the 1990s, or the early 2000s rather than from the 1970s and 1980s, reflecting time periods when federal-level tobacco-related controversies most often occurred. By topic, the matches include the advertising and sale of cigarettes, smoking in public places or in the workplace, smoking by minors, legal liability and lawsuit issues, tax hikes, and a few miscellaneous topics. Some poll to policy matches, such as the Master Settlement Agreement, were highly visible but most matches received very little media attention. By outcome, about half (47 percent) of these fifty-nine proposals became federal policy and about half (53 percent) failed. By the policy-making forum, some measures were debated in Congress, others within the federal agencies, others through litigation, and several through a combination thereof.

Overall Results

American public opinion was more often favorable to tobacco control proposals than were federal-level policy-makers. Poll majorities (or occasionally, pluralities) supported 70 percent of these fifty-nine proposed tobacco control measures and opposed only 27 percent of these measures; the polls were closely divided or inconsistent on the remaining 3 percent of these measures. By comparison, for 47 percent of these matches a new tobacco control restriction occurred as the "final" policy result but for the remaining 53 percent of these matches the status quo prevailed (that is, no new tobacco control measure occurred).

About three-fifths (59 percent) of these fifty-nine tobacco control decisions were consistent with American public opinion, 37 percent of the outcomes were inconsistent with the polls, and the remaining 3 percent were "unclear." Excluding instances of evenly-divided or conflicting poll results, 61 percent of these tobacco control outcomes were consistent with public opinion and 39 percent were inconsistent. This 61 percent figure is very similar to prior estimates of national-level poll to policy agreement. Monroe (1979, 1998) reported that 63 percent of national policy outcomes across a broad range of policies were consistent with the polls between 1960 and 1979 and that 55 percent were consistent between 1980 and 1993.[26] Marshall (1989, 2008) reported that 63 percent of U.S. Supreme Court decisions were consistent with the polls between 1934 and 1986 and that 61 percent of Supreme Court decisions were consistent with the polls between 1986 and 2005.

That federal-level tobacco control decisions agree with American public opinion about as often as do most other policies is surprising for two reasons. First, all these fifty-nine measures involve a newly-proposed tobacco control measure and American politics is well-known for its status quo tendencies. Second, the tobacco industry is well-organized, wealthy, politically influential, and fully capable of protecting its interests (Baumgartner and Jones 1993; Brandt 2007; Kessler 2001: 198–213; Kluger 1997). Gilens and Page (2014) recently suggested that economic interest groups can usually successfully defend their interests against the average citizen, especially when interest groups are defending the status quo. The discussion below compares the influence on policy-making of public opinion versus the tobacco industry.

As chapter 1 described, several recent accounts of representation examine not just nationwide (or collective) attitudes; they also compare the views of different groups such as the rich and the poor. The evidence presented here is admittedly limited but generally reflects what has been reported elsewhere (Gilens 2012b). The wealthiest and the poorest Americans often hold similar views on most tobacco control disputes (that is, five-sixths of the time, or fifty of fifty-nine instances).[27] When group attitudes differ, federal-level tobacco control decisions more often reflect the views of wealthier Americans than of poor Americans, doing so in seven versus two instances, respectively.

Regrettably, pollsters seldom ask identically-worded poll questions both before and after a "final" policy decision occurs, and did so for only nine of these fifty-nine poll to policy matches. Examining poll shifts on these identically-worded, before-versus-after poll questions allows a very limited test of whether tobacco-related policy decisions influence public opinion. The results are very modest. Pre- to post-decision poll support on tobacco control policies shifted an average of only nine-tenths of 1 percent annually toward the "final" policy outcome. This suggests that federal-level tobacco control policy decisions do not greatly influence American public opinion, at least not so in the short term. Stated otherwise, there is virtually no evidence to support the manipulation model. The remainder of this section describes and evaluates nine hypotheses as to why some proposed tobacco control measures succeed but others fail.

The Poll Majority Hypothesis

The first hypothesis is simple and intuitively obvious: a tobacco control proposal will more often become policy if most Americans support the policy. Most studies on democratic responsiveness support this hypothesis (Burstein 2003; Monroe 1979, 1998; Page and Shapiro 1983; Shapiro 2011: 985). Table 5.1 reports the findings. As expected, popular tobacco control proposals significantly more often become public policy than do unpopular proposals. If more Americans *favor* a tobacco control measure than oppose it, the chances for success are 56 percent. If the reverse is true, that is, if more Americans *oppose* than favor a proposed tobacco control policy, the chances for success are only 19 percent.

The Bias Against Change

A simple summary measure describing the relationship between public opinion and public policy outcomes is the "bias against change." This measure compares the percentage of times that a proposed policy measure *fails* if more Americans oppose it than favor it (here, 81 percent) minus the percentage of times that a proposed policy measure *succeeds* if more Americans favor it than oppose it (here, 56 percent). This figure is typically a positive percentage, reflecting the status-quo tendency of American politics (Erikson 2015; Monroe 1979, 1998). The 25 percent bias against change figure for tobacco control policies (or 81 percent minus 56 percent equals 25 percent) is typical of results reported by past studies. This suggests that tobacco control policy-making has a status quo bias roughly as large as that found across all federal-level policy-making.[28] This does not mean that cigarette manufacturers, the now-defunct Tobacco Institute, and all the industry's political action committees, lawyers, and lobbyists, were without influence. Yet the industry has not been much more successful than the average in preventing unfriendly policy changes. The discussion below expands upon this finding.

Table 5.1. Policy outcomes and poll support for tobacco control proposals

	Poll Preference:	
	Status Quo	Change
Policy Outcome:		
Status Quo	81%	44%
Change	19%	56%
Total	(100%)	(100%)

The Public Mood Hypothesis

The "public mood" is a well-known measure that taps over-time swings in Americans' liberal-versus-conservative policy attitudes (Stimson 1991, 1999; Stimson, MacKuen, and Erikson 1995; Erikson, MacKuen, and Stimson 2002). Elected officials, bureaucrats at the agencies, and even federal judges tend to reflect the current public mood in their decision-making either because they sense and share current political views, because defying public opinion may lead to losses in upcoming elections, or because unpopular actions are likely to be overturned by other policy-makers. Since the public mood measure does not include any tobacco policy-related poll questions, it allows a fair test of whether policy-makers react to the public's liberal-versus-conservative views when deciding on tobacco control policies. These fifty-nine decisions were split into two groups based on whether public opinion was more liberal or more conservative when the decision was made.[29] Not surprisingly, the bias against change is higher (32 percent) when the public mood was more conservative than when the public mood was more liberal (only 15 percent). When the public mood was more conservative only 39 percent of tobacco control proposals succeeded, but when the public mood was more liberal 57 percent of tobacco control proposals succeeded. In short, swings in liberal-versus-conservative sentiment usefully predict whether tobacco control measures succeed or fail.

The Policy Forum Hypothesis

Tobacco control advocates have long viewed Congress as tobacco-friendlier than are the federal agencies or the federal courts, largely so because of the diligent efforts of U.S. Senators and Representatives from tobacco-producing states and the tobacco industry's lobbying and fund-raising efforts (Baumgartner and Jones 1993: 90–93, 114–17; Brandt 2007; Fritschler 1983; Kelder and Daynard 1997b: 66–70; Kluger 1997; Taylor 1985; Taylor 2003; Studlar 2002: 54, 98; Yang and Novotny 2009). Others attribute the tobacco industry's successes in Congress more to the members' conservative, pro-business, and anti-regulation ideologies (Wright 2004) and in some cases to the members' own smoking habits (Burden 2007). By comparison, several federal agencies typically support tobacco control policies, some agencies occasionally and others repeatedly so, and among these the Federal Trade Commission, the Federal Communications Commission, the Interstate Commerce Commission, the Food and Drug Administration, and the National Cancer Institute (Fritschler and Rudder 2007: 110, 170–72; Studlar 2014).

Is Congress actually the tobacco-friendliest policy-making forum? Most of these fifty-nine policies were pursued in only one forum, that is, either through Congress, the agencies, or else through the federal courts and litigation. Some were pursued through multiple forums, for example, the FDA's attempt to regulate tobacco products during the 1990s then involving the FDA and the federal courts and a decade later achieved by a 2009 Congressional act. Thirty-four of these fifty-nine tobacco control decisions were pursued through Congress, fourteen through the federal agencies, and nineteen through litigation.[30]

Examined in two different ways, Congress has indeed been the tobacco-friendliest forum. First, Congress supported tobacco control policies only half (50 percent) of the time. By comparison, the federal courts and the litigation process supported tobacco control policies 63 percent of the time.[31] Federal agencies supported tobacco control policies even more often—86 percent of the time. Second, the bias against change figures for Congress, the federal courts, and the agencies are strikingly different. For Congress the bias *against* change figure is 58 percent—an unusually large figure indicating that Congress is much tobacco-friendlier than is American public opinion. For the federal courts the opposite pattern occurs—there is actually a small bias *for* change of 17 percent.[32] For the federal agencies the bias *for* change is even larger—85 percent. The conventional wisdom is correct. The tobacco industry fares much better in Congress; tobacco control supporters fare better at federal agencies and in federal court.

The Time Period Hypothesis

This test compares the status quo bias for earlier years (the 1960s, 1970s, and 1980s) versus later years (the 1990s, 2000s, and 2010s). For three reasons the bias against change is predicted to be larger during the earlier years. First, tobacco control advocates were then less well organized than in later years. Second, scientific evidence and public knowledge about the ills of smoking was less complete in earlier than in later years. Third, earlier presidents and Congresses were tobacco-friendlier than in later years. As expected, a bias against change occurs during both time periods but is larger for the earlier years—33 percent during the 1960s, 1970s, and 1980s versus 21 percent thereafter.

The Salience Hypothesis

Some tobacco control controversies receive a great deal of media attention—none more so than the battle over the Master Settlement Agreement during the 1990s—but most such disputes receive little news coverage. This test compares the bias against change, using as a cutoff whether the dispute received at least six news mentions in the *New York Times*. As expected, the status quo bias is greater for less visible policy disputes. The bias against change is 35 percent for less visible disputes versus 23 percent for more visible disputes. Just as with many other issues (Burstein 2003; Lax and Phillips 2012; Monroe 1998: 20–22; Page and Shapiro 1983; Shapiro 2011), public opinion more greatly influences tobacco policy-making if the media heavily covers a dispute. If media coverage is slight or nonexistent, the status quo bias is stronger.

The Policy Type Hypothesis

Tobacco control advocates have pursued different policies including taxes hikes, limits on the sale or the advertising of cigarettes, bans on smoking in public places, limits on smoking by minors, financial damages for those who become ill or die from smoking, and several other policies. Do the chances of successfully enacting a tobacco control policy depend upon what type of policy is being pursued? Across each of the four most common tobacco control policies a moderately large status quo bias exists. The bias against change is 50 percent for tax hikes; 44 percent for limits on cigarette sales and advertising; 25 percent for bans on smoking in public places; and 33 percent for limits aimed at minors.[33] In short, a status quo bias is typical for all the most common approaches to tobacco control.

The Gridlock Hypothesis

Many political observers now view the federal government as prone toward partisan gridlock—that is, Republicans and Democrats are polarized along conservative-versus-liberal lines and disinclined to compromise (Crotty 2014). In this view whenever political control over the White House and Congress is divided between Republicans and Democrats, gridlock and a strong status quo bias result. The gridlock hypothesis is tested in three ways. The first and broadest version of this hypothesis examines all fifty-nine tobacco control policy decisions but here little support for the gridlock hypothesis appears.

A second and narrower version of the gridlock hypothesis is that tobacco control efforts will more often succeed when Democrats control the White House and both the U.S. Senate and House. This reflects the view that Republicans less often support tobacco control proposals than do Democrats. Little support appears for this version of the gridlock hypothesis. The bias against change is actually slightly larger (33 percent versus 22 percent) when Democrats control both Congress and the White House than when Republicans control both Congress and the White House or with divided party control.[34]

A third version holds that the gridlock hypothesis applies only to a subset of tobacco control policies, those decisions made by the elective branches and not to those made by federal agencies and federal courts. Some support appears for this version of the gridlock hypothesis. When tobacco control policies are decided by Congress and the White House, and when one party controls both branches, the bias against change is small (only 9 percent). Under these same conditions but with divided party control over Congress and the White House, the bias against change is 27 percent. As a caveat, this test excludes about half of tobacco control proposals during the last half century.

The gridlock hypothesis is intriguing but of limited scope and best explains the unusually small status quo bias for tobacco control decisions made by the elective branches when the same political party controls the White House and Congress. Periods of one-party control over both Congress and the White House have occurred roughly a third of the time since 1964. When this happens the status quo bias in tobacco control policy-making is unusually small.

The Industry Support Hypothesis

The tobacco industry opposed most of these fifty-nine tobacco control measures, but was divided or even supportive on some policies. As an example of a split within industry ranks, Philip Morris/Altria supported but other cigarette manufacturers opposed the 2009 tobacco control act. A rare instance of industry support for a tobacco control measure was the industry's support for Congress' 1965 package warning requirement. This hypothesis tests the impact of the tobacco industry's position at the time that the final policy decision occurred. The industry's position is quite important in tobacco control policy outcomes. The bias against change is 36 percent when the industry uniformly opposed a tobacco control proposal but only 7 percent when the industry was split on or supportive of a policy.

The Stand-Alone Hypothesis

Many of these fifty-nine tobacco control proposals are "stand-alone" measures—that is, only one measure was being debated or litigated at the time. For example, the 1965 cigarette package warning label was not tied to any other tobacco control proposal. By contrast, several tobacco control measures were combined into a larger piece of legislation. For example, the proposed (and failed) Clinton health care plan, among its many provisions, included a proposed tax hike on cigarettes; both the 1998 Master Settlement Agreement and the 2009 Family Smoking Prevention and Tobacco Control Act also contained multiple tobacco control measures. Stand-alone tobacco control proposals are predicted more often to succeed because multi-part measures give the industry more potential issues with which to kill a proposal. As predicted, the bias against change is only 20 percent for stand-alone tobacco control proposals, versus 33 percent for multi-part proposals.

Combining the Predictors

To explain which tobacco control proposals succeed and which fail, these nine hypotheses were tested in a variety of statistical models each with two or more predictors. The best-fit logit model includes just two predictors: first, whether more Americans favor than oppose the measure, and second, whether the tobacco industry is split or supportive rather than uniformly opposed. This two-variable model correctly predicts 66 percent of the outcomes of these fifty-nine tobacco control proposals, a significant improvement over the 53 percent base rate. Alternatively, combining the public mood indicator with the tobacco industry's position also successfully explains whether a tobacco control proposal will succeed or fail.[35] Stated otherwise, if both public opinion and the tobacco industry oppose a tobacco control policy, there is only a 20 percent chance that policy will occur. If public opinion favors but the tobacco industry opposes a policy, those odds become 51 percent. If public opinion opposes but the tobacco industry is split or supportive, the odds are 69 percent. If public opinion favors a tobacco control policy and if the industry is either split or supportive, the odds of that policy being enacted are 91 percent.

To summarize: both public opinion and the tobacco industry's position well explain a tobacco control proposal's chances of success. Adding other predictors do not improve upon this model.

CONCLUSION: AMERICAN PUBLIC OPINION AND TOBACCO CONTROL POLICIES

Tobacco control efforts at the federal level have a long and complicated history (Yang and Novotny 2009; Fritschler and Rudder 2007). Anti-smoking advocates' efforts sometimes succeed, sometimes not. Some proposals are broad in scope, others narrow. Some tobacco control proposals are considered by Congress and the White House, others by the federal agencies, others through litigation, and some through multiple forums. Some proposals enjoy widespread poll support, some not. Enough of these efforts succeeded that cigarettes are now highly taxed, highly regulated, and highly stigmatized—a far cry from the conditions of half a century ago. This chapter offers two conclusions about the link between public opinion and federal tobacco control policies.

First, public opinion matters. If more Americans support than oppose a proposed tobacco control measure, the chances greatly improve that a proposal will be enacted. In this tobacco control policies are not unique. Many studies show that American public opinion is by no means the sole influence on policy-making, but in most accounts (cf. Gilens and Page 2014) neither is public opinion irrelevant. Even when considering the tobacco industry's position, majority public opinion remains a significant predictor of tobacco control policy outcomes. Whether these results are particularly encouraging to those who believe that public opinion should influence public policy is a matter of interpretation.

Second, the status quo bias for tobacco control policy-making is neither much different nor much larger than for all federal policy-making. This does not mean that the tobacco industry was or now is without influence. By all accounts the industry's lobbyists, lawyers, grass-roots support, and fundraising efforts were and still are diligent, skillful, and well-funded. Yet the tobacco industry also has many skillful and determined enemies. Over the last half century the tobacco industry's influence over federal policy-making does not stand out as unique. The tobacco industry's record cannot be accurately assessed solely by looking backwards to the 1960s and 1970s nor by looking at its successes in Congress—the tobacco-friendliest era and forum.

NOTES

1. This chapter is based, in part, on descriptions in Brandt (2007), Derthick (2002, 2005), Fritschler and Rudder (2007), Kluger (1997), Rabin and Sugarman (2001), Studlar (2002), and Warner (2006).

2. In 1993 the Federal Trade Commission voted three to two not to ban the Joe Camel ads, but in 1997 reversed its position and reached an agreement with R. J. Reynolds to withdraw the ads, an agreement included in the 1998 Master Settlement Agreement; the FTC then dismissed the case. This poll-to-policy match is counted as of the FTC's 1997 agreement with R. J. Reynolds. For a discussion of youth-oriented tobacco advertising, see Wolfson (2001: 36–38); Snell (2005); Elkin and Wilson (2010); Pierce and Gilpin (1995); and Pierce, Gilpin, and Farkas (1998).

3. For evidence on American attitudes during the mid-1980s see Lieberman Research, Inc. (1986).

4. For evidence that depictions of smoking on television and in film declined since the 1950s see Jamieson and Romer (2010, 2015); for an assessment of the impact of such depictions see Gibson and Maurer (2000).

5. The 1998 Master Settlement Agreement earlier sharply reduced the number of cigarette vending machines.

6. In 2014 Gallup reported smoking rates varied widely across the states, from a low of 12 percent in Utah and 15 percent in California to a high of 27 percent in Mississippi and 30 percent in West Virginia and in Kentucky.

7. Regrettably, no poll questions exist on several early federal actions restricting smoking in specific public places, including a 1964 Public Health Service ban on the free distribution of cigarettes in Indian and PHS hospitals; a 1973 Federal Aviation Authority requirement for separate seating sections for smokers and nonsmokers on airplanes; a 1973 Interstate Commerce Commission policy limiting smokers to the rear fifth of seats on commercial interstate busses and a 1976 policy limiting smoking on trains. These fifty-nine poll-to-policy matches are a diverse but nonrandom sample of tobacco control issues.

8. Smokers sometimes avoid tax hikes by buying from duty-free stores or Indian reservations and offset higher taxes by purchasing multipacks or by shopping at discount tobacco-only stores (Cornelius et al. 2015); see also Chaloupka et al. (2002).

9. Wilson et al. (2004) estimate the loss of life expectancy from lost income due to tobacco taxes at only three to sixteen days, a small fraction of lost life expectancy resulting from cigarette smoking.

10. Several accounts describe tax hikes as the largest single reason for declining smoking rates (e.g., Levy et al. 2000, 2005, 2007, and 2010).

11. The large per-pack price increases that resulted from the 1998 Master Settlement Agreement were not tax hikes but had a similar effect on smoking rates. Estimates of the price elasticity of cigarette smoking generally fall within the range of .3 or .4; that is, a 10 percent increase in per-pack prices causes a 3 to 4 percent decrease in smoking due to fewer cigarettes being smoked per smoker, increased quitting rates, and lower initiation of smoking. Price elasticity varies considerably across age groups and is highest among younger smokers (Gruber 2001, 2002; Ross and Chaloupka 2003, 2004).

12. By raising tobacco prices, the federal government's quota and price support program slightly raised the cost of cigarettes and thereby decreased consumption. Even so, tobacco control advocates opposed the program because it provided government support for tobacco growing and because the program solidified the economic ties between tobacco farmers and cigarette manufacturers (Warner 2006: 45–47).

13. Viscusi (2002: 33–100) argued that the states' estimates of their tobacco-related costs conveniently ignored both revenues from cigarette taxes and cost savings from smokers' early death; under some conditions smoking was "a financial profit center, not a costly imposition" (Viscusi 2002: 75).

14. The 1997 Global Settlement Agreement is sometimes called the Proposed Resolution. The Master Settlement Agreement refers to the final 1998 agreement.

15. The 1997 Global Settlement Agreement included FDA oversight of the tobacco industry, stronger health warnings, tighter restrictions on youth access, and financial penalties if youth tobacco usage did not decrease; these provisions were not included in the 1998 Master Settlement Agreement. Several of the 1997 agreement's proposed restrictions on advertising were included in the 1998 agreement (Studlar 2002: 102–11; Givel and Glantz 2004).

16. Derthick (2002, 2005) and Daynard et al. (2001) examine the 1998 agreement's many provisions. Studlar (2002: 102–11) and Givel and Glantz (2004) compare the 1997 Global Settlement, the U.S. Senate version, and 1998 Master Settlement Agreement. The 1998 agreement's terms effectively raised the per-pack price by about forty cents, although the average per-pack price actually rose by ninety-four cents within two years (Wolfson 2001: 210; Viscusi 2002/2003: 63; Sloan, Mathews, and Trogdon 2004: 359). Coupons and retail discounting reduced the price hikes' impact. Even so, the 1998 agreement did not harm major cigarette manufacturers' profits or investor returns (Sloan, Mathews, and Trogdon 2004).

17. In 1996 Philip Morris had 46 percent of U.S. market share with RJR at 28 percent, Brown & Williamson at 18 percent, Lorillard at 8 percent, and Liggett at 2 percent. After some restructuring by 2015 Altria had 50 percent of U.S. market share, with Reynolds American at 28 percent, Lorillard at 13 percent, Imperial Tobacco at 4 percent, and other companies at 6 percent.

18. This classification is a "congruence" study, one that compares policy-specific poll questions with policy decisions. "Trend" or "dynamic representation" studies (e.g., Lax and Phillips 2012: 149–50; Stimson 1991, 1999; Stimson, MacKuen, and Erikson 1995, 2002; Erikson, MacKuen, and Stimson 2002) compare over-time poll changes with changing policy decisions, but require consistently-worded poll questions across time, a condition rarely met for poll questions on tobacco-related issues.

19. The matching poll question is "*. . . the tobacco companies should be regulated by the Food and Drug Administration: strongly agree, agree, disagree, strongly disagree?*"—69 percent agree, 25 percent disagree, 6 percent don't know. EDK Associates, 10/18–20/1999.

20. Nationally representative polls describe attitudes for Americans nationwide but not for individual states or localities or for demographic groups such as men versus women.

21. A "final" policy decision is one that prevails for at least five years during which the policy debate becomes largely inactive. If after a five-year lag the policy debate again becomes active and if timely polls are then available, another poll match may occur.

22. For example, a 15-cent-a-pack tax increase on cigarettes was classified as consistent with public opinion, although the matching poll question asked about a larger increase: "*Two senators, a Republican and a Democrat, have proposed increasing cigarette taxes by forty-three cents a pack and giving much of the money raised to help states provide health insurance for insured children. Based on this description, do you favor or oppose this plan?*" NBC/*Wall Street Journal*, 4/26–28/ 1997—72 percent favor, 24 percent oppose, 4 percent not sure.

23. For fifty of these fifty-nine cases the matching poll question occurred before the final policy decision, reflecting a common survey research practice to ask poll questions only during ongoing policy debates.

24. This situation rarely occurred and typically includes federal court rulings on agency policies, or a few instances in which one policy-maker deferred to another which soon thereafter made a policy decision. For example, in 1964 the Federal Trade Commission considered a package warning requirement, but under political pressure deferred to Congress which in 1965 enacted that requirement; herein, both the FTC and Congress were considered to take a pro-tobacco control position.

25. The Affordable Care Act's financial penalty for smokers was poll-matched as of the bill's passage in 2010 although the actual regulations were not written until 2013. The tobacco addiction coverage poll match was coded as of the federal agency rules written in 2010 for Medicare and in 2011 for Medicaid.

26. During the 1960 to 1993 time period 67 percent of tobacco control policies were consistent with the polls—a figure slightly higher than Monroe's 1960 to 1993 estimates of 59 percent across all policy areas.

27. This analysis relies upon the income categories offered by pollsters themselves. Generally the wealthiest Americans number about one-quarter of poll respondents and the poorest Americans about one-fifth of Americans. The position favored by a majority (or occasionally, a plurality) of respondents in each income group was classified as the group's policy preference which was then classified as being either consistent or inconsistent with the policy outcome. The remaining middle income respondents' views rarely disagreed with wealthier Americans, doing so only five of fifty-nine times; in four of those five instances the views of wealthier Americans prevailed.

28. Monroe (1998: 18) reports an average bias against change of 17 percent during the 1960 to 1979 period and of 25 percent during the 1980 to 1993 period; both figures are reported for a wide variety of policies. The largest bias against change (of 77 percent and 100 percent, respectively) were for political reform issues.

29. Periods of a conservative public mood had a score of fifty-nine or lower; a liberal public mood was of sixty or higher (Stimson 1991, 1999). Using this cutoff thirty-one of these fifty-nine policy decisions occurred during conservative periods and 28 occurred during liberal periods.

30. The forum in which a decision is actively pursued is based on where the tobacco industry and tobacco control supporters focused their efforts.

31. These results include both federal court rulings and other decisions achieved through litigation such as the 1998 Master Settlement Agreement. Unfortunately there are few poll matches for the federal courts and very few from the post-2009 time period.

32. Findings of a bias *for* change are unusual in American policy-making (Monroe 1998: 18).

33. As a caveat, the number of cases within each of these four categories is small, ranging from ten cases for bans on smoking in public places to twenty-five cases for restrictions on sales and advertising.

34. The lack of support for this hypothesis may result from the many tobacco-friendly, mostly Southern Democrats who served in Congress until the 1980s or in the case of Lyndon Johnson and Jimmy Carter who served as president.

35. The two-predictor binary logit model is: -.856 +.834 (if the polls favored the measure) and +1.357 (if the tobacco industry was split or supportive); standard errors are .399, .357 and .674, respectively; the constant and predictors are all significant at the .05–level. Using the "public mood" measure (Stimson 1991, 1999) almost as successfully predicts tobacco control proposals' success or failure as do policy-specific poll questions. Stated otherwise, a tobacco control measure's likelihood of being enacted is about equally well explained by public attitudes toward the issue or by Americans' liberal-conservative swings.

SIX

Public Opinion, Juries, and Courts

As Alexis de Tocqueville wrote in 1835, "(t)here is hardly a political question in the United States which does not sooner or later turn into a judicial one." Lawsuits have long been an important part of American policymaking, much more so than in other countries (Mather 2009). Tobacco control is no exception to this pattern. A few examples show how far-ranging tobacco litigation has been. In 1911 the U.S. Supreme Court's ruling that the then-powerful tobacco trust be broken up led to a fierce competition among cigarette companies and to a rapid rise in the number of cigarette smokers. During the 1950s and 1960s ill smokers or their heirs began filing lawsuits against cigarette manufacturers. The tobacco industry itself filed or threatened to file lawsuits against many local, state, or federal restrictions on smoking. During the 1990s prominent trial lawyers joined with state attorneys general to recover the states' costs for tobacco-caused health care resulting in an out-of-court settlement, the 1998 Master Settlement Agreement. In 2000 cigarette manufacturers won a five to four decision at the U.S. Supreme Court, forestalling for nine years the Food and Drug Administration's attempt to regulate cigarettes. Some juries awarded financial damages, often including substantial punitive damages, to individual smokers or to groups of smokers. After the 2009 tobacco control act was enacted, some cigarette manufacturers successfully challenged in federal court several new regulations.

How did the American public react to all this litigation? This chapter asks three questions. First, do tobacco litigation outcomes reflect prevailing American public opinion? Second, has tobacco litigation affected Americans' views toward the tobacco industry? Third, what does public opinion portend for future tobacco litigation?

Why public opinion might influence judicial decisions, or vice versa, merits a brief discussion. Federal judges are appointed for life terms, not popularly elected; so, too, are most state judges appointed rather than elected. Judges typically explain their rulings in terms of statute or past judicial rulings, and seldom explicitly consider current polls. Under these conditions federal and state judges might appear to be relatively free agents, capable of simply ignoring current public opinion. Further, federal and state judges rarely make any great efforts to influence public opinion in favor of their rulings. Indeed American judges have very few effective ways to influence public opinion even if they desired to do so. Nor does the media heavily or long cover more than a few court rulings, thereby doing little to inform or influence public opinion about judicial decisions.

All this notwithstanding, a great deal of empirical research suggests that most judicial decisions reflect timely public opinion and poll trends. Epstein and Martin (2010) and Shapiro (2011) recently reviewed this research. New judicial appointments bring the federal courts back into line with current public opinion. Some sitting judges markedly change their voting patterns over time and when they do, usually in ways that better reflect timely public opinion. A few judges have themselves suggested that large shifts in public opinion do not pass by unnoticed the bench. Many years ago U.S. Supreme Court justice Benjamin Cardozo (1921: 168) wrote that "the great tides and currents which engulf the rest of men do not turn aside in their course and pass the judges by." In this view judges sense and share, or at least defer to popular majorities (Rehnquist 1986).[1] Judges have good reasons to pay attention to public opinion. Executives and legislatures less often overturn popular judicial rulings than unpopular decisions. Higher-level courts more often reverse lower court decisions when the lower court's decision disagreed with current poll majorities (Marshall 2008). Further, the judicial precedents and statutes upon which judges typically rely in making decisions often reflect current public opinion. So, too, jury rulings may (or may not) reflect current American attitudes. Court decisions may agree with current public opinion for completely different reasons without any clear intent to do so by juries or judges; this chapter describes just such an apparent case of "coincidental" representation. That court decisions more often agree with public opinion than not is by now a well-supported finding.

By contrast, findings on the American courts' ability to influence (or manipulate) mass public opinion is very mixed. A great deal of experimental research and some studies on local public opinion shows that judicial decisions can possibly influence public opinion. However, research on actual poll shifts show that court rulings seldom favorably influence public opinion on the issue in dispute, at least not so in the short term (Page, Shapiro, and Dempsey 1987: 33; Marshall 1989, 2008: 131–37). None of these findings are based on tobacco-related lawsuits. This chapter considers whether these well-established conclusions accurately describe tobacco control litigation.

PUBLIC OPINION AND THE THREE WAVES OF TOBACCO LITIGATION

Beginning during the 1950s, as an increasing number of scientific studies tied cigarette smoking to lung cancer and to heart disease, numerous sick or dying smokers or their heirs filed lawsuits against the tobacco industry (Rabin 1992: 855–63). During the 1950s and 1960s over one hundred individual lawsuits were filed charging the industry with negligence or with failing at an implied warranty by causing smoking-related illnesses and deaths (Glantz et al. 1996: 235–87; Rabin 1993; Schwartz 1993). Yet none of the plaintiffs succeeded during this "first wave" of tobacco litigation. The tobacco industry fully realized its enormous potential liability and turned to its well-financed and skillful attorneys who insisted on costly and time-consuming pretrial motions and depositions. If these costs and delays did not kill the lawsuit, the industry's attorneys insisted on full court hearings. If still necessary the industry's attorneys pursued lengthy and costly post-decision appeals. The industry made no pretrial settlement offers (Glantz et al. 1996: 235–87; Guardino and Daynard 2005). Few plaintiff attorneys, most of whom were in solo practice or in small firms, could afford to take these case to trial; as a result very few of these lawsuits even reached the trial stage (Garner 1980). If a case did make it to trial, the industry's expert witnesses disputed the scientific evidence that smoking was harmful, that cigarette manufacturers could have foreseen that it was, and that a particular plaintiff's illnesses resulted from his or her smoking (Player 1998: 312–15; Proctor 2011; Schwartz 1993). Further, the idea that using an ordinary, widely sold commercial product might cause serious long-term harm was not yet a commonly-held legal or public view. Nor were cigarette manufacturers necessarily held responsible for selling a harmful product unless the company knew that cigarette smoking was harmful and this the companies strongly disputed. Another obstacle for plaintiffs arose soon after the 1964 Surgeon General advisory committee's report was issued when Congress in 1965 mandated warning labels for cigarette packages. The American Law Institute's 1965 restatement on tort law held that if a product was commonly known as harmful, the consumer was responsible for the resulting harm.

By the mid-1960s the first wave of tobacco litigation failed to produce a single payout for plaintiffs. Some years then passed before the "second wave" of lawsuits By the 1980s the American public was more familiar with dangerous and toxic products such as asbestos, DES, Agent Orange, or Dalkon Shields. By this time some courts were applying the plaintiff-friendlier standards of comparative fault and of strict liability to corporations that sold dangerous products. Still, most of the 175 to 200 second-wave cases on behalf of individual plaintiffs were brought by solo practitioners or by small law firms few of whom had the financial and legal abilities to pursue complex cases (Rabin 1992; 1993: 115).[2] By contrast, the tobacco industry's attorneys could afford to make these lawsuits "extremely burdensome and expensive" (Rabin 1992: 868).

Second-wave tobacco litigation proved to be no more successful for plaintiffs than was the first. By this time tobacco companies' attorneys could argue that the federally-mandated cigarette package warning adequately alerted smokers that smoking was risky; that federal law preempted such lawsuits; and that the risks of smoking were common knowledge, a view also accepted by several federal appeal courts, state courts, and state legislatures (Player 1998: 314–20; Rabin 1992, 1993). The companies' attorneys argued that cigarette smoking in the face of federally-mandated package warnings and constant publicity was an individual choice, and that smokers should bear the consequences of their own freedom of choice (Rabin 1993: 114, 124–25). The comparative fault doctrine encouraged cigarette company lawyers to make jurors fully aware of a defendant's personal foibles and failures (Myers 1998). Tobacco attorneys sometimes argued that package warnings preempted lawsuits brought in state courts. Nor was whistle-blower evidence yet available that smoking was addictive and that cigarette companies targeted minors. In the *Cipollone* case, a rare New Jersey verdict that partly went against a cigarette manufacturer, the verdict was overturned upon appeal and then further appealed to the U.S. Supreme Court.[3] The Supreme Court's 1991 decision allowed some smoker' lawsuits, at least those that argued over hard-to-prove fraud or express warranty claims. However, all except pre-1969 failure-to-warn tort claims based on state laws were barred (Henderson and Twerski 2010; Schwartz 1993: 149–53). The *Cipollone* lawsuit itself was eventually abandoned when the plaintiff's law firm judged any further litigation too expensive to pursue. Despite its failure the *Cipollone* case resulted in a significant breakthrough when plaintiff's legal discovery produced and made public thousands of previously-secret tobacco industry documents (Brandt 2007: 327–34; Daynard and Morin 1988). In short, from the 1950s through 1992 none of the lawsuits brought by individual smokers won any monetary damages (Mather 1998: 904). Its own substantial legal costs notwithstanding, the tobacco industry paid nothing in damages to sick or dying smokers or to their heirs (McCann, Haltom, and Fisher 2013: 291–93).

The few lawsuits that reached a jury trial faced another serious problem: large majorities of Americans held individual smokers, not the cigarette manufacturers responsible for smoking-related illnesses. The view that individuals are responsible for their own choices, including illnesses, accidents, and death, is not new. During the mid- to late 1800s popular opinion, legal doctrine, and courtroom practices made it difficult for injured or dead workers to collect damages from their employers (Hans 2000: 5–10). Helping to continue that tradition are the modern tort reform movement, media coverage that focuses on high-dollar jury awards and on sizeable attorney fees (Haltom and McCann 2004), the widely-held public view that there is too much personal injury litigation, jurors' tendency to scrutinize more closely the plaintiff than the defendant, favorable public views toward business, beliefs that large jury awards will lead to higher prices, and U.S. Supreme Court limits on punitive damage awards (Hans 2000: 10–17, 58–67, 71–78, 84, 175–77, 209–24). On the other hand, corporations that recklessly endanger their customers or that with held evidence about faulty products elicit less sympathy from jurors (Hans 2000: 47–49, 114–18, 136, 166).

Table 6.1 reports several nationwide poll question, mostly from the 1990s, on whether the smoker or the tobacco industry should bear the responsibility for smoking-related illnesses and death. By a two or three to one margin Americans held individual smokers responsible for their smoking-related illnesses. This may be surprising since tobacco industry was widely unpopular, since news coverage is negative toward the industry (Smith, Wakefield, and Edsall 2006), and since public awareness that cigarette smoking caused serious health problems was high. Many Americans also held other beliefs that discouraged large jury awards on behalf of ill, dying, or dead smokers. In a September 1999 Decision Quest survey, for example, 56 percent of Americans said that *"large jury awards usually get upheld on appeal"* and only 22 percent said (correctly) that large jury awards are usually thrown out or reduced upon appeal.

The results reported in Table 6.1 did not change greatly in later surveys. In Gallup's polling the percentage of Americans who said that they mostly or completely blamed cigarette companies *"for the health problems faced by smokers in this country"* was only 25 percent in 1997 and 24 percent in 2008. The percentage who mostly or completely blamed smokers was 64 percent in 1997 and 66 percent in 2008. Despite all the criticisms of the tobacco industry and despite the industry's admission that cigarettes were cancer-causing and addictive, there was virtually no change in American attitudes on who was to blame for smoking-related illnesses.

To be sure, a jury is very different than a public opinion poll. A jury is locally, not nationally selected. Jurors are far fewer in number than are respondents in a nationwide poll. Jurors are subject to extensive questioning before being seated. Jurors are more often older and middle-class than is an average American. Unlike respondents in a public opinion poll, jurors listen to evidence about the health consequences of smoking, learn about an individual smoker's life, hear from expert witnesses about scientific evidence, and sit through lengthy testimony and cross-examinations. Unlike poll respondents, jurors deliberate one with another. Further, poll questions have their limits. None of the poll questions in Table 6.1 is worded so as to ask about the relative share of blame each party bears. Even so, those poll results show that most Americans were not initially sympathetic to an individual smoker's claims. Statistically there is less than a 5 percent likelihood that at least seven of twelve jurors randomly drawn from the U.S. population would favor claims holding a

Table 6.1. Attitudes on who is responsible for smoking-related illnesses and death

	Nationwide poll results
"Do you think tobacco companies should or should not be legally responsible for deaths caused by smoking?" Gallup, July 1988	16% should, 79% should not, 5% don't know
"Do you think cigarette companies should be held legally responsible if they are sued by the families of smokers who died of smoking-related causes or does the fact that the companies put warning notices on cigarette packs excuse them from responsibility?" Gallup, October 1991	13% held responsible, 66% warning notices excuse companies, 17% not responsible for other reasons, 4% don't know/refused
Same question, Gallup, March 1997	28% held responsible, 52% warning notices excuse companies, 14% not responsible for other reasons, 6% don't know/refused
"Thinking for a minute now about who is more responsible for smoking habits – do you think it is the smokers themselves who are most responsible for their own habit because they can choose whether or not to smoke, or do you think that it is the tobacco industry which is most responsible for people's smoking habits because it promotes a product that is known to be addictive?" Marttila & Kiley, April 1993 (national registered voters)	76% smokers, 17% tobacco industry, 5% both, 1% not sure
"Around the country, smokers and former smokers are suing tobacco companies for compensation for smoking-related illnesses and some tobacco companies are considering settling these lawsuits before they go to trial. Who do you think is more responsible for these smoking-related illnesses: the people who smoke or the tobacco companies?" Fox News, April 1997	67% people who smoke, 19% tobacco companies, 13% neither or both, 1% not sure
"Do you think tobacco companies should be held legally responsible for smoking related illnesses and deaths, or not?" CBS News Poll, May 1997	24% yes, 71% no, 5% don't know
"Do you think that a person who starts smoking today, knowing that smoking can cause cancer, should or should not be able to sue the tobacco companies if they become ill from smoking later on in life?" NBC News/*Wall Street Journal* Poll, April 1998	8% should be able to sue, 90% should not, 2% not sure

"Please tell me which of these two statements you agree with more: Smoking is a bad habit and our society should do everything possible to stamp it out, or smoking may be a bad habit but everyone should have the right to make his or her own choices about whether to smoke or not?" *Time*/CNN/Yankelovich, April 1998	26% stamp it out, 72% personal choice, 2% not sure
"In your opinion, should the tobacco companies have to pay money damages to people who develop smoking-related illnesses, or not?" ABC News, October 1999	34% yes, 60% no, 3% depends, 3% no opinion

cigarette manufacturer responsible for smoking-caused illnesses. There is essentially no likelihood that all twelve randomly-drawn jurors would do so. These odds do not greatly increase within any region or demographic group.

Nearly all first and second-wave jury decisions were consistent with nationwide poll results. Most Americans believed that individual smokers were responsible for their own illnesses and until the late 1990s and thereafter the tobacco industry never paid any damages in these cases. Since few individual smokers' lawsuits actually went to trial, however, the link between public opinion and legal outcomes is largely happenstance or "coincidental." Public policy agreed with majority public opinion, but not because public opinion had much direct influence on the decisions. In the well-known statistical saying: correlation is not causality.

In 1994 a "third wave" of tobacco litigation began to emerge. This era of tobacco litigation was very different from the two earlier waves. More cases were pursued by well-funded plaintiff attorneys who sometimes worked together or in the case of the Master Settlement Agreement lawsuit worked with state attorneys general. Some lawsuits were class action lawsuits; many more were individual cases; and some were brought on behalf of the states, labor unions, or health insurance companies (Daynard 1994; Henderson and Twerski 2010: 74–76). In Minnesota litigation forced the tobacco industry to make public thousands of previously secret industry documents, a move that in time led to the legacy web site's on-line collection of several million documents (Hurt and Robertson 1998). In a few states, most notably Florida, the state legislature rewrote state law to make the tobacco industry's legal position more difficult. Some third wave litigation charged the tobacco industry with criminal misconduct in lying about or withholding evidence of the dangers of smoking (Koenig and Rustad 1998; McCann, Haltom, and Fisher 2013). A new and untested legal theory argued that cigarette manufacturers had unjustly enriched themselves at the expense of state governments or of insurance companies who paid the medical bills for sick and dying smokers, and that the cigarette manufacturers should repay these costs.[4] So basing a state's lawsuit to recover the costs of treating sick smokers offered a major benefit for plaintiffs since the tobacco companies' lawyers could not argue that the ills of smoking resulted from a smoker's own freedom of choice and should be an individual's burden. As Mississippi's legal team described their lawsuit: "the state of Mississippi has never smoked a cigarette." When local public opinion polls in Mississippi suggested that this novel legal theory would not impress a jury, the state's attorney general, Michael Moore, filed the case before a judge (Fritschler and Rudder 2007: 118–21: Orey 1999: 268–69). The unjust enrichment theory, along with public nuisance, indemnity, and deception were all used against the industry (Gifford 2010: 120–33). The states' lawsuits proved to be very successful, even as several class action lawsuits failed.[5]

By the mid-1990s other circumstances had also changed. Whistleblower evidence became available that cigarette manufacturers knew that nicotine was addictive and marketed its cigarettes to children (Mollenkamp et al. 1998: 37–48; Kelder and Daynard 1997a, 1997b). Lawsuits against the industry led to the release of thousands, then millions of pages of previously-secret industry documents, further damaging industry claims that smokers were simply exercising their "freedom of choice" to smoke (Ciresi, Walburn, and Sutton 1999). News coverage was very negative toward the tobacco industry (Haltom and McCann 2004; McCann, Haltom, and Fisher 2013; Mather 1998: 923). A February 1994 Day One ABC News program alleged that cigarette manufacturers "spiked" the nicotine in cigarettes. During an April 1994 Congressional hearing several tobacco company executives, televised and under oath, denied that cigarettes were deadly and addictive—arguments that most Americans rejected and that conflicted with the companies' internal documents. The number of lawsuits pending against the tobacco industry rose from under 100 in 1993 to over 800 by 1998 (Mather 1998: 911–12). Some tobacco critics were optimistic that third-wave litigation would greatly raise the industry's costs and the price of cigarettes, frighten off investors, lower cigarette consumption, and seriously damage cigarette manufacturers (Kelder and Daynard 1997a: 183).

American public opinion was less one-sided and more mixed on class action lawsuits and on lawsuits brought by governments than on lawsuits brought by individual smokers. As Table 6.2 reports, on class action and government-brought lawsuits, the tobacco industry's poll support ranged between roughly two-fifths to three-fifths of the public. On four of six of these poll questions—all except the Justice Department's financial penalties and payments for the poor under the Master Settlement Agreement—a majority or a plurality of Americans held a position that was consistent with the eventual outcome.

Litigation continued despite the 1998 settlement between cigarette manufacturers and the states. The Master Settlement Agreement did not

Table 6.2. Attitudes toward tobacco-related class action and government lawsuits

	Nationwide poll results
"All in all, do you think it would be a good thing or a bad thing for the tobacco companies in this country to be driven out of business by lawsuits?" Gallup/CNN/*USA Today* Poll, May 1997	42% good thing, 54% bad thing, 4% don't know/refused
"Do you think that cigarette makers should be given immunity from future legal claims if they agree to restrictions on sales and advertising and if they pay smokers for existing claims?" *Business Week*/Harris Poll, June 1997	49% no, 45% yes, 6% no opinion
". . . agree or disagree. . . . Tobacco companies should be required to refund states for the cost of medical care for poor people who contract diseases related to smoking?" NBC News/*Wall Street Journal* Poll, July 1997	41% agree, 54% disagree, 5% not sure
"Under the settlement by the big tobacco companies to settle state lawsuits, no group of people could join together to sue the tobacco companies over smoking-related illnesses. Do you think reaching a nationwide settlement is worth giving the tobacco companies this legal protection or not?" Associated Press, August 1997	31% worth it, 54% not worth it, 3% depends, 13% don't know
"As you may know, this week the U.S. Justice Department filed a lawsuit against the tobacco industry seeking to recover billions of dollars in federal health costs for smoking-related illnesses. The tobacco companies being sued have stated the charges have no merit and should be dismissed. Which side do you agree with more in this lawsuit—the Justice Department or the tobacco companies?" Gallup, September 1999	51% DOJ, 42% tobacco companies, 2% both, 2% neither, 4% no opinion
"As you may know, a Florida jury ordered tobacco companies to pay $145 billion in damages to Florida smokers who have been made sick by smoking. Would you say you approve or disapprove of this decision by the Florida jury?" Gallup, July 2000	37% approve, 59% disapprove, 4% no opinion

preempt current or preclude future individual or class action lawsuits, did not limit the size of damage awards, and did not set a cap on the tobacco industry's total or annual payouts. Third-wave tobacco litigation included two important cases from Florida, the *Broin* and the *Engle* cases, both brought by the Rosenblatt's family-run law firm. A class action lawsuit filed in 1991, *Broin v. Phillip Morris et al.*, was pursued on behalf of "innocent" third parties, some 60,000 flight attendants who were exposed to secondhand smoke from passengers. By October 1997 the tobacco industry for the first time signed off on a $300 million settlement to fund scientific and medical research on tobacco-related diseases.[6] Although in dollar amount the *Broin* settlement was far smaller than the Master Settlement Agreement, it was the tobacco industry's first-ever settlement agreement in a class action lawsuit and hinted that the industry's position had weakened.

More litigation followed. In California, Florida, and Oregon and occasionally in other states some juries handed multimillion dollar awards to ill, dying, or dead smokers or their heirs. Many awards included large punitive damage awards against the cigarette manufacturers although these were often reduced post-trial (DelRossi and Viscusi 2010; Douglas, Davis, and Beasley 2006; Rabin 1999; Viscusi 2002: 45).[7] In 1996 a jury awarded $750,000 in compensatory damages but no punitive damages to Grady Carter, a Florida smoker and lung cancer victim. The Carter award was upheld on appeal and paid with accrued interest. In 1995 a California jury awarded a smoker $1.3 million in compensatory damages and $700,000 in punitive damages with $3 million later paid, including interest. In 1999 a California jury awarded a smoker $1.5 million in compensatory damages plus a $50 million punitive award, reduced upon appeal to $16.7 million and paid. An Oregon lawsuit led to an award of $1.6 million in compensatory damages and $79.5 million in punitive damages. In 2001 a Los Angeles case led to $5.5 million in compensatory damages plus a $3 billion punitive damage award, eventually paid as $82 million. A 2002 Los Angles jury went further and awarded $850,000 in compensatory damages plus a $28 billion punitive damages award against Philip Morris, reduced after lengthy appeals to $28 million. As noted, most of these large jury awards were reduced in size but upheld upon appeal and eventually paid. Between 1999 and 2005 plaintiffs won 31 of 75 cases that reached a verdict, with payments to seven plaintiffs totaling $115 million (Douglas, Davis, and Beasley 2006: iv11–iv12). Admittedly, this dollar amount is relatively small compared to the payout in the Master Settlement Agreement and far smaller than the industry's own legal expenses estimated at half a billion dollars annually during the 2000 to 2004 period (Douglas, Davis, and Beasley 2006: iv13–iv14).

By far the largest number of third wave individual lawsuits filed against the cigarette manufacturers or that came to trial were from Florida. In 1994 a large class action lawsuit, the *Engle* case, was filed on behalf of sick, dying, or dead Florida smokers. Six years later a Dade County, Florida jury awarded a record-breaking $145 billion in punitive damages in the *Engle* lawsuit against the tobacco industry. The *Engle* class action lawsuit, estimated to include well over half a million Florida smokers, was later decertified when a Florida Supreme Court decision held that the smokers varied too greatly to bring a class action lawsuit. Even so, the Florida Supreme Court upheld the factual findings of guilt as applied to the tobacco companies and allowed about nine thousand individual cases to be filed by January 2008 on behalf of sick and dead smokers. In 2013 and 2014 the U.S. Supreme Court declined to overturn two jury awards to smokers, thus rejecting tobacco company appeals over procedural issues. Under the *Engle* procedures a smoker need not prove the tobacco companies' actions but must only show that he or she was addicted and unable to quit smoking and that cigarettes led to illness or death. By mid-2014 about a hundred of an estimated three thousand remaining individual *Engle* lawsuits had been decided in Florida courtrooms. Over half of the state court outcomes favored the plaintiffs and, when favorable to plaintiffs, awards averaged about $4.5 million with another estimated $1 million in costs per case for the tobacco companies' attorneys. Some awards were much larger although likely to being reduced upon appeal. In 2014 a smoker's widow and children won a jury award of $17 million in compensatory damages, plus a $23.6 billion punitive damage award, an amount almost certain to be reduced upon appeal.[8] By early 2015 the tobacco companies' payouts approached a billion dollars, with hundreds more lawsuits pending, mostly in Florida. One analyst estimated the tobacco companies' liabilities at up to $25 billion, a large dollar figure, but still relatively small compared to the industry's valuation.[9]

Large jury awards in Florida, California, Oregon that favor individual or class action lawsuits raise an interesting question. Is public opinion toward tobacco litigation in these three states vastly different than that in other states? Some nationwide polls can be broken down and the results compared by states. Table 6.3 presents evidence for several poll questions on tobacco litigation, comparing residents' attitudes in California, Oregon, and Florida to attitudes in other states. Perhaps surprisingly since all three states had visible and active anti-smoking programs, public opinion in California, Oregon, and Florida is not consistently more hostile to the tobacco industry than that in other states. For tobacco control advocates the message may be that if unfavorable state court rulings and state laws were overcome, juries in many states might assess large compensatory or punitive damages to ill, dying, or dead smokers and to their heirs.

In 1995 the U.S. Department of Justice seemed poised to enter into tobacco litigation with a criminal investigation (Douglas, Davis, and Beasley 2006), but that investigation eventually petered out. In 1999, nearly at the end of the Clinton Administration, the U.S. Justice Department filed a civil lawsuit to recover the federal government's tobacco-related health care costs, to restrain the tobacco industry from continuing to commit fraud, and to force the industry to disgorge $280 billions of dollars in past profits (LaFrance 2000; Howells 2011: 159–64). The federal government's lawsuit largely failed just as had all the other Clinton-era initiatives. In 2000 the cost recovery claims were dismissed upon appeal; in 2005 so were the disgorgement claims. In 2006 federal district judge Gladys Kessler issued a lengthy ruling in favor of the federal government on several remaining claims. That decision barred the tobacco companies from continuing to make deceptive claims about the health risks of cigar-

Table 6.3. Comparing attitudes in Florida, California, and Oregon versus other states

	Florida, California, and Oregon	Remainder of the U.S.
"Which of the following statements best describes your view of who's to blame for the health problems faced by smokers in this country? The tobacco companies are completely to blame, the tobacco companies are mostly to blame, smokers are mostly to blame, smokers are completely to blame?" Gallup, September 1999	33% tobacco companies, 50% smokers, 17% equally and other	29% tobacco companies, 56% smokers, 15% equally and other
"As you may know, this week the U.S. Justice Department filed a lawsuit against the tobacco industry seeking to recover billions of dollars in federal health costs for smoking-related illnesses. The tobacco companies being sued have stated the charges have no merit and should be dismissed. Which side do you agree with more in this lawsuit—the Justice Department or the tobacco companies?" Gallup, September 1999	60% DOJ, 32% tobacco companies, 8% other	50% DOJ, 42% tobacco companies, 7% other
"As you may know, a Florida jury ordered tobacco companies to pay $145 billion in damages to Florida smokers who have been made sick by smoking. Would you say you approve or disapprove of this decision by the Florida jury?" Gallup, July 2000	36% approve, 60% disapprove, 4% other	39% approve, 59% disapprove, 4% other

ettes; banned the companies from using terms such as "light," "ultra-light," or "mild" to describe their products; ordered the cigarette manufacturers to make corrective statements in newspapers, on television, and on their web sites; and ordered litigation documents to be made public and available on company web sites for another decade (Douglas, Davis, and Beasley 2006). Seemingly some parts of Judge Kessler's decision were important, but none greatly affected Americans' beliefs about the ills of smoking or greatly shifted public opinion toward possible restrictions on smoking.

Eleven years passed after the 1998 Master Settlement Agreement and nine years passed after the tobacco industry's narrow win at the U.S. Supreme Court in *FDA. V. Brown & Williamson* (2000). In 2009 Congress passed and President Obama signed the Family Smoking Prevention and Tobacco Control Act. As chapter 5 describes, the 2009 act was controversial both within the tobacco industry and within the public health community. Some critics of the tobacco industry believed that the act would lead to lengthy court challenges and to adverse rulings. Their suspicions were well-founded. By mid-2015 the FDA had lost several key lawsuits.

The FDA's losses included federal court decisions barring the regulation of e-cigarettes under the tougher federal standard for drugs and devices, rather than under more lenient standard for tobacco products; barring graphic pictorial health warnings that would have covered half of the front and rear of cigarette packages and a fifth of cigarette advertisements; delaying a report on the effects of menthol in cigarettes; and barring a "plain packaging" restriction on the colors and images used on cigarette packages.[10]

LITIGATION AND PUBLIC OPINION TOWARD THE TOBACCO INDUSTRY

As chapter 4 describes, American public opinion toward the tobacco industry grew increasingly negative from the mid-1960s to the 1980s. This occurred after the "first wave" of tobacco litigation failed and largely before the "second wave" began and which in time also failed. The hundreds of lawsuits brought by sick or dying smokers or by their heirs played no significant role in declining public support for the tobacco industry. Few first and second wave lawsuits reached the trial stage; none produced a payoff for the smoker; few received much publicity. Early scientific evidence, media attention, and grass-roots activism were far more important in creating a negative image for the industry.

By the early 1990s when third wave litigation got underway, public opinion already poorly viewed the cigarette manufacturers. Third wave litigation corresponds to an increased awareness that secondhand smoke was *"very harmful"* and to growing public support for banning cigarette smoking in the workplace, in restaurants, and in hotels and motels. Otherwise, third wave litigation did not clearly worsen the industry's already poor image among Americans. A Harris poll series found little change in public perceptions of the industry between 1998 and 2009. In March 1998 only 32 percent of Americans said that the tobacco companies generally do a good job of serving their customers and in August 2009 that figure was 31 percent. In short, although the tobacco companies continue their standing as Americans' least popular large industry, litigation had little to do with this. Arguably, part of the reason why litigation had limited impact on the industry's image is that most Americans disagreed with individual smokers' lawsuits. Most Americans also opposed blockbuster jury awards such as the Florida *Engle* decision in 2000. Government-sponsored lawsuits such as the Master Settlement Agreement and the U.S. Justice Department's lawsuit, were of only middling popularity. Litigation over the 2009 tobacco control act was relatively low-profile and unfortunately has been little polled.

PUBLIC OPINION AND THE FUTURE OF TOBACCO LITIGATION

Whether tobacco litigation has a bright or a long-term future is at best doubtful and for reasons that have little to do with public opinion. Class action tort claims on behalf of smokers and third-party payer claims brought by states or by insurance companies face great and perhaps insurmountable difficulty with adverse precedents and seem unlikely to succeed (Henderson and Twerski 2010). Outside Florida and a few other states the number of individual cases has dropped and may continue to do so. The tobacco industry's capable attorneys[11]; the industry's willingness to spend large dollar amounts in discovery, during trial or, if necessary, upon appeal; and the U.S. Supreme Court's decisions that limit punitive damage awards (Viscusi and McMichael 2014) effectively limit the number of these lawsuits. State legislatures that rely on cash payouts from the Master Settlement Agreement often try to protect their payouts from lawsuits that threaten their cash flow; state courts do so, as well (O'Connell 2004; Viscusi and McMichael 2014: 371–37). As of mid-2015 no state other than Florida has seen an explosion of smoking-related claims. Nor have lawsuits brought by smokers of "light" cigarette so far made much progress. Lawsuits seeking to force cigarette manufacturers to cover the costs of medical monitoring for future illnesses have had limited success. Nor do more than a few lawsuits brought overseas seem promising of success. Efforts by cigarette manufacturers to present themselves as contrite and responsible corporations, cigarette manufacturers' potential to claim to be government-regulated or even government-approved, the large number of smoking cessation products and treatments available, and the steady dwindling number of older smokers who began smoking before package warnings were required effectively reduce the number of smoker-related lawsuits in future years (Henderson and Twerski 2010).

Americans' attitudes toward blame for smoking-related health problems typically change only slowly. Rarely do dramatic events result in rapid attitude change. As Table 6.1 reports, the percentage of Americans who believe that cigarette companies should be held legally responsible for smoking-related illnesses, notwithstanding federally-mandated package warning labels, increased from 13 percent in 1991 to 28 percent in 1997. This suggests that American public opinion can respond to high-profile events such as whistle-blower evidence on addiction, Congressional hearings, and perhaps even to the lawsuits filed during these years. This particular poll change was large by American standards—averaging almost 3 percent a year. Yet the trend did not continue thereafter according to a 1997–2008 Gallup Poll series, discussed above, on whether smokers or tobacco companies bore more blame for smoking-related health problems. No later events apparently had much affected American attitudes.

Nor will generational replacement soon change Americans' tendency to blame smokers for smoking-related health problems. In a Gallup survey in 2000, for example, 40 percent of the youngest American adults, those eighteen to twenty-nine years old, completely or mostly blamed the tobacco companies. By contrast, only 28 percent of those who were thirty to forty-nine years old blamed the tobacco companies. For those fifty to sixty-four years old the percentage was 29 percent and for those sixy-five years old or older the percentage was 20 percent. Younger Americans do more often blame tobacco companies for the ills of smoking. Yet even if these generational differences continue into the future, it will be many decades until most Americans blame the tobacco companies for the ills of smoking.[12]

Tobacco litigation proceeds on many fronts and with no end to litigation presently in sight. Following passage of the 2009 Family Smoking Prevention and Tobacco Control Act new lawsuits predictably followed.[13] In 2011 the Food and Drug Administration lost an effort to ban electronic cigarettes and accessories (or e-cigarettes) as an unapproved drug-device product; instead the FDA was permitted only to regulate the then-new product as a tobacco product although e-cigarettes do not contain tobacco. In 2012 the FDA lost its bid to ban color and imagery on cigarette packages (the so-called "plain packaging" requirement), lost its bid to prohibit statements that a tobacco product is safe or safer as a result of FDA regulation, and at least temporarily lost its bid to require graphic pictorial warnings on half of the front and rear surfaces of cigarette packages and on a fifth of cigarette advertisements. The FDA also lost a suit over possible conflicts-of-interest among members of a advisory committee. The tobacco industry has argued with mixed success over whether the 2009 tobacco control act preempts local signage regulations, whether flavored but non-menthol tobacco products may be banned, and whether coupon redemption can be regulated or banned. Regrettably, timely national polls are not available on these issues.

CONCLUSION: LITIGATION, PUBLIC OPINION, AND TOBACCO CONTROL

The last half-century of tobacco litigation was in some ways important, especially so the "third wave" of tobacco litigation that began during the mid-1990s. In dollar amounts the states were by far the most successful plaintiff—winning payments estimated at a quarter of a trillion dollars over twenty-five years and then to be continued in perpetuity. Most class action lawsuits against the tobacco industry failed. Several dozen individual smokers won their lawsuits against the industry, most of them in

Florida, Oregon, and California (Viscusi 2002: 45). Some plaintiff attorneys profited greatly (Derthick 2005: 192–98; Viscusi 2002: 49–55) just as long have the industry's own law firms (Pringle 1998: 230). Beyond the Master Settlement Agreement this litigation has so far cost the industry somewhat over a billion dollars in payouts plus several times as much in the industry's own legal bills. These costs along with an extra margin of profit were passed along to smokers. The tobacco industry is a skillful survivor. Six decades of litigation have neither seriously financially damaged the tobacco industry nor led to the near-disappearance of smoking.

Dollar amounts are not the only measure by which to judge the success of litigation. Cigarette manufacturers were forced sharply to reduce their advertising and marketing profiles. The industry was forced to provide and to make available on-line several million pages of previously-secret internal documents, some of which damaged the industry's reputation (Ciresi et al. 1999). The Master Settlement Agreement caused the price of cigarettes to rise sharply. Cigarette smoking rates continued a slow long-term decline. Rising cigarette prices and lower smoking rates led to a decline in smoking-related diseases, just as industry critics have long hoped (Daynard 1988). Arguably, the industry's legal costs, rising public disapproval, and negative media coverage led the largest cigarette manufacturer, Philip Morris/Altria, to support the new federal regulatory scheme enacted in 2009.

Court-watchers disagree on whether litigation is a successful tobacco control strategy. Some observers including Mather (1998); Taylor (1984); Coller, Harrison, and McInnes (2002: 989); Daynard and LeGresley (2012); Hanson and Logue (1998); Jacobson and Warner (1999); Jacobson and Soliman (2002); Kelder and Daynard (1997); Howells (2011); and Parmet and Danard (2000), view tobacco litigation as a modestly effective strategy at least compared to the meagre results from Congress or from state legislatures. Wagner (2007) argues that litigation usefully benefits the legislative and administrative process by providing information about industry practices, by increasing media attention, by increasing public awareness, and by allowing injured parties to recover damages. Parmet (1999: 1692–96) adds that American courts are often important actors in public health policy, that courts are less easily influenced by well-funded lobbyists than are legislatures, and that court rulings can influence legislative and agency decisions. From this perspective third-wave tobacco litigation was a partial success by forcing the tobacco industry to change its marketing and advertising practices, to limit its lobbying efforts, and to pay billions of dollars to the states.

Other critics, among them Derthick (2002, 2005), Godshall (1999), Gifford (2010), LaFrance (2000), Melnick (1999) Traylor (2010), and Viscusi (2002), take a more negative view.[14] To these critics "adversarial legalism" seriously distorts the constitutional system, forces mostly-low-income smokers to bear the costs of legal settlements, ensures the legal and financial survival of large cigarette manufacturers, rarely yields any cash payouts to sick smokers or to their heirs, and reduces smoking rates only marginally and slowly. Unlike litigation over other harmful products, six decades of tobacco litigation neither forced cigarettes from the marketplace not led to any obvious reductions in the harmfulness of cigarettes.[15] Berman (2009) argues that some federal court rulings in the tobacco cases actually harmed both plaintiffs in other lawsuits and health-focused regulatory agencies. Nor has tobacco litigation provided a coherent future national health policy (LaFrance 2000: 193). As Coller, Harrison, and McInnes (2002) note, the much-touted Master Settlement Agreement failed fully to recover the past or future health costs from smoking.[16] In reviewing the pros and cons of litigation as a tobacco control strategy, Jacobson and Warner (1999: 798) call litigation "a second-best solution."

This chapter asked three questions. First, are tobacco litigation outcomes consistent with nationwide public opinion? For individual lawsuits the answer is a qualified yes. Nationwide poll majorities have never favored this type of litigation, and with notable exceptions, the vast majority of individual smokers' lawsuits failed. Admittedly, most individuals' lawsuits failed because they were underfunded, suffered from inept lawyering and never reached the trial stage. This outcome is consistent with widely- and long-held American views that favor individual responsibility.

The link between American public opinion and class action or government lawsuits on behalf of individual smokers is more mixed.[17] Nationwide public opinion opposed the initial Florida *Engle* class action decision in 2000, and that decision was later decertified with about three thousand individual claims proceeding to trial. As of mid-2015 two-thirds of the *Engle* progeny cases that reached a verdict favored the plaintiff. Public opinion is closely divided on litigation involving state or federal governments. A slight (51 to 42 percent) poll majority favored the U.S. Department of Justice's 1999 lawsuit, but that lawsuit was so greatly reduced in scope by the time it was decided in 2006 that it no longer involved many "billions of dollars" in damages. The U.S. Supreme Court's five to four *Brown & Williamson* decision against the U.S. Food and Drug Administration disagreed with poll majority. The polls were mixed and mostly negative on the Master Settlement Agreement as a whole, although favorable to several specific provisions.

On the second question—whether lawsuits influenced American public opinion—little evidence suggests that tobacco litigation much affected Americans' attitudes toward the tobacco industry. The first and second waves of litigation were low-key, unsuccessful, and little covered by the news media and cannot explain the tobacco industry's declining popularity between the 1950s and the 1980s. By the mid-1990s when the third wave of tobacco litigation began, the tobacco industry already had very poor approval ratings. Thereafter the industry's approval ratings remain largely unchanged. At most third-wave litigation played some part in public beliefs that secondhand smoke was harmful. Ironically, other than the *Broin* case third-wave lawsuits did not focus on secondhand smoke.[18]

What does all this say about the third question raised in this chapter concerning the future tobacco litigation? To be sure, few public opinion polls are available from which to draw firm conclusions. Assuming that most of the future lawsuits against the tobacco companies will be brought on behalf of individual smokers, the polls are not very supportive. In a 1998 NBC/*Wall Street Journal* survey, for example, only one in twelve Americans said that a person who starts smoking today and knows that smoking can cause cancer (as nearly all Americans do) should be able to sue the tobacco companies for the damages to their health. Chapter 7 turns to American public opinion and the end-of-smoking debate.

NOTES

1. U.S. Supreme Court justices can also write disparagingly about public opinion. Justice Rehnquist, for example, wrote that "the Court's duty is to ignore public opinion and criticism on issues that come before it," dissenting, in *Planned Parenthood of Southeastern Pennsylvania v. Casey* (1992).

2. LaFrance (2000: 190–91) puts the number of tort claims filed by private citizens in state courts against the tobacco companies between 1954 and 1994 at approximately 813. Only twice did court verdicts favor plaintiffs and both decisions were substantively reversed upon appeal.

3. The U.S. Supreme Court's decision in *Cipollone* was of special concern to the tobacco industry which tracked its impact on public opinion through focus groups; see The Wirthlin Group's "The Cipollone Supreme Court Decision: A Pulseline Analysis," dated June 1992, and related documents , available in the on-line Legacy archive.

4. The unjust enrichment concept is often attributed to Donald Garner (1977, 1980); see Pringle (1998: 28–31) and Mollenkamp et al. (1998). The quote about Mississippi having never smoking a cigarette has been attributed to various plaintiff lawyers and to Michael Moore, the Mississippi attorney general (Mollenkamp 1998: 29).

5. The *Castano* nationwide class action lawsuit was decertified by a federal appeals court and was thereafter largely unsuccessful as class action litigation in state courts (Pringle 1998: 170, 258–82; Henderson and Twerski 2010).

6. Under the *Broin* settlement, no dollars went directly to the flight attendants, but attendants with certain tobacco-related illnesses can pursue a lawsuit under expedited rules without being required to prove the causal relationship at trial (Brandt 2007: 406–09).

7. Punitive damage awards against the tobacco industry usually led to prolonged litigation about the propriety and size of the awards. These payouts are of recent vintage. Not until the 2005 was the first such award in *Henley v. Philip Morris* actually paid (Berman 2009: 48–49).

8. In *BMW of North America, Inc. v. Gore* (1996), *State Farm v. Campbell* (2003), and *Philip Morris USA v. Williams* (2007) the U.S Supreme Court ruled that punitive damage awards should seldom exceed nine times the amount of compensatory damages and should not punish defendants for actions beyond the present lawsuit (Viscusi 2004; Viscusi and McMichael 2014).

9. In February 2015 Lorillard, Reynolds American, and the Altria group settled for $100 million some 400 federal court cases that had not yet gone to trial. That settlement left unresolved an estimated three thousand individuals 'cases still pending in Florida

state courts. A 2013 decision by Liggett to settle 4,900 pending individual cases in Florida was pegged at $110 million.

10. For a review of these and other post-2009 lawsuits, see the Tobacco Control Legal Consortium's litigation update, dated September 24, 2014, www.publichealthlawcenter.org. In January 2016 a federal appeals court ruled in favor of a FDA report on menthol, overturning a district court ruling that the panel's members had conflicts of interest.

11. For a review of arguments by tobacco industry attorneys, see Cummings, Brown, and Douglas (2006).

12. Younger Americans more often favor legal actions against cigarette companies than do older Americans. For example, in a July 2000 Gallup question asking about the *Engle* case's $145 billion jury award against cigarette manufacturers, 44 percent of those aged eighteen to twenty-nine approved of the decision but only 34 percent of those aged fifty or older did.

13. For a review, see "Litigation Update: Recent Cases that Implicate the Family Smoking Prevention and Tobacco Control Act—September 24, 2014," on-line by the Tobacco Control Legal Consortium, accessed June 10, 2015.

14. These views reflect Gerald Rosenberg's (1991: 97–103; 2008) now-classic argument that litigation can seldom force major policy or social changes absent the support of elected and bureaucratic policy-makers; see also Nathanson (1999).

15. In other areas of product liability a frequent argument is that litigation or the prospect thereof forces manufacturers to reduce the risks of injury resulting from the use of the products (Teret and Jacobs 1989), but in tobacco litigation no such evidence is presently available (Rabin 2008: 1745–47).

16. Estimates of the share of all U.S. health care costs that result from cigarette smoking range from 6.5 percent to 14.4 percent (Coller, Harrison, and McInnes 2002; Warner et al. 1999; Miller et al. 1998, 1999).

17. Very few class action lawsuits against the tobacco industry have succeeded outside the United States. Two recent class action lawsuits brought in Quebec, decided in June 2015 partly in favor of smokers who developed throat cancer, lung cancer, or emphysema, carried an estimated penalty at up to $12 billion. As of mid-2015 the *Blais* and *Letoruneau* rulings against the Canadian operations of three large global tobacco companies were on appeal.

18. Between Gallup's March 1994 survey and its June 1997 survey, Americans' beliefs that secondhand smoke is harmful to adults rose from 36 percent to 55 percent, but thereafter rose little further.

SEVEN

Public Opinion, Public Policy, and the End of Smoking

Cigarette smoking has a long and complicated history in American politics and with American public opinion. So far this account has described the first four of five stages of tobacco control policy-making. During the first half of the 1900s cigarette smoking became a common and little questioned behavior among Americans. By 1949 nearly half of Americans said that they had smoked cigarettes during the past week.[1] During the 1950s the scientific evidence linking cigarette smoking to lung cancer and heart disease began to mount. In 1964 the U.S. Surgeon General's advisory committee released its game-changing report on smoking. Thereafter, a growing number and variety of protests against "the single most deadly consumer product ever made" (Proctor 2011) led to many new tobacco control policies. Over the next half century cigarettes became a highly taxed, highly regulated, and highly stigmatized product. The fifth stage of tobacco control began more recently and features three tobacco control efforts and a new regulatory regime.

Over time improving knowledge of the health risks of cigarette smoking and a growing number of policies that discourage smoking caused a slow and steady drop in the percentage of Americans who smoke cigarettes. Even so, the drop in smoking prevalence remains incomplete. A well-known federal government report in 1990 set a goal that only 12 percent of Americans be smokers by the year 2010.[2] However, by 2014 nearly one in six Americans is a current smoker. Compared to Americans' smoking prevalence in 1949, this represents a drop of over half over the last half century. Gallup estimated the percent of Americans who currently smoked cigarettes at 44 percent in 1949 compared to 19 percent in 2015. The CDC estimated smoking prevalence at 42 percent in 1965 compared to 17 percent in 2015. By a different measure, the number of cigarettes annually consumed by American adults, per capita, dropped from 4,345 in 1963 to 1,236 in 2011 (Warner et al. 2014; Levy, Mumford, and Gerlowski 2007).[3] The number of cigarettes smoked daily by current smokers declined from 34 cigarettes in 1980 to 18 in in 2011. By Gallup's figures in 1949 42 percent of current smokers said that they smoked less than a pack a day; that figure increased to 68 percent in 2014.[4] Figure 7.1 depicts the decline in Americans' smoking prevalence based both on Gallup's figures from 1944 to 2014 and on CDC and National Health Interview Surveys from 1965 to 2013.[5]

American public opinion and public policy reacted to the evidence about the dangers of cigarette smoking in a slow and sequenced manner. During the 1950s a growing number of scientific reports on the health dangers of smoking, although alarming and prescient, neither greatly raised public awareness about the health risks of smoking nor caused any major changes in public policy. A decade passed until the U.S. Surgeon General's 1964 advisory committee's report effectively set off the process of attitude and policy change. Americans' beliefs that smoking was a cause of lung cancer increased almost immediately, followed by steady increases during later decades. Beliefs also rose that cigarette smoking was a cause of heart disease, although not so quickly or fully as did beliefs on lung cancer. The rate of change in Americans' health beliefs about the many ills of smoking was fairly steady although slow, usually about 1 percent a year and rarely as much as 3 percent a year. In a few

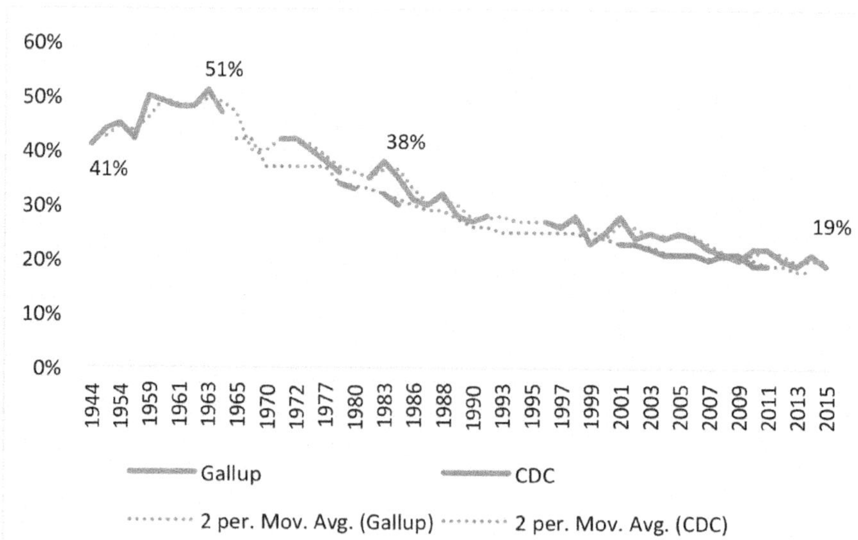

Figure 7.1. Smoking Prevalence, 1944–2015, Gallup and CDC estimates.

instances high-profile government reports or exposes and the ensuing media coverage sparked large belief change, that is, poll changes exceeding 3 percent a year. More important than high-profile events were the efforts of anti-smoking activists and the schools, whose impact is also rarely dramatic in the short term. Lawsuits, Congressional debates, and presidential and bureaucrats' actions seldom have any large and immediate impact on Americans' health beliefs or on their policy views. Within a decade of the 1964 Surgeon General's report Americans' attitudes toward smokers and toward the tobacco industry itself also grew increasingly negative. As with health beliefs, once underway, these attitude changes continued for many more years.

During the mid-1970s grass-roots activists turned to state and local governments and to issue elections to raise taxes on cigarettes and to ban smoking in public places. Although these early efforts had a mixed record of success and failure, the movement often enough succeeded that it worsened the image of the tobacco industry and of smokers and raised public awareness on secondhand smoking. During the 1990s trial lawyers and state attorneys general in 1998 reached a settlement with cigarette manufacturers to pay the states a quarter-trillion dollar over a quarter century. These lawsuits succeeded in winning a large settlement from cigarette manufacturers although had little apparent impact on Americans' views of the tobacco industry. The fifth and most recent stage of tobacco control policy and public opinion, described in this chapter, dates from about the turn of this century

In past tobacco control efforts Congress and the White House seldom led and were often surprisingly belated or ineffective in their response to the ills of smoking. True, a few federal policies or actions, most notably the 1964 Surgeon General's report, package warnings, the fairness doctrine, and the broadcast ban, occurred during the 1960s. As well, tobacco controls and taxes were often debated within the federal agencies or by Congress and the White House. Yet until 2009 Congress and the White House produced surprisingly few tobacco control policies of much importance. Forty-five years after the 1964 Surgeon General's advisory committee issued its report on smoking, Congress finally passed and President Obama signed into law a significant although flawed regulatory scheme for cigarettes, discussed in chapter 5 and further below. The 2009 bill is an anomaly since the federal government seldom takes the lead in tobacco control policy-making. More often tobacco control efforts were led by grass-roots activists at the state and local level.

The decline in Americans' rates of cigarette smoking depicted in Figure 7.1 has already yielded important health benefits. By one estimate 800,000 lung cancer deaths within the United States were averted due to the reductions in smoking behavior that occurred between 1975 and 2000 (Moolgavkar et al. 2012).[6] As impressive as is that number, three times that many lung cancer deaths might have been averted if all smokers had immediately quit smoking in response to the Surgeon General's 1964 report. One simulation model estimated that if no further policy changes are forthcoming, annual smoking-attributable deaths in the United States will fall from about 416,000 in 2000 to 350,000 by 2040. In a better-case scenario smoking-attributable deaths may fall to an estimated 250,000 annually by 2040 with cigarette taxes increased by a dollar per pack and adjusted to inflation, with comprehensive clean air requirements, with a vigorous mass media campaign, with a total ban on cigarette advertising, with complete smoking cessation coverage, and with strict youth access rules (Levy, Mumford, and Pesin 2003; Cummings 2002b; see also Bowser, Canning, and Okunogbe 2016).[7]

PUBLIC POLICIES AND THE END OF SMOKING?

During the early 2000s three major advances occurred in the long-running debate over cigarette smoking. These three advances are not isolated one from another, but occurred in different settings and so are discussed separately. The first is the passage of the 2009 Family Smoking Prevention and Tobacco Control Act. The 2009 tobacco control act resulted from an unusual combination of circumstances. In 2000 the U.S. Supreme Court's 5-to-4 ruling in *FDA v. Brown & Williamson* struck down the FDA's effort to regulate tobacco products. The Supreme Court's ruling forced tobacco control advocates to seek clearly-expressed Congressional authority for FDA oversight. The Supreme Court's ruling in 2000 came at the end of the Clinton presidency, which was marked by a friendly but ineffective stance on tobacco control efforts, and at the beginning of the George W. Bush presidency, which was seldom and only minimally friendly to tobacco control. The ensuing wait for a new regulatory regime lasted exactly as long as did President Bush's two terms in the White House.

Support for FDA regulation over tobacco products came from another source. Beginning in the mid-1990s Philip Morris, renamed Altria in 2003 and by then clearly the nation's largest cigarette manufacturer, sought to improve its troubled corporate image and to gain the benefit of a predictable if not overly strict federal regulation (Derthick 2012; Smith and Malone 2003a, 2003b).[8] Altria's change-of-course did not reflect an industry-wide consensus. All the other large cigarette manufacturers opposed the new federal regulatory effort. The drive to win Congressional approval for FDA oversight stalled until for reasons completely unrelated to tobacco control the Democratic Party swept the 2006 and 2008 congressional elections and the 2008 presidential election.[9] In June 2009 Congress passed and President Obama signed a bill finally giving the FDA a measure of oversight over tobacco products.

Most of the nation's leading tobacco control advocates, including the American Cancer Society, the American Lung Association, the American Heart Association, and the Campaign for Tobacco Free Kids, supported passage of the 2009 tobacco control bill. Long-time tobacco control supporters U.S. Senator Ted Kennedy and U.S. Representative Henry Waxman backed the bill. On the key Congressional votes the new legislation handily passed, by 307 to 97 in the House of Representatives and by 79 to 17 in the Senate. In some ways the new legislation gave tobacco control advocates a significant victory. Among its provisions, the bill banned tobacco advertising within 1,000 feet of schools and playgrounds; banned terms such as "light," "mild," or "low tar" that implied cigarettes were safe to smoke; mandated that the FDA must by 2012 design and approve large graphic warnings with pictures and words on cigarette packs; created a scientific advisory board to advise the FDA on future regulations; banned cigarette vending machine sales except in adults-only facilities; banned tobacco brand sponsorships of nearly all sports and entertainment events; banned free giveaways of cigarettes; banned brand-name promotional items; banned tobacco product sales to minors; and banned any new tobacco products from coming onto the market unless that product could show a health benefit to smokers and nonsmokers alike. The tobacco industry was required to pay an estimated $70 million over a decade to cover the costs of the FDA's regulatory efforts.

Even so, the 2009 tobacco control act made several important concessions to cigarette manufacturers (Givel 2005, 2007; Glantz, Barnes, and Eubanks 2009). The act barred the FDA from requiring a prescription to purchase tobacco products; allowed the FDA to reduce but not to eliminate nicotine levels in cigarettes; and prohibited a ban on face-to-face sales in any particular category of retail outlet, for example, pharmacies or stand-alone smoke shops. The FDA cannot ban all cigarettes, all smokeless tobacco products, all little and non-little cigars, or all roll-your-own tobacco products. The bill banned most flavorings such as licorice, cherry, cinnamon, or coffee, but allowed the continued use of menthol. The bill ensured that the tobacco industry would be well-informed about any new regulations, since three non-voting tobacco industry representatives sit on the FDA's twelve-member scientific advisory committee. Although new tobacco products became difficult to bring onto the market, existing tobacco products, harmful as they may be, were effectively grandfathered in. The bill preempted most state and local tobacco product regulations. Although little publicized in 2009, the legislation also set out legal standards that, when applied by skeptical or tobacco-friendly federal judges, effectively doomed several proposed regulations (Outterson 2011). These standards require providing pre-regulatory scientific evidence that new regulations will cause those who now use tobacco products to stop using those products and that nonsmokers will not start using such products; technical achievability; and the impact on international trade, the economy, and contraband. Nor did (or could) the bill overturn the U.S. Supreme Court's business-friendly rulings on commercial free speech that gave corporations a right to litigate on key issue such as whether companies could continue to use long-familiar colors and logos on cigarette packs; whether cigarette manufacturers must, over their objections, include large graphic pictorial warnings about the health risks of smoking on cigarette packages; or even whether cigarette manufacturers can claim that their products are government regulated or approved. Cigarette manufacturers also benefitted when the 2009 bill's passage forestalled Congressional ratification of an even less tobacco-friendly international treaty, the Framework Convention for Tobacco Control, discussed just below. Arguably, cigarette manufacturers benefitted by being regulated by the FDA, a federal agency often perceived as overextended, underfunded, and politically weak (Chaloupka et al. 2015; Gottlieb 2014; Malone 2015a; Weissert and Weissert 2002: 163–64; Zeller 2012).

A second recent development is a growing international effort to reduce the prevalence and harm of cigarette smoking. Until the 1990s tobacco control efforts typically occurred on a country-by-country basis. Yet many issues involved in tobacco control are global in nature, among them the growing smoking prevalence in the developing world, rising death rates, cross-border media and internet advertising, mergers and acquisitions among cigarette manufacturers, and cigarette smuggling (Bialous and Peeters 2012; Drope and Lencucha 2014; Warner and Tam 2012). In 1994 serious efforts began to develop an international tobacco control program. This effort was backed by top officials at the World Health Organization and the World Bank who were in large part motivated by estimates that, absent stronger efforts at tobacco control, up to a billion persons worldwide will die of tobacco-related causes during the twenty-first century (Britton and Edwards 2007; Peto and Lopez 2001; Thun et al. 2012). About half of these deaths will be among persons aged thirty-five to sixty-nine years of age and with grave economic costs (Peto et al. 1996). By one estimate worldwide smoking prevalence could be reduced from about 24 percent in 2010 to 13 percent in 2030 with strong tobacco control measures including a 100 percent price increase for cigarettes. With no new tobacco controls, worldwide smoking prevalence rates might fall from only 24 percent in 2010 to 22 percent in 2030 (Mendez, Alshanqeety, and Warner 2013).

Efforts to develop an international treaty took about a decade. By 2003 the World Health Assembly had laid out a Framework Convention on Tobacco Control (FCTC) that individual countries could ratify. By February 2005 a sufficient number of countries had ratified the treaty to bring it into effect. By early 2015 one hundred and eighty countries had ratified the treaty, representing 90 percent of the world's population and including all the most prosperous countries such as Canada, the United Kingdom, Japan, France, and Germany, all except the United States. As of mid-2015 only sixteen U.N. member states had not ratified the treaty, among the larger nations the United States, Indonesia, Cuba, and Argentina. A delegation from the United States participated in early discussions and initially signed the agreement, but neither President Bush nor Obama sent the treaty to the U.S. Senate where its prospects for ratification seemed unlikely. As a result, the United States remains outside the FCTC and with a weaker set of tobacco control programs.

The FCTC was the first World Health Organization treaty to address a non-communicable disease. The treaty is legally binding on ratifying countries but not all the provisions must be immediately adopted. Even so, the FCTC set off new tobacco control efforts. By 2015 four-fifths of reporting ratifying nations had strengthened their existing tobacco control laws or adopted new laws. The average rate of implementation of the treaty's several substantive parts was nearly 55 percent (Nikogosian and Costa e Silva 2015).[10] Some FCTC provisions reflect goals already found in many American local, state, and federal laws: higher taxes on tobacco products (Chaloupka, Yurekli, and Fong 2012); disclosure of tobacco product ingredients; increased public awareness of the consequences of smoking; restrictions on sales to minors; more widely-available addiction and cessation programs; a ban on tobacco advertising; and limits on secondhand exposure to tobacco smoke in indoor workplaces, public transit, and indoor public places (Hyland, Barnoya, and Corral 2012).

Two key FCTC provisions exceed current U.S. practices. The FCTC's provision requiring that contacts between the tobacco industry and policy-makers be limited clearly conflicts with current American lobbying practices and with the tobacco industry's three nonvoting seats on the FDA's advisory scientific advisory committee. The FCTC also mandates large health warnings covering at least thirty percent of cigarette packages, but a similar provision was in 2012 at least temporarily struck down by a U.S. federal judge. Outside the United States the graphic warnings provision has been adopted by several dozen countries.

The third key development is the emergence of an "end-of-smoking" movement beginning in the mid-1990s. The term describes a wide variety of proposals aimed at greatly reducing current and future smoking rates (Institute of Medicine 2007; Warner 2013). The movement aims to lower smoking prevalence to only 10 percent or even lower within the next one or two decades. The most ambitious such proposals would reduce smoking rates to under 5 percent (Malone, McDaniel, and Smith 2014b; Beaglehole et al. 2011) or in a few accounts completely to eliminate the smoking of combustible tobacco. The end-of-smoking movement has many supporters both within the United States and abroad, but it is not primarily a poll-driven effort. Some end-of-smoking proposals enjoy only middling or less poll support. On many proposals little or no reliable polling data exist. The end-of-smoking debate is most often carried on among academics and scientists whose aim is to influence policy-makers in the

United States and elsewhere. The many end-of-smoking proposals reflect a common view that present-day tobacco control policies will not greatly or soon reduce current smoking rates or lower the health costs of cigarette smoking. To do better will require undermining within the foreseeable future the "structural, political and social dynamics that sustain the tobacco epidemic" (Malone, McDaniel, and Smith 2014a, 2014b). One prominent tobacco control advocate, Ruth Malone (2014) described endgame proposals as non-incremental efforts that aim virtually to eliminate tobacco usage and its related diseases and deaths, rather than continuing to envision tobacco control efforts "as an ongoing war of attrition."

Some end-of-smoking proposals expand upon traditional approaches to tobacco. Two such examples include requiring graphic pictorial warning labels on cigarette packages and requiring that cigarettes be sold in plain packages without any well-known and colorful company brand logos. The 2009 tobacco control act required the FDA to propose graphic warnings that cover the top half of the front and back sides of cigarette places and 20 percent of the area of cigarette ads. Several cigarette manufacturers, not including Altria, promptly challenged in federal court the proposed FDA graphics. Despite clear Congressional authorization in the 2009 tobacco control legislation, adverse federal court rulings killed both the plain packaging requirement and the FDA's then-proposed set of graphic warnings. Even so, the graphic warning's basic constitutionality was upheld. The FDA may yet produce an acceptable set of re-designed graphic warnings but as of 2015 the FDA has not yet announced a new set of proposed graphic warnings for cigarette packs. As a result, as of 2015—six years after the 2009 tobacco control act was passed—the United States has one of the world's smallest, oldest, and least visible warnings, ones that appear only in small print, without pictures, are unchanged in recent years, and that appear only on the side of the cigarette package. By comparison, as of 2014 some sixty countries or jurisdictions, prominent among them Canada and Australia, require a graphic warning that covers at least half of the cigarette package's front and back. That number of countries is up from only twenty-four such countries in 2008 and is steadily rising (Myers 2014). In a November 2010 Pew survey conducted by Princeton Survey Research Associates, public awareness of graphic warnings was low, likely so because the warnings were never implemented. Only 17 percent of Americans said that they had heard "*a lot*" and another 38 percent said that they had heard "*a little*" about the FDA's "*new graphic warning labels for cigarette packs*." Small-scale surveys and experimental studies suggest that most U.S. smokers and nonsmokers favor Canadian-style graphic warning labels.

Several end-of-smoking proposals aim to regulate further the marketing and sales of tobacco products. Some of these proposals enjoy majority poll support. A proposal by Gartner and McNeill (2010) would ban publicly-visible sales displays of cigarette packs (the so-called "power wall") in retail stores. In a 2013 Quinnipiac survey 59 percent of Americans who were registered voters supported and 39 percent opposed a proposal from then-mayor of New York City Michael Bloomberg that "*stores be required to keep cigarettes out of sight to discourage young people from smoking*."[11] A national survey conducted in 2011 reported that just over half of American adults either would not allow the sale of tobacco products in grocery stores (24 percent would not) or else would require that these products be hidden from view (another 30 percent). For pharmacies and drug stores the figures were slightly higher (31 percent and 26 percent, respectively). Support for point-of-sale restrictions was much higher among nonsmokers than among smokers (Patwardhan, McMillen, and Winickoff 2013). In a 2013 nationwide survey 71 percent of American adults favored raising the legal age to buy tobacco to 21 with poll majorities in all groups favoring the idea (Winickoff et al. 2015). Several cities and on January 1, 2016 Hawaii have such restrictions.

Many other end-of-smoking proposals have been offered. Under the provisions of the 2009 tobacco control act the U.S. Food and Drug Administration can reduce but not completely eliminate the nicotine levels of cigarettes. As of 2015 the FDA has not implemented this strategy. Benowitz and Henningfield (1994, 2013) advocate significantly lowering nicotine levels in cigarettes since the addictive quality of cigarettes would be greatly reduced or even eliminated by reducing nicotine levels from the current levels of 10 to 15 mg of nicotine per cigarettes to a tenth or less of that level.[12] McNeill, Hammond, and Gartner (2015) urge a phased-in ban on combustible tobacco products and favor moving customers to "cleaner" nicotine products, a ban on all marketing of tobacco products, and a plain packaging requirement. Gray et al. (2005) and Britton and Edwards (2007) also recommend a switch to "cleaner" and less harmful nicotine products. Only a little polling data is available. In one national survey just under half of Americans supported the FDA immediately decreasing the nicotine in cigarettes; another fifth of Americans favored gradually decreasing nicotine over the next fifteen years (Connolly et al. 2012). Greater poll support exists when the question describes the goal of reducing under-age smoking. When asked whether the FDA should reduce the nicotine in cigarettes if it would cause fewer kids to become addicted, nearly four-fifths of Americans were in favor.

Some end-of-smoking advocates favor a ban on menthol, a widely-used flavoring that reduces the harshness of cigarette smoking, thereby encouraging youthful experimentation and reducing cessation (Giovino et al. 2015; Levy et al. 2011a, 2011b). Menthol was expressly permitted under the 2009 tobacco control act and is especially popular among young smokers and African-American smokers. Simulations suggest that if menthol were banned, smoking initiation would decrease and cessation would increase, thus averting between 300,000 to 600,000 smoking-attributable U.S. deaths by the year 2050 (Levy et al. 2011b). In one 2009 national survey respondents were first asked whether *"cigarettes with added flavorings like cherry, chocolate, lime and mint should be prohibited"* and 70 percent of respondents agreed. Respondents were then asked whether *"menthol cigarettes should be prohibited just like other flavored cigarettes"* and just over half (56 percent) agreed. Support for a ban was high among blacks (68 percent in favor), among those who had never smoked (67 percent), among those sixty-five years old or older (70 percent), women (65 percent), and among those with less than a high school education (71 percent) (Winickoff et al. 2011). In a study of two major metropolitan areas support (at 79 percent and 60 percent, respectively) for reducing nicotine was higher than support for reducing or removing menthol (Bolcic-Jankovic and Biener 2015).

In other end-of-smoking proposals Callard, Thompson, and Collishaw (2005) urge the transfer of cigarette sales from for-profit companies to non-profit corporations that have a public health mandate. Khoo et al. (2010) propose that those born after the year 2000 not be allowed to buy tobacco products. Chapman and Liberman (2005) urge that smokers be licensed. Hall and West (2008) urge that the production and sale of smoked tobacco products be phased out over two decades in favor of safer smokeless tobacco and medicinal nicotine products.[13] Thompson et al. (2010) propose using a "sinking lid" on the supply and availability of tobacco products to make such products less easily available and more expensive. Gartner and McNeill (2010) urge, among other strategies, a ban on smoking in cars, a reduction in the local density of retail outlets that sell cigarettes,[14] and that mandatory anti-smoking ads be shown before any movies that depict smoking. Warner and Mendez (2010) advocate a variety of state and local initiatives, including bans on smoking in cars with children present, bans on smoking in apartments and on university campuses, and bans on smoking on sidewalks or in parks. Borland (2003) proposes transferring all cigarette marketing and wholesale activities to a newly-created public agency that has a mandate to provide reduced-harm cigarettes.[15] Other proposals, including some made for countries other than the United States and which are not immediately likely within the United States, include reducing the known carcinogens and lowering the pH of cigarettes, requiring a prescription to purchase cigarettes, and capping the prices or profits of cigarette manufacturers (Doval 2013; Gilmore, Branston, and Sweanor 2010; Malone 2015b). Reliable polling data on American attitudes toward these proposals are not now available.[16]

Tobacco control advocates disagree on how likely these proposals are to succeed in reducing smoking prevalence. Myers (2013) questions whether any of these new proposals will succeed as well as have the six traditional (or "proven") tobacco control strategies: higher taxes, stronger warning labels, smoke-free air laws, aggressive public education campaigns, packaging restrictions, and restrictions on tobacco industry marketing.[17] Several traditional tobacco strategies enjoy popular support. In recent polls about half to three-quarters of Americans favored specific proposals for tax hikes on cigarettes. In mid-2009 a series of Kaiser Health tracking polls pegged at between 63 percent and 71 percent public support for *"increasing the cigarette tax . . . to help pay for health care reform and to provide coverage for more of the uninsured."* In a 2008 Harvard/Kaiser poll 72 percent of respondents rated favorably a proposal to increase the cigarette tax *"to help pay for expanding health insurance for the uninsured"*; this was the most popular of several possible funding sources for health insurance. Support for increasing the cigarette tax was highest among groups with a low smoking prevalence—those with more than an undergraduate college education, those making $50,000 or more a year, liberals, and Democrats.

Poll support for further tax hikes is sensitive to question wording and to issue framing. In Gallup surveys that gave respondents a choice between alternative policies, slightly under half (46 percent in 2002 and 48 percent in 2005) of Americans favored *"raising cigarette taxes by substantial amounts to discourage smoking"* while about half of Americans (50 percent in 2002 and 49 percent in 2005) opposed raising these taxes *"because doing so would unfairly discriminate against smokers."* With a different question wording slightly more than half (55 percent in 2002 and 53 percent in 2005) of adults favored substantial tax hikes *"to help state and local governments pay for the health costs related to smoking"* and fewer respondents (39 percent in 2002 and 43 percent in 2005) opposed tax hikes because they would *"unfairly discriminate against smokers."* The higher level of public support for the latter question wording suggests that the more popular frame is a tax hike described as a means to offset the health costs of smoking; even so worded, public support for tax hikes on cigarettes barely reaches a majority. Describing tobacco control measures as a way to reduce minors' smoking also increases poll support (Farley et al. 2015).

Since the 1970s limiting or banning cigarette smoking in public places has been a popular "proven" strategy for tobacco control advocates. Smoking bans in public places are a rare instance of tobacco control measures that are growing more popular. In Gallup surveys between 2001 and 2015 public support for making *"smoking in all public places . . . totally illegal"* rose from 39 percent to 58 percent, an average annual rate of increase of 1 to 2 percent. Opposition dropped from 60 percent to 44 percent over that time period. An average annual poll change of 1 or 2 percent is not large, but, even so, support for banning smoking in public places is the only instance of a tobacco control measure that has become markedly more popular in recent years. About the same rate of change appears on several more narrowly-worded poll questions. Support for totally banning smoking in hotels and motels rose from 10 percent in 1987 to 36 percent in 2010. Support for totally banning smoking in workplaces rose from 17 percent to 44 percent between 1987 and 2010. Support for a total ban in restaurants rose from 17 percent in 1987 to 59 percent in 2010. Support for a total smoking ban in bars rose from 23 percent in 2003 to 31 percent in 2010. Not surprisingly, many tobacco control supporters continue to seek bans on cigarette smoking in public places and even in ostensibly private places, such as within apartments in multifamily housing, where nonsmokers may be affected (Wilson et al. 2014).

A few smoking-related proposals do not come from tobacco control advocates. Seldom, if ever do tobacco control advocates seek to make health insurance more costly or to make jobs more difficult to obtain for smokers. Even so, the steadily rising costs of employer-paid health care and the higher costs of employing smokers encourages many employers to make raise the costs of health insurance for employees who smoke. An increasing number of employers refuse to hire smokers.[18] Poll support for raising health insurance rates for smokers is much higher than for allowing companies to refuse to hire smokers. In recent Gallup surveys over half of Americans favored higher health insurance rates for people who smoke although that percentage declined from 65 percent in 2003 to 58 percent in 2014. Poll support for charging higher rates for smokers is highest among those with high incomes and among those with an undergraduate college degree or more, both groups in which there are relatively few smokers. Poll support for allowing companies to refuse to hire smokers is much lower—only 13 percent in favor in 2005 and only 14 percent in favor in 2014.[19] How effectively either of these two practices would reduce smoking rates is unclear.

The most ambitious end-of-smoking proposals call for completely prohibiting the cigarette trade. The prohibition position is not a commonly-sought remedy for the ills of smoking. The failed experiment to prohibit the manufacture, sale, and transportation of alcoholic beverages during the 1920s and early 1930s, still often taught in schools and recounted in the media, probably discourages many tobacco control advocates from urging the prohibition of tobacco products. So, too, may the reality that one-sixth of Americans still smoke cigarettes, that the tobacco industry is a financially lucrative industry that pays large amounts in taxes and in Master Settlement Agreement dollars, and that the cigarette trade is well protected by its lobbyists and lawyers (Hall and West 2008). A few proposals call for phasing out tobacco products; among the best known is Robert Proctor who concludes his recent book, *Golden Holocaust* (2011: 556–61) with a call for abolishing the manufacture and sale of cigarettes.[20]

The immediate prohibition of smoking is not popular among Americans. A series of Gallup Poll questions asks whether *"smoking in this country (should) be made totally illegal, or not?"* Support for prohibition rose very slowly over the last quarter of a century—from only 14 percent of Americans in favor in 1990 to 24 percent in favor in 2015. Not only did few Americans favor a complete ban; support for tobacco prohibition rose at an average rate of only 1 percent every two to three years. About three-fourths or more of Americans opposed such a ban.[21] There was apparently never much public support for completely prohibiting smoking. In a federal government-sponsored survey conducted in 1964 only 22 percent of Americans favored a complete ban on the sale of cigarettes. Drastic policy changes that are supported by only a fifth or fewer of Americans seldom occur. By an even older historical comparison, current poll support for the total prohibition of smoking is much lower than was support for reinstating a ban of alcohol during the mid-to-late 1930s just after the Twenty-first Amendment to the U.S. Constitution repealed prohibition.[22] Poll support for phasing-out cigarettes over time is higher than support for an immediate ban. In a 2011 national survey about half of Americans favored banning cigarettes by the next decade (Connolly et al. 2012).

PUBLIC OPINION AND THE FUTURE OF TOBACCO CONTROL

Over the last half century tobacco control advocates have enjoyed many successes, including higher prices for cigarettes, the public release of the tobacco industry's previously-secret internal documents, a reduced advertising and marketing profile for the industry, large cash payments from the industry to the states and to a few smokers, and far fewer public places where smoking is permitted (Malone and Warner 2012). Since the 1950s the percentage of Americans who smoke cigarettes has slowly and steadily dropped by over half. Journalists and political scientists no longer use the term "iron triangle" to describe a cozy and mutually-supportive relationship between Congress, the federal agencies, and the tobacco industry. Americans today are far better informed about the health risks of smoking than were Americans half a century ago. Against a long-established, well-funded, and well-organized oligopoly, this is no small progress.

How fully Americans support further tobacco control efforts, however, is unclear. That most Americans view cigarette smoking as a serious health problem is not in question. In Gallup surveys between 2002 and 2014 about four-fifths of Americans described smoking as "*very harmful*" to smokers themselves. Over half of Americans (56 percent in 2002 and 57 percent in 2014) said that secondhand smoking was "*very harmful*" to adults. Most Americans (57 percent in 2003, 66 percent in 2005, and 67 percent in 2012) called cigarettes as an "*extremely*" or "*very serious problem*" to society.

Even so, public opinion support for the tobacco control movement's efforts is in several important ways mixed. Smoking does not rank at the top of Americans' health concerns. Since 1987 Gallup Poll has regularly queried Americans about *"the most urgent health problem facing the country at the present time."* Through 2014 no more than 2 percent of Americans named smoking as a most urgent health problem. If cancer and heart disease, the two illnesses most often linked to cigarette smoking, were also counted, that figure would rise considerably but still declined from 23 percent in 1987 to 12 percent in 2013 and 2014. Other surveys report similar results. A 2013 Pew Research Center poll question asked Americans to rate the seriousness of seven health problems. Cancer and obesity were rated as an *"extremely"* or *"very serious problem"* by 79 percent of Americans. Cigarette smoking, alcohol abuse, and AIDS were lower rated, at 53 percent, 53 percent, and 51 percent, respectively. The 2013 Pew rating for smoking (at 53 percent) indicates a drop in perceptions of smoking as a serious problem, compared to a 72 percent figure in a 2004 ABC News/Time poll. A 2013 Kaiser/Harvard/Robert Woods Johnson survey asked Americans to rate the importance of fifteen health problems as to its priority *"for federal spending in 2013."* The option of *"reducing smoking and tobacco use"* was tied for the next-to-lowest rank with only 26 percent of respondents described it as *"one of the top"* priorities. Other polling evidence is also mixed. In a 2012 Gallup survey about half (55 percent) of Americans said that it is either *"extremely"* or *"very important"* to have *"federal government programs that address health risks associated with . . . smoking."* For obesity and excessive alcohol consumption, the figures were 57 percent and 48 percent, respectively. Among health experts obesity is increasingly more often cited as a pressing health problem (Sturm 2002).

Nor is there growing public support among Americans for many key tobacco control measures. On consistently-worded poll questions over time, only on banning cigarette smoking in public places has poll support clearly increased over the last two decades.[23] From a polling perspective the early 2000s were a disappointment for the tobacco control movement.

Exactly why Americans' support for tobacco control efforts has stalled is not completely clear, but several possible reasons can be offered. Ironically, as smoking rates continue to decline, fewer Americans and their families are personally affected by the ills of smoking. This is particularly so for affluent Americans. In Gallup surveys the percentage of Americans who agreed that *"smoking (has) ever been a cause of serious health problems in your family"* dropped from 45 percent in 1999 to 40 percent in 2014. The percentage of Americans who say that it has not been a serious family problem rose from 54 percent to 58 percent. Higher income Americans are now less likely to experience smoking-related health problems in their families. In a 2011 Gallup survey, for example, only 41 percent of those with family incomes over $50,000 a year said that they had experienced smoking-related family problems; among those with lower incomes 47 percent said that they had. These demographics are important since the affluent are the most politically active and influential. Smoking may be among the most frequent and preventable causes of disease and death but its toll is less and less evenly distributed across American society.

Tobacco control efforts now suffer from a dearth of popular and high-profile celebrities, exposes, and events. Among the best-known of anti-smoking figures, former U.S. Surgeon General C. Everett Koop died in 2013; David Kessler, a former Commissioner of the U.S. Food and Drug Administration, has largely moved on to other pursuits; Henry Waxman, a California Democrat who served for forty years in the U.S. House of Representatives and who often took the lead on tobacco control issues, retired in 2015. No equally visible anti-smoking advocates have yet replaced these figures. Further, very few "blockbuster" news events have recently occurred. The high-dollar state government lawsuits against the tobacco industry of the 1990s are now nearly two decades in the past. The 2009 federal tobacco control act, itself of only middling popularity, relegated federal-level tobacco control efforts to a low-profile future of agency rule-making and federal court hearings. An FDA-produced set of graphic warnings for cigarette packages that won federal court approval might well be a breakthrough to greater media and public attention but as of 2015 that has not yet happened. An insurance premium rate hike for enrolled smokers was included in the 2010 Affordable Care Act, popularly known as Obamacare, but received little media attention and the Obamacare plan itself was not very popular in the polls. The steady trickle of large courtroom awards in favor of ill, dying, or dead smokers and against the cigarette companies are not particularly popular. None of U.S. Surgeon General's recent reports have won much media attention or greatly influenced public opinion.

Its opponents from within the tobacco industry have long derided tobacco control efforts as "paternalism" or even as embodying "the nanny state" that seeks to regulate personal choices of adults. Tobacco control efforts increasingly confront social norms that favor greater individual freedom over personal and health choices. Consider, for example, the steady increase in support for legalizing the personal use of marijuana. In Gallup surveys the percentage of Americans who favored making the use of marijuana legal rose from 12 percent in 1969 to 51 percent in 2014—an average increase of about 1 percent a year and with a slightly greater rate of change during the 2000s. Pew and General Social Survey results show similar trends.[24] Support for legalizing marijuana has risen among all generations, and most rapidly so among younger Americans. Among millennials, those born from 1981 to 1997, the Pew/GSS figures for legalization rose from 34 percent in 2008 to 68 percent in 2015—an annual rate of change of nearly 5 percent. To be sure, tobacco and marijuana are very different products in their histories, legal status, consumer appeal, and economics (Burnham 1993; Courtwright 2001; Goodman, Lovejoy, and Sherrat 1995). Yet a growing sentiment for less government involvement in personal behavior does not augur well for tobacco control efforts and may in part explain the stagnating support for further government measures to reduce cigarette smoking.

The sentiment that government regulations can overreach is an important part of modern American public opinion. Since 1992 Gallup has regularly asked respondents to choose between two opposing positions on how actively the government should be involved in the country's problems. Poll support for a less active government is usually the more popular position. The percentage who said that "*government is trying to do too many things that should be left to individuals and businesses*" averaged a little over half of Americans, reached to a high of 61 percent in 2012 and was 54 percent in September 2014. Support for the opposing view, that government "*should do more to solve our country's problems,*" averaged about 40 percent, reached a plurality or a small majority only during the 1992 economic recession and shortly after the 9/11 terrorist attacks, and was at 41 percent in September 2014. As these poll results suggest, end-of-smoking advocates confront not only a difficult policy-making environment in Washington DC, but also majority or plurality public opinion that is reluctant to enlarge government. Arguably, the passage of the 2009 tobacco control bill itself reduced media and public interest in tobacco control.

These survey results are in addition to the waxing and waning of political support for tobacco control. Over the last two decades tobacco control supporters won strong but ineffective support from the Clinton White House, very little support at all from the George W. Bush White House, and only early and partially effective support from the Obama White House. Congress has backed the tobacco control movement only occasionally in the last two decades. The final verdict on the FDA's post-2009 efforts is still out, but even a very charitable view of the FDA's regulatory and legal track record so far is very poor. So, too, is the federal courts' recent post-2009 record of support for tobacco control efforts very mixed. Other issues such as health care coverage and foreign crises more typically dominate the news. Whether the 2016 or 2018 or 2020 election results will be more favorable for tobacco control advocates than were national elections since 2008 is unclear. Several energetic political movements, among them Libertarians and the Tea Party movement, are not inclined to support tobacco control. Nor is it yet clear how new and increasingly popular consumer products, particularly e-cigarettes, will affect the prevalence of smoked tobacco products.[25] Further, cigarette manufacturers remain well-funded and politically skillful and have in the past proven surprisingly capable of weathering major challenges (Jones 1997; Miles 1982; Pollock 1996).

All this suggests that the "ongoing war of attrition" between tobacco control advocates and the cigarette trade is far from over. Over the past six decades the tobacco control movement's many successes were not accomplished simply or easily. Both American public policy and American public opinion changed slowly but profoundly. Cigarette smoking came to be viewed as a harmful, stigmatized, and deviant, albeit still legal behavior. As this struggle moves into future decades, public policy and public opinion changes will continue to evolve, but how quickly and how fully is as yet unclear.

NOTES

1. "*Have you, yourself, smoked any cigarettes in the past week?*" 44 percent yes, 56 percent no. Gallup Poll, 10/30–11/4/1949.

2. The goal was outlined in a 1990 report, commonly called Healthy People 2000 or 2010, issued by the U.S. Department of Health and Human Services, Public Health Service, Centers for Disease Control, Office on Smoking and Health; see *The health benefits of smoking cessation: a report of the Surgeon General*. Atlanta Georgia.

3. Absent tobacco control efforts Americans' annual cigarette consumption, per capita, might have reached 5,907 cigarettes by 2011—almost five times the actual consumption (Warner et al. 2014: 85).

4. See Hughes (2000) for a discussion of the health benefits of reducing the number of cigarettes smoked daily.

5. Gallup's figures are based on the question "*Have you yourself smoked any cigarettes in the past week?*" and include 1959-to-1964 figures that may be found in the online Legacy Tobacco Documents archive. The CDC figures are based on current smoking behavior every day or some days and whether a respondent has smoked one hundred cigarettes during his or her lifetime.

6. Over the 1964-to-2012 period an estimated eight million premature smoking-attributable deaths were avoided through tobacco control efforts (Holford et al. 2014). During this time period Americans' life expectancy at age forty increased by 7.8 years for men and by 5.4 years for women, of which 2.3 years for men and 1.6 years for women resulted from tobacco control programs.

7. U.S. adult smoking prevalence may not fall to 10 percent until about the year 2050 even with a 25 percent improvement in initiation and cessation rates (Warner and Mendez 2010).

8. Philip Morris' support for FDA regulations was thoroughly tested through polls and focus groups; for examples see the many documents by Frederick polls and KRC Research & Consulting starting in 2000.

9. In both 2006 and 2008 less than 1 percent of Americans mentioned tobacco or smoking as their most important problem during October and November pre- or post-election polls.

10. Even so, FCTC supporters concede problems resulting from low levels of spending on tobacco control programs (Nagler and Viswanath 2013); from limited access to smoking cessation programs; from internet advertising (Elkin and Wilson 2010; Freeman and Chapman 2009); from limited compliance in large and populous countries, particularly China (Jin 2014); and from increasingly-popular products such as smokeless tobacco, hookahs and water pipes (Nikogosian and Costa e Silva 2015). For an estimate that FCTC measures had by 2013 averted 7.5 million deaths worldwide, see Levy et al. (2013)

11. In 2014 the large retail chain CVS Pharmacy ended cigarette sales. For evidence from New Zealand that banning retail displays of cigarette packs is popular, see Whyte, Gendall, and Hoek (2014).

12. Recent research (Donny et al. 2015) suggests that smoking very low nicotine cigarettes reduces the number of cigarettes smoked daily, reduces nicotine exposure, and does not increase compensation or withdrawal-related discomfort or safety.

13. For survey evidence that tobacco control advocates hold mixed to negative views of several alternatives to smoked tobacco products, see Warner and Martin (2003).

14. For evidence that high retail density of stores that sell tobacco products encourages youthful initiation of cigarettes and e-cigarettes, see Cantrell et al. (2015).

15. For a criticism of this proposal see Liberman (2006).

16. In a New York City survey three-fifths or more of residents favored prohibiting stores located near schools from selling tobacco, favored a ban on pharmacies selling tobacco products, favored raising the minimum age to purchase cigarettes from 18 to 21, favored requiring retailers to keep tobacco products out of customers' view, and favored raising taxes per pack (Farley et al. 2015).

17. The "proven" tobacco control measures' impact on smoking prevalence is also far better studied than are newer proposals. Levy, Chaloupka, and Gitchell (2004) report that tax hikes and clean air laws are especially effective in reducing smoking prevalence.

18. Berman et al. (2012) estimate the average annual excess costs of employing a smoking employee at $5,816—a heavy cost particularly for low-wage employees among whom smoking remains common.

19. State laws vary on whether a smoker can be denied employment. A Gallup question asks whether a respondent would be more likely, less likely or whether it would make no difference in a hiring decision "*if you were in a position to hire someone for a job and you learned that the person smoked.*" A quarter (24 percent) of respondents said "*less likely*" in the most recent (2010) survey.

20. For a list of twenty other tobacco control proposals see Proctor (2011: 549–56); see also Daynard (2009).

21. A 2006 Zogby survey reported higher levels of support for a future ban. Among registered and likely voters 45 percent supported and 52 percent opposed "*a federal law making cigarettes illegal within the next five to ten years.*"

22. In Gallup Polls between 1936 and 1940 support for reinstating the prohibition of alcoholic beverages ranged between 30 percent and 36 percent. No reliable nationwide polls are available between 1920 and 1933 when Prohibition was in effect.

23. For polling evidence on smoking bans in public places see also Thompson, Wilson, and Edwards (2009).

24. The Gallup, Pew, and General Social Survey question is "*Do you think the use of marijuana should be made legal, or not?*" In the Pew poll series the percentage of Americans saying "yes, legal" rose from 41 percent in 2010 to 53 percent in 2015. In the GSS series that percentage rose from 18 percent in 1973 to 43 percent in 2012.

25. For evidence that about a third of e-cigarette smokers do not currently smoke tobacco-based cigarettes see McMillen et al. (2015). For a review of the development of e-cigarettes see Chen and Husten (2014). For survey data see Wackowsky and Delnevo (2015). *Nicotine & Tobacco Research* published numerous articles on e-cigarettes, particularly in 2014 and 2015.

EIGHT

Bringing Public Opinion Back Into Tobacco Control Policy

That American tobacco control policy has greatly changed over the last century is clear. That American public opinion has played an important part in these policy changes often escapes attention. Many excellent studies on tobacco control have focused on tobacco industry strategies, on bureaucratic conflicts, on lawsuits, on the financial costs and the medical harm of cigarette smoking, on the efforts of tobacco control activists and interest groups, or on state and local-level tobacco control efforts. In these accounts American public opinion sometimes plays only a minor role and sometimes almost no role at all. This book reconsiders the importance of American public opinion in tobacco control policy.

Two major conclusions stand out. The first is that public opinion reacts in understandable and predictable ways to key events and group strategies. On balance, the evidence presented here offers a relatively optimistic view of the role that American public opinion plays in tobacco control policy. Over recent decades Americans became vastly better informed about the health risks of cigarette smoking, less favorable toward the tobacco industry, less accepting of cigarette smokers, and more supportive of many restrictions on cigarettes. This change occurred largely as a result of mounting scientific evidence about the ills of cigarette smoking, rising media coverage, and a grass-roots tobacco control movement. These attitude changes did not occur rapidly, but they were sweeping and sustained.

The changes in American attitudes on tobacco control policy were sequenced and dynamic. Americans' scientific beliefs were the earliest to begin changing, a process that began in the early 1950s, stalled, and were then spurred on in 1964 when an advisory group assembled by the U.S. Surgeon General's office released its landmark report. Within a decade thereafter the image of cigarette manufacturers had sharply deteriorated, and the stigma attached to smoking increased. With a few exceptions important tobacco control policies followed, not preceded this transition in attitudes. Once underway, these attitude changes were never reversed.

Many years ago Benjamin Page and Robert Shapiro (1982, 1992) argued that when considered collectively Americans' policy attitudes are meaningful, stable, and sensible. Americans' attitudes react in a reasonable and predictable fashion to changing circumstances and new information. True, these opinion changes are seldom rapid and the process of attitude change sometimes can even seem "inertial." The pattern that Page and Shapiro described also appears in tobacco control policy. On Americans' scientific beliefs, on the tobacco industry's image, on the stigma of smoking, and on specific policies, public opinion usually changes very slowly. Large and rapid changes that equal or exceed 3 percent annually are the exception, not the rule. Yet slow rates of change should not obscure how large are the attitude changes that occurred over the last two-thirds of a century.

Americans' changing attitudes on tobacco control mostly resulted from new scientific evidence, media coverage, and grass-roots activism. The changes on scientific beliefs, images, and policy disputes are consistently negative toward cigarette smoking. Indeed, whenever faced with a visible public debate, the tobacco industry has proven surprisingly inept at managing public opinion. This was not for a lack of effort on the industry's part. The tobacco industry clearly believed that public opinion was important. At one time or another the tobacco industry hired nearly all of the nation's best pollsters in its efforts to reframe cigarette smoking. The industry enjoyed some successes at influencing public opinion, for example, in sustaining a controversy over the harm of cigarette smoking from 1954 until 1962 and in early state and local issue elections on tobacco control. At that time the industry's opponents were ill-prepared and poorly funded. The tobacco industry's several policy successes resulted more from its prowess at fundraising and lobbying than from its ability to sway public opinion. Since the 1960s in no instance has American public opinion, over time, changed to become more favorable to the tobacco industry.

The second conclusion offered here is that some linkage models of public opinion and public policy better explain the tobacco control situation than do other. That several different linkage models are helpful is not surprising. Since the 1950s modern tobacco control policy-making has involved many different issues, many different political actors, and many different forums. It seems unrealistic to expect that one model alone would adequately describe the entire spectrum of tobacco control efforts.

V. O. Key's early and well-known argument that public opinion operates as an outer boundary for public policymaking receives some support although, taken alone, Key's argument is only a very incomplete description of tobacco control policy. When public opinion overwhelmingly and consistently opposed a proposed tobacco control policy—for example, on a complete ban on the sale of cigarettes—such unpopular proposals were not seriously debated and never enacted. At the other extreme, once enacted, few if any popular tobacco control policies have ever been repealed. The fairness doctrine is an early and arguable exception, but unfortunately public views on the 1967 Federal Communication Commission decision were apparently never polled. Tax hikes, bans on public smoking, restrictions on sales and advertising, once enacted and popular in the polls, endure as public policy. As Key himself acknowledged, the outer boundaries of public acceptance are not static and can change over time.

The candidate-centered "electoral connection" is a long-standing and important theory, but is only modestly useful in considering tobacco control policy. Until Bill Clinton's presidency during the 1990s, American presidents carefully avoided taking a public position on the cigarette issue. Nor was tobacco control a high-ranking "most important problem" to American voters. The two American presidents who supported major tobacco control initiatives, Bill Clinton and Barack Obama, were initially elected much more for their health care promises and when the American economy was in an economic recession. Alone among presidents, only Bill Clinton raised tobacco control as even a minor theme in his successful reelection campaign. Further, all of President Clinton's tobacco control initiatives failed. The electoral connection best explains the steadfast opposition to tobacco control measures by members of Congress from tobacco growing districts and states. Scattered examples do appear that members of Congress considered the electoral consequences of their vote on tobacco control disputes. In 1998, for example, the tobacco industry used its polling to reassure wavering U.S. Senators that killing the proposed Global Settlement Agreement would not harm their reelection prospects. For federal judges and top-level federal bureaucrats, none of whom face elections, the candidate-centered electoral connection theory is an even less useful linkage theory.

Direct issue elections at the state and local level offer an alternative and useful election-connection linkage model for public opinion and tobacco control policy. Beginning anew in the 1970s anti-smoking activists often turned to these elections, sometimes successfully enacting tax hikes, bans on smoking in public places, and funding for anti-smoking education programs. When they succeeded, anti-smoking activists heightened the stigma of smoking, raised awareness of the harm of smoking, increased the price and inconvenience of smoking, and thereby reduced smoking rates. As a limitation, only about half of the American states allow citizen-initiated issue elections.

The sense and share linkage model posits that key policy-makers are influenced by the same events and the same media coverage as are ordinary Americans. Ideally, this model could be supported by timely surveys of policy-makers' opinions, but elite-level interviews are seldom available and actions must serve as indicators of elite opinion. Several examples appear. After the 1964 Surgeon General's advisory committee report was issued to high levels of media coverage, top officials at the Federal Trade Commission and in several states soon threatened to require a stringent cigarette warning label for cigarette packages. Although the FTC backed down under Congressional and industry pressure, their threats and poll support caused the industry to make a strategic concession and Congress to enact the first package warning requirement. Chapter 5 better tests the sense and share model, and suggests that while Congress had a strong bias against change, in the federal courts there was a small bias for change and in the federal agencies a pronounced bias for change.

Two important instances of strategic concessions appear, including the package warning example discussed just above. The other example is Philip Morris' well-researched about-face on federal regulations that led to the 2009 Family Smoking Prevention and Tobacco Control Act. The 2009 act produced a new federal regulatory regime but one with several weak provisions that relegated tobacco control policy-making to a slow-moving and low-profile future at the U.S. Food and Drug Administration and in related federal court challenges. The 2009 act is an unusual case. Except for Philip Morris, the major cigarette manufacturers opposed the legislation and mounted the ensuing lawsuits. Public opinion was mixed on the 2009 tobacco control bill as a whole, favorable to many of its parts, very hostile to the tobacco industry and well-informed on the harm of cigarette smoking.[1] Several state-level examples of strategic concessions occurred as the industry offered to accept weak statewide regulations on smoking in return for preempting tougher local regulations.

By far the greatest amount of polling evidence for any linkage model is on the manipulation model. Most important tobacco control events had little or no apparent short-term effects on public opinion. Neither the 1957 and 1959 U.S. Surgeon General's statements on cigarette smoking, nor the 1962 British report, the Federal Trade Commission's early on-and-off-again ban on health claims in cigarette advertising, nor the steady stream of scientific reports during the mid-1950s and the early 1960s, nor the 1971 broadcast ban greatly increased Americans' beliefs that cigarette smoking was a cause of lung cancer or heart disease. A few of the U.S. Surgeon General's reports on smoking influenced Americans' scientific beliefs, but most did not. None of these events can compare to the impact of the 1964 report from the Surgeon General's advisory committee. To this day that report stands out as a unique event in the history of tobacco control, at least in its immediate effect on Americans' scientific beliefs.

The tobacco industry's oft-reputed success at managing public opinion should be reconsidered. Interest groups sometimes convey mass public opinion into public policy but often interest groups act as a barrier between public opinion and public policy (Erikson and Tedin 2015: 301–04; Gilens and Page 2014). The tobacco industry is commonly described as the latter. The evidence on the industry's ability to manage public opinion is quite mixed. At times the industry's well-polled efforts to influence public opinion seemingly succeeded. From 1954 through 1962 the industry's public relations strategy of "creating controversy"—an effort aided by the newly-introduced filter cigarettes and by inconsistent federal actions—slowed what had been from 1950 to 1954 rising beliefs that cigarette smoking caused lung cancer and heart disease. After 1964 the tobacco industry's success at managing nationwide public opinion sharply deteriorated. During the 1970s the tobacco industry's image deteriorated and the stigma of smoking increased, in both cases about as rapidly and consistently as possible given the slow-moving tendencies of American public opinion. Industry efforts to reframe cigarette smoking were a partial success. The industry's polling and focus group work identified three frames—the limited-government frame, the freedom-of-choice frame, and the fairness-for-smokers frame—that proved useful to the industry in state and local ballot elections, on the average reducing by twelve to fifteen percent the early poll support for tax hikes or public smoking bans. Sometimes this was sufficient to defeat tobacco control ballot initiatives although by the 1990s more often not. Arguably, the tobacco industry sometimes manages public opinion even more indirectly. By thus far keeping graphic warning labels from appearing on cigarette packages, for example, the industry probably reduced public awareness about those labels, prevented whatever increased beliefs about the ills of cigarette smoking that might occur, and precluded any resulting drop in cigarette smoking. These industry successes are not minor, but they should not disguise the adverse attitude shifts toward the industry itself and toward smokers, on the medical harm of smoking, and on many tobacco control policies.

The term "manipulation" is seldom applied to the efforts of scientists and grass-roots activists whose efforts nonetheless sometimes influence American attitudes if slowly so. From 1950 and 1954 new scientific evidence and media attention on the ills of cigarette smoking contributed to Americans' rising beliefs that smoking was harmful. The 1964 U.S. Surgeon General's report was based on the results of several thousand scientific studies. So were later Surgeon General reports, a few of which increased public beliefs in harm of cigarette smoking. The social cascade model, discussed below, makes a strong case for the influence of scientific evidence on public opinion and public policy.

Grass-roots activists and educators can also influence attitudes, although, as for scientists, their influence is more long-term than immediate. Several examples appear. Beginning during the 1950s health activists focused their efforts on the schools, leading to a rising awareness among youth of the harm of smoking. Changes in young Americans' scientific beliefs did not immediate cause a large shift in poll samples of American adults, but these changes did affect the polls as generational replacement occurred. The rising awareness of the harm of secondhand smoke is another such example. At a much earlier time the vigorous anticigarette movement of a century ago left behind a cohort of Americans that smoked less and better recognized the harm of smoking than did better educated Americans born over the next several decades.

Little evidence exists that the federal courts, the president, and Congress influenced Americans' scientific beliefs, the image of cigarette manufacturers, the stigma of smoking, or policy preferences on specific issues. Many lawsuits were filed by sick or dying smokers during the first and second wave of tobacco litigation, but these lawsuits all failed, were not particularly popular, seldom reached the trial stage, received little media attention, and these lawsuits do not correspond to the time periods during which the tobacco industry's image declined and the stigma of smoking increased. During the 1990s high-profile lawsuits, Congressional hearings, and whistleblower evidence modestly influenced Americans' beliefs about who is responsible for tobacco-related illnesses. By the time that the third wave of tobacco lawsuits arose during the 1990s Americans' scientific beliefs, the industry's image, and the stigma of smoking had already greatly changed. When polls are available both before and after federal-level tobacco control decisions, the polls barely changed—at a rate of less than 1 percent annually—in favor of the policy decision. Congress' 1971 "broadcast ban" slightly lowered the rise in Americans' knowledge of the harm of cigarette smoking. As discussed earlier in this chapter, most presidents avoided taking clear public positions on tobacco control issues, serving as a reminder that actions are necessary to influence public opinion.

Manipulating American public opinion is not a simple or quick matter. The results here are mostly as Page, Shapiro, and Dempsey (1987) long ago suggested. Interest groups, Congress, and the federal courts seldom influence public opinion. Popular presidents do but only if they make a sustained effort. Scientific experts and high-profile media coverage that offers clear and one-sided accounts can successfully shift poll numbers. To the latter list might be added the efforts of grass-roots activists and educators. Poll shifts are usually modest in size and more often slow than quick. When changes in public opinion do occur, these changes are more often narrow than broad in scope.

Modest support for the coincidental representation thesis appears. When the policy references of wealthy, middle-class, and poor Americans differ, the preferences of the wealthy usually prevail. This pattern is not unique to tobacco control policy. As a caveat, most

Americans' policy preferences do not differ by a respondent's level of affluence. Only on one in six of the federal-level tobacco control policies examined here did preferences differ by income. Lawsuits offer a very different instance of coincidental representation. Most individual and class action lawsuits brought by ill or dying smokers failed, mostly because of the financial costs and legal difficulties involved in these lawsuits, not simply because public opinion was unsympathetic.

The thermostatic model, although elsewhere useful, does not well describes public opinion on tobacco control policy. Since the 1960s Americans' scientific beliefs in the harm of cigarette smoking steadily rose. Americans' images of smokers and Americans' views of cigarette manufacturers steadily worsened. On preferences for specific tobacco control policies, identically worded poll questions, over time, are not often available, and the conclusions are necessarily more tentative. Yet for major tobacco control policies—including tax hikes, tobacco price supports, and limits on smoking in public places—poll support steadily if slowly increased notwithstanding a growing number of tobacco control policies enacted at the federal and state level. No evidence suggests that enacting new tobacco control policies leads to a backlash and to lower public support for future tobacco control policies.

The circumstances under which tobacco control decisions occur are also important. By the evidence presented here the policy-making forum involved matters a great deal. The federal courts and the federal agencies often accept tobacco regulations in advance of public opinion and are far friendlier to tobacco control policies than is Congress. Highly-salient tobacco control policies are less prone to a status quo bias than are low-salience policies. Periods of divided political control between Republicans and Democrats produce a higher status quo bias, at least when the elective branches are the policy-makers. In all this tobacco control policies are not unique.

Throughout this book the view that tobacco control policy-making is a long and often greatly drawn-out process comes through strongly and repeatedly. Public opinion has also greatly changed over recent decades. Several linkage models usefully explain parts of the relationship between public opinion and tobacco control policy-making. A very useful perspective is that of a social cascade with one or more punctuated equilibrium and tipping points. This perspective focuses attention on the changing relationship between public policy, key events, media coverage, industry and antismoking strategies, and public opinion and calls particular attention to the sequence of events involved. As described earlier, the relationship between public opinion and public policy is by no means static, but highly dynamic over time. Several attitudes are important to examine, including scientific beliefs and images, and not simply the public's policy preferences. The sequence of actions and reactions for tobacco control should not be expected to be identical to that found on other social cascades. Indeed, they are not.

This book draws its conclusions from examining American public opinion and tobacco control policy-making over the last century. The modern tobacco control movement reemerged over six decades ago and is still far from eliminating the smoking of combustible tobacco and the harm that results therefrom. Two major conclusion are offered here. First, Americans' smoking-related attitudes, viewed collectively, have reacted slowly but in sensible, predictable, and rational ways to important events. Second, public opinion has played an important role in deciding the outcomes of smoking-related issues. To summarize: American public opinion deserves to be brought back into the study of tobacco control policy-making.

NOTE

1. A third and more arguable case may be made for the industry's acceptance of the Global Settlement Agreement and the Master Settlement Agreement since the threat of large financial damages loomed should the states' attorney generals and trial lawyers prevail, regardless of public opinion.

Bibliography

Abrams, Jeanne E. 2013. "'Spitting is Dangerous, Indecent, and against the Law!' Legislating Health Behavior during the American Tuberculosis Crusade." *Journal of the History of Medicine and Allied Sciences* 68: 416–50.

Adler, Isaac. 1912. *Primary Malignant Growths of the Lungs and Bronchi*. New York: Longmans, Green, and Company.

Alamar, Benjamin and Stanton A. Glantz. 2006. "Effect of Increased Social Unacceptability of Cigarette Smoking on Reduction in Cigarette Consumption." *American Journal of Public Health* 96: 1359–63.

Albers, Alison B., Michael Siegel, Debbie M. Cheng, Lois Biener, and Nancy A. Rigotti. 2007. "Effect of Smoking Regulations in Local Restaurants on Smokers' Anti-Smoking Attitudes and Quitting Behaviours." *Tobacco Control* 16: 101–06.

Alchon, Suzanne Austin. 2003. *A Pest In The Land: New World Epidemics in a Global Perspective*. Albuquerque, NM: University of New Mexico Press.

Al-Delaimy, Wael K., John P. Pierce, Karen Messer, Martha M. White, Dennis R. Trinidad, and Elizabeth A. Gilpin. 2007. "The California Tobacco Control Program's Effect on Adult Smokers: Daily Cigarette Consumption Levels." *Tobacco Control* 16: 91–95.

American Cancer Society. 1969. "The Teenager Looks At Cigarette Smoking." New York: American Cancer Society.

American National Election Study. 2012. "Trust the Federal Government 1958–2008." Available at www.electionstudies.org/nesguide/toptable/tab5a_1.htm.

Apollonio, Dorie E. and Lisa A. Bero. 2007a. "The Creation of Industry Front Groups: The Tobacco Industry and 'Get Government Off Our Back.'" *American Journal of Public Health* 97: 419–27.

———. 2007b. "Industry Front Groups: A Tobacco Case Study." *Journal of Consumer Protection and Food Safety* 2: 341–48.

Apollonio, D. E. and R. E. Malone. 2009. "Turning Negative into Positive: Public Health Mass Media Campaigns and Negative Advertising." *Health Education Research* 24: 483–95.

Arnett, John. 1962. "Youth Confronts the Cigarette." *Journal of the American College Health Association* 11: 159–61.

"*Attitudes of Young American Adults: A Survey Conducted For The Saturday Evening Post, August 1961*." 1961. Princeton, NJ: Public Opinion Surveys.

Austin v. State of Tennessee, 179 U.S. 343 (1900).

Badger, Anthony J. 1980. *Prosperity Road: The New Deal, Tobacco, and North Carolina*. Chapel Hill, NC: University of North Carolina Press.

Balbach, Edith D. and Stanton A. Glantz. 1998. "Tobacco Control Advocates Must Demand High-Quality Media Campaigns: The California Experience." *Tobacco Control* 7: 397–408.

Balbach, Edith D., Michael Traynor, and Stanton A. Glantz. 2000. "The Implementation of California's Tobacco Tax Initiative: the Critical Role of Outsider Strategies in Protecting Proposition 99." *Journal of Health Politics, Policy and Law* 25: 689–715.

Balbach, E. D., R. J. Gasior, and E. M. Barbeau. 2002. "Tobacco Industry Documents: Comparing the Minnesota Depository and Internet Access." *Tobacco Control* 11: 68–72.

Bansal-Travers, Maansi, David Hammond, Philip Smith, and K. Michael Cummings. 2011. "The Impact of Cigarette Pack Design, Descriptors, and Warning Labels on Risk Perception in the U.S." *American Journal of Preventive Medicine* 40: 674–82.

Barker, Kevin Gauntt. 2009. "Thank You For Regulating: Why Philip Morris' Embrace of FDA Regulation Helps the Company but Harms the Agency." *Administrative Law Review* 61: 197–224.

Barnes, D. E. and L. Bero. 1998. "Why Review Articles on the Health Effects of Passive Smoking Reach Different Conclusions." *Journal of the American Medical Association* 279: 1566–70.

Bartels, Larry M. 2008. *Unequal Democracy: The Political Economy of the New Gilded Age*. Princeton, NJ: Princeton University Press.

Barth, Ilene. 1997. *The Smoking Life*. Columbia, MS: Genesis Press.

Bartrip, Peter. 1998. "Pushing the Weed: The Editorializing and Advertising of Tobacco in the Lancet and the British Medical Journal, 1880–1958." In *Ashes to Ashes: The History of Smoking and Health*, edited by Stephen Lock, Lois Reynolds and E.M. Tansey, 100–29. Atlanta, GA: Rodopi.

Baud, Michiel. 2005. "South and Central America." In *Tobacco in History and Culture: An Encyclopedia, Vol. 2*, edited by Jordan Goodman, 570–74. Detroit, MI: Charles Scribner's Sons.

Baumgartner, Frank R. and Bryan D. Jones. 1993, 2009. *Agendas and Instability in American Politics*. Chicago: University of Chicago.

Baumgartner, Frank R., Suzanna L. DeBoef, and Amber E. Boydstun. 2008. *The Decline of the Death Penalty and the Discovery of Innocence*. New York: Cambridge University Press.

Bayer, Ronald. 2008. "Stigma and the Ethics of Public Health: Not Can We But Should We." *Social Science & Medicine* 67: 463–72.

———. 2010. "Stigma and the Ethics of Public Health Redux: A Response to Bell et al." *Social Science & Medicine* 70: 800–01.

——— and James Colgrove. 2002. "Science, Politics, and Ideology in the Campaign Against Environmental Tobacco Smoke." *American Journal of Public Health* 92: 949–54.

Beaglehole Robert, Ruth Bonita, Richard Horton, et al. 2011. "Priority Actions for the Non-Communicable Disease Crisis." *Lancet* 377: 1438–47.

Begay, Michael E., Michael Traynor, and Stanton A. Glantz. 1993. "The Tobacco Industry, State Politics, and Tobacco Education in California." *American Journal of Public Health* 83: 1214–20.

Bell, Kirsten, Amy Salmon, Michele Bowers, Jennifer Bell, and Lucy McCullough. 2010. "Smoking, Stigma and Tobacco 'Denormalization': Further Feflections on the Use of Stigma as a Public Health Tool." *Social Science & Medicine* 70: 795–99.

Benedict, Carol. 2005. "Therapeutic Uses." In *Tobacco in History and Culture: An Encyclopedia, Vol. 2*, edited by Jordan Goodman, 609–15. Detroit, MI: Charles Scribner's Sons.

Benowitz, Neal L. and Jack E. Henningfield. 1994. "Establishing a Nicotine Threshold for Addiction: The Implications for Tobacco Regulation." *New England Journal of Medicine* 331: 123–25.

———. 2013. "Reducing the Nicotine Content to Make Cigarettes Less Addictive." *Tobacco Control* 22: i14–i17.

Berinsky, Adam J. 1994, 2004. *Silent Voices: Opinion Polls and Political Participation in America*. Princeton, NJ: Princeton University Press.

——— and Donald R. Kinder. 2006. "Making Sense of Issues Through Media Frames: Understanding the Kosovo Crisis." *Journal of Politics* 68: 640–56.

Berkson, Joseph. 1946. "Limitations of the Application of Fourfold Table Analysis to Hospital Data." *Biometrics* 2: 47–53.

———. 1955. "The Statistical Study of Association Between Smoking and Lung Cancer." *Proceedings of the Staff Meetings of Mayo Clinic* 30: 319–48.

———. 1958. "Smoking and Lung Cancer: Some Observations on Two Recent Reports." *Journal of the American Statistical Association* 53: 28–38.

Berman, Micah L. 2009. "Smoking Out the Impact of Tobacco-Related Decisions on Public Health Law." *Brooklyn Law Review* 75: 1–61.

———, Rob Crane, Eric Seiber, and Mehmet Munur. 2013. "Estimating the Cost of a Smoking Employee." *Tobacco Control* 23: 428–33.

Bero, Lisa A. 2005. "Tobacco Industry Manipulation of Research." *Public Health Reports* 120: 200–08.

——— and G. Kennedy. 1999. "Print Media Coverage of Research on Passive Smoking." *Tobacco Control* 8: 254–60.

Berridge, Virginia. 1998. "Science and Policy: The Case of Postwar British Smoking Policy." In *Ashes to Ashes: the History of Smoking and Health*, edited by Stephen Lock, Lois Reynolds, and E. M. Tansy, 143–62. Amsterdam: Rodopi.

———. 2007. "Medicine and the Public: The 1962 Report of the Royal College of Physicians and the New Public Health." *Bulletin of the History of Medicine* 81: 286–311.

Bethencourt, Francisco. 2005. "Portuguese Empire." In *Tobacco in History and Culture: An Encyclopedia, Vol. 2*, edited by Jordan Goodman, 440–46. Detroit, MI: Charles Scribner's Sons.

Bialous, Stella Aguinaga and Stanton A. Glantz. 1999. "Arizona's Tobacco Control Initiative Illustrates the Need for Continuing Oversight by Tobacco Control Advocates." *Tobacco Control* 8: 141–51.

Bialous, Stella Aguinaga, Brion J. Fox, and Stanton A. Glantz. 2001. "Tobacco Industry Allegations of 'Illegal Lobbying' and State Tobacco Control." *American Journal of Public Health* 91: 62–67.

Bialous, Stella Aguinaga, and Silvy Peeters. 2012. "A Brief Overview of the Tobacco Industry in the Last 20 Years." *Tobacco Control* 21: 92–94.

Bjornson, W. R. and C. Sahr. 1997. "Tobacco Tax Initiative—Oregon 1996." *Morbidity and Mortality Weekly Report* 46: 246–47.

Bleda, Paul R. and Paul H. Sandman. 1977. "In Smoke's Way: Socioemotional Reactions to Another's Smoking." *Journal of Applied Psychology* 62: 452–58.

Blendon, Robert J. and John T. Young. 1998. "The Public and the Comprehensive Tobacco Bill." *JAMA* 280: 1279–84.

Blum, Alan. 2014. "Blowing Smoke: The Lost Legacy of the 1964 Surgeon General's Report on Smoking and Health." *Oncology* 2014: 418–22.

Bogart, Laura and Douglas Delahanty. 2004. "Psychosocial Models." In *Handbook of Clinical Health Psychology*, edited by Thomas Boll, Vol. 3: 214–28. Washington, DC: American Psychological Association.

Bogen, Emil. 1929. "The Composition of Cigarets and Cigarette Some." *JAMA* 93 1110–14.

Bolcic-Jankovic, Dragana and Lois Biener. 2015. "Public Opinion About FDA Regulation of Menthol and Nicotine." *Tobacco Control* 24: 543–46.

Borden, Neil H. 1944. *The Economic Effects of Advertising*. Chicago: Irwin.

Borland, Ron. 2003. "A Strategy for Controlling the Marketing of Tobacco Products: A Regulated Market Model." *Tobacco Control* 12: 374–82.

———, Hua-Hie Yong, Nick Wilson, Geoffrey T. Fong, David Hammond, K. Michael Cummings, Warwick Hosking, and Ann McNeill. 2009. "How Reactions to Cigarette Health Warnings Influence Quitting: Findings from the ITC Four-Country Survey." *Addiction* 104: 669–75.

Bowler, Shaun and Todd Donovan. 1994. "Information and Opinion Change on Ballot Propositions." *Political Behavior* 16: 411–35.

———. 2004. "Measuring the Effect of Direct Democracy on State Policy: Not All Initiatives Are Created Equal." *State Politics & Policy Quarterly* 4: 345–63.

——— and Caroline J. Tolbert, eds. 1998. *Citizens as Legislators: Direct Democracy in the United States*. Columbus: Ohio State University.

Bowser, Diane, David Canning, and Adeyemi Okunogbe. 2016. "The Impact of Tobacco Taxes on Mortality in the USA, 1970–2005." *Tobacco Control* 25: 52–59.

Brandt, Allan M. 1990. "The Cigarette, Risk, and American Culture." *Daedalus* 119: 155–76.

———. 2007. *The Cigarette Century*. New York: Basic Books.

Britton, John and Richard Edwards. 2007. "Tobacco Smoking, Harm Reduction, and Nicotine Product Regulation." *Lancet* 371: 441–45.

Brodie, Mollyann, Claudia Deane, and Sarah Cho. 2011. "Regional Variations in Public Opinion on the Affordable Care Act." *Journal of Health Politics, Policy and Law* 36: 1097–103.

Burden, Barry C. 2007. *Personal Roots of Representation*. Princeton, NJ: Princeton University Press.

Burney, Leroy E. 1957. "Excessive Cigarette Smoking: Statement." *Public Health Reports* 72: 786.

———. 1959. "Smoking and Lung Cancer." *Journal of the American Medical Association* 171: 1829–36.

Burnham, John C. 1989. "American Physicians and Tobacco Use: Two Surgeons General, 1929 and 1964." *Bulletin of the History of Medicine* 63: 1–31.

———. 1993. *Bad Habits: Drinking, Smoking, Taking Drugs, Gambling, Sexual Misbehavior and Swearing in American History*. New York: New York University Press.

Burstein, Paul. 1998. "Bringing the Public Back In: Should Sociologists Consider the Impact of Public Opinion on Public Policy?" *Social Forces* 77: 27–62.

———. 2002. "Public Opinion and Congressional Action on Labor Market Opportunities, 1942–200." In *New Directions in Public Opinion*, edited by Adam J. Berinsky, 86–105. New York: Routledge.

———. 2003. "The Impact of Public Opinion on Public Policy: A Review and an Agenda." *Political Research Quarterly* 56: 29–40.

———. 2006. "Why Estimates of the Impact of Public Opinion on Public Policy are Too High: Empirical and Theoretical Implications." *Social Forces* 84: 2273–89.

Calfee, John E. 1985. "Working Paper # 134: Cigarette Advertising, Health Information and Regulation Before 1970." Washington, DC: Bureau of Economics, Federal Trade Commission.

———. 1986. "The Ghost of Advertising Past." *Regulation* 10 (November/December): 35–45.

Callard, C., D. Thompson, and N. Collishaw. 2005. "Transforming the Tobacco Market: Why the Supply of Cigarettes Should be Transferred from For-Profit Corporations to Non-Profit Enterprises with a Public Health Mandate." *Tobacco Control* 14: 278–83.

Campbell, Andrea Louise. 2012. "Public Opinion and Public Policy." In *New Directions in Public Opinion*, edited by Adam J. Berinsky, 271–91. New York: Routledge.

Campbell, Angus, Philip E. Converse, Warren E. Miller, and Donald Stokes. 1960. *The American Voter*. New York: Wiley.

Cantor, David and Carsten Timmermann. 2005. "Lung Cancer." In *Tobacco in History and Culture: An Encyclopedia, Vol. 1*, edited by Jordan Goodman, 329–35. Detroit, MI: Charles Scribner's Sons.

Cantrell, Jennifer, Jennifer L. Pearson, Andrew Anesetti-Rothemel, Haijun Ziao, Thomas R. Kirchner, and Donna Vallone. 2015. "Tobacco Retail Outlet Density and Young Adult Tobacco Initiation." *Nicotine & Tobacco Research* 2015: 1–8.

Cardozo, Benjamin N. 1921. *The Nature of the Judicial Process*. New Haven, CT: Yale University Press.

Cavari, Amnon. 2012. "The Short-Term Effect of Going Public." *Political Research Quarterly* 66: 336–51.

Chaloupka, Frank J., Melanie Wakefield, and Christina Czart. 2001. "Taxing Tobacco: The Impact of Tobacco Taxes on Cigarette Smoking and Other Tobacco Use." In *Regulating Tobacco*, edited by Robert L. Rabin and Stephen D. Sugarman, 39–56. New York: Oxford University Press.

Chaloupka, F. J., K. M. Cummings, C. P. Morley, and J. K. Horan. 2002. "Tax, Price and Cigarette Smoking: Evidence from the Tobacco Documents and Implications for Tobacco Company Marketing Strategies." *Tobacco Control* 11: i62–i72.

Chaloupka, Frank J., Ayda Yurekli, and Geoffrey T. Fong. 2012. "Tobacco Taxes as a Tobacco Control Strategy." *Tobacco Control* 21: 172–80.

Chaloupka, Frank J., Kenneth E. Warner, Daron Acemoglu, Jonathan Gruber, Fritz Laux, Wendy Max, Joseph Newhouse, Thomas Schelling, and Jody Sindelar. 2015. "An Evaluation of the FDA's Analysis of the Costs and Benefits of the Graphic Warning Label Regulation." *Tobacco Control* 24: 112–19.

Chapman, S., R. Borland, M. Scollo, et al. 1999. "The Impact of Smoke-Free Workplaces on Declining Cigarette Consumption in Australia and the United States." *American Journal of Public Health* 89: 1018–23.

Chapman, S. and Liberman, J. 2005. "Ensuring Smokers are Adequately Informed: Reflections on Consumer Rights, Manufacturer Responsibilities, and Policy Implications." *Tobacco Control* 14: 873–74.

Chen, Li-Lun and Corinne G. Husten. 2014. "Introduction to Tobacco Control Supplement." *Tobacco Control* 23: ii1–ii3.

Chong, Dennis and James N. Druckman. 2010. "Dynamic Public Opinion: Communications Efforts over Time." *American Political Science Review* 104: 663–80.

Christensen, Jon. 2008. "Smoking Out Objectivity: Journalistic Gears in the Agnotology Machine." In *Agnotology: The Making and Unmaking of Ignorance*, edited by Robert N. Proctor and Londa Schiebinger, 1–36. Stanford CA: Stanford University Press.

"Cigarette Smoking in the United States, 1986." 1987. *Morbidity and Mortality Weekly Report* 36: 581–85.

Ciresi, Michael V., Roberta B. Walburn, and Tara D. Sutton. 1999. "Decades of Deceit: Document Discovery in the Minnesota Tobacco Litigation." *William Mitchell Law Review* 25: 477–566.

Cohen, Joel B. 1989. "Counting Advertising Assertions to Assess Regulatory Policy: When It Doesn't Add Up." *Journal of Public Policy and Marketing* 8: 24–29.

Coller, Maribeth, Glenn W. Harrison, and Melayne Morgan McInnes. 2002. "Evaluating the Tobacco Settlement Damage Awards: Too Much or Not Enough?" *American Journal of Public Health* 92: 984–89.

Comin, Francisco. 2005. "State Tobacco Monopolies." In *Tobacco in History and Culture: An Encyclopedia, Vol. 2*, edited by Jordan Goodman, 599–602. Detroit, MI: Charles Scribner's Sons.

Connolly, Gregory N., Ilan Behm, Cheryl Healton, and Hillel Alpert. 2012. "Public Attitudes Regarding Banning of Cigarettes and Regulation of Nicotine." *American Journal of Public Health* 102: e1–2.

Converse, Jean M. 1987. *Survey Research in the United States: Roots and Emergence 1890–1960*. Berkeley: University of California Press.

Converse, Philip E. 1964. "The Nature of Belief Systems in Mass Publics." In *Ideology and Discontent*, edited by David E. Apter, 206–64. New York: Free Press.

Cook, Fay Lomax and Edith J. Barrett. 1992. *Support for the American Welfare State: The Views of Congress and the Public*. New York: Columbia University Press.

Cornelius, Monica E., Pete Driezen, Andrew Hyland, Geoffrey T. Fong, Frank J. Chaloupka, and K. Michael Cummings. 2015. "Trends in Cigarette Pricing and Purchasing Patterns in a Sample of US Smokers: Findings from the ITC US Surveys 2002–2011." *Tobacco Control* 24: iii4–10.

Cortas, Chandi W. and Colin L. Talley. 2006. "'Appropriate Remedial Action?' Medical Students, Medical Schools, and Smoking and Health Education in New York and the United States, 1964–1987." *Journal of the History of Medicine and Allied Sciences* 62: 316–35.

Courtwright, David T. 2001. *Forces of Habit: Drugs and the Making of the Modern World*. Cambridge, MA: Harvard University Press.

———. 2005. "'Carry on Smoking,' Public Relations and Advertising Strategies of American and British Tobacco Companies since 1950." *Business History* 47: 421–32.

Crane, Jonathan. 1991. "The Epidemic Theory of Ghettos and Neighborhood Effects on Dropping Out and Teenage Childbearing." *American Journal of Sociology* 96: 1226–59.

Crawford, Michael. 1998. *The Origins of Native Americans: Evidence from Anthropological Genetics*. Cambridge: Cambridge University Press.

Cross, Gary. 2001. "Corralling Consumer Culture: Shifting Rationales for American State Intervention in Free Markets." In *The Politics of Consumption*, edited by Martin Daunton and Matthew Hilton, 283–300. Oxford: Berg.

Crotty, William, ed. 2014. *Polarized Politics: The Impact of Divisiveness in the US Political System*. Boulder, CO: Lynne Rienner.

Cullman, Joseph F., III. 1998. *I'm a Lucky Guy*. New York: Philip Morris.

Cummings, K. Michael. 2002. "Programs and Policies to Discourage the Use of Tobacco Products." *Oncogene* 21: 7349–64.

———. 2006. "Consumer Acceptable Risk: How Cigarette Companies Have Responded to Accusations That Their Products are Defective." *Tobacco Control* 15: iv84–iv89.

———, Anthony Brown, and Clifford E. Douglas. 2006. "Consumer Acceptable Risk: How Cigarette Companies Have Responded to Accusations that Their Products are Defective." *Tobacco Control* 15: iv84–iv89.

———, C. P. Morley and A. Hyland. 2002. "Failed Promises of the Cigarette Industry and Its Effect on Consumer Misperceptions About the Health Risks of Smoking." *Tobacco Control* 11: i110–i117.

Davis, Ronald M. 1995. "Tobacco Policy Research Comes of Age." *Tobacco Control* 4: 6–9.

———, Gayle M. Boyd, and Charlotte A. Schoenborn. 1990. "'Common Courtesy' and the Elimination of Passive Smoking." *JAMA* 263: 2208–10.

Daynard, Richard. 1988. "Tobacco Liability Litigation as a Cancer Control Strategy." *Journal of the National Cancer Institute* 80: 9–13.

———. 1994. "The Third Wave of Tobacco Products Liability Cases." *Trial* 30: 34–40.

———. 2009. "Doing the Unthinkable (and Saving Millions of Lives)." *Tobacco Control* 18: 2–3.

——— and Laurie Morin. 1988. "The Cipollone Documents: Following the Paper Trail to Tobacco Industry Liability." *Trial* 50: 2450–54.

———, Eric LeGresley, Wendy Parmet, Graham Kelder, and Patricia Davidson. 2001. "Implications for Tobacco Control of the Multistate Tobacco Settlement." *American Journal of Public Health* 91: 1967–71.

——— and Eric LeGresley. 2012. "Product Liability." *Tobacco Control* 21: 227–28.

DeBoer, Connie. 1977. "The Polls: Nuclear Energy." *Public Opinion Quarterly* 41: 402–11.

——— and Ineke Catsburg. 1988. "The Impact of Nuclear Accidents on Attitudes Toward Nuclear Energy." *Public Opinion Quarterly* 52: 254–61.

DeCicca, Philip, Don Kenkel, and Alan Mathios. 2008. "Cigarette Taxes and the Transition from Youth to Adult Smoking: Smoking Initiation, Cessation, and Participation." *Journal of Health Economics* 27: 904–17.

DelRossi, Alison F. and W. Kip Viscusi. 2010. "The Changing Landscape of Blockbuster Damages Awards." *American Law and Economics Review* 12: 116–61.

Derthick, Martha A. 1979. *Policymaking for Social Security*. Washington, DC: Brookings Institution.

———. 2002, 2005. *Up In Smoke: From Legislation to Litigation in Tobacco Politics*. Washington, DC: CQ Press.

———. 2012. "From Litigation to Legislation in Tobacco Politics: The Surrender of Philip Morris." *Political Science Quarterly* 127: 401–15.

Dewhirst, Timothy. 2005. "Public Relations." In *Tobacco in History and Culture: An Encyclopedia, Vol. 2*, edited by Jordan Goodman, 473–79. Detroit, MI: Charles Scribner's Sons.

DiFranza, J. R. and G. F. Dussault. 2005. "The Federal Initiative to Halt the Sale of Tobacco to Children—The Synar Amendment, 1992–2000: Lessons Learned." *Tobacco Control* 14: 93–98.

Dikötter, Frank. 2005. "China." In *Tobacco in History and Culture: An Encyclopedia, Vol. 1*, edited by Jordan Goodman, 129–35. Detroit, MI: Charles Scribner's Sons.

Dillow, Gordon L. 1981. "Thank You For Not Smoking." *American Heritage* 1981 (Feb/March): 94–107.

"Doctors Have Changed Their Smoking Habits." 1957. *Resident Physician* 3 (11): 51–63.

Doll, Richard and A. Bradford Hill. 1950. "Smoking and Carcinoma of the Lung: Preliminary Report." *British Medical Journal* 2: 739–48.

———. 1952. "A Study of the Aetiology of Carcinoma of the Lung." *British Medical Journal* 2: 1271–86.

———. 1954. "The Mortality Of Doctors In Relation To Their Smoking Habits: A Preliminary Report." *British Medical Journal* 1: 1451–55.

———. 1956. "Lung Cancer And Other Causes Of Death In Relation To Smoking: A Second Report On The Mortality Of British Doctors." *British Medical Journal* 2: 1071–81.

Doll, Sir Richard. 1998. "The First Reports on Smoking and Lung Cancer." In *Ashes to Ashes: The History of Smoking and Health*, edited by Stephen Lock, Lois Reynolds and E. M. Tansey, 130–40. Atlanta, GA: Rodopi.

———. 1998. "Uncovering the Effects of Smoking: Historical Perspective." *Statistical Methods in Medical Research* 7: 87–117.

———, Richard Peto, Jillian Boreham, and Isabelle Sutherland. 2004. "Mortality in Relation to Smoking: 50 Years' Observations on Male British Doctors." *British Medical Journal* 328: 1519–27.

Domhoff, G. William. 2002. "The Power Elite, Public Policy, and Public Opinion." In *Navigating Public Opinion*, edited by Jeff Manza, Fay Lomax Cook, and Benjamin I. Page, 124–37. New York: Oxford University Press.

———. 2013. *Who Rules America: The Triumph of the Corporate Rich*. 7th ed., New York: McGraw-Hill.

Donny Eric, Rachel Denlinger, Jennifer Tiday, Joseph Kepmeiners, Neal Benowitz, Ryan Vandrey, Mustafa al'Absi, Steve Carmella, Paul Cinciripini, Sarah Dermody, David Drobes, Stephen Hecht, Joni Jensen, Tonya Lane, Chap T. Le, F. Joseph McClernon, Ivan Montoya, Sharon Murphy, Jason Robinson, Maxine Stitzer, Andrew Strasser, Hilary Tindle, and Dorothy Hatsukami. 2015. "Randomized Trial of Reduced-Nicotine Standards for Cigarettes." *New England Journal of Medicine* 373: 1340–49.

Doron, Gideon. 1979. *The Smoking Paradox: Public Regulation in the Cigarette Industry*. Cambridge, MA: Abt Books.

Douglas, Clifford E. 1993. "Punish the Smoking Industry, Not the Smoking Individual." *Tobacco Control* 2: 239–41.

———, Ronald M. Davis, and John K. Beasley. 2006. "Epidemiology of the Third Wave of Tobacco Litigation in the United States, 1994–2005." *Tobacco Control* 15: iv9–iv16.

Doval, Hernan C. 2013. "How to End the Tobacco Epidemic: What Tobacco Control Strategy Should be Used?" *Argentine Journal of Cardiology* 81: 425–32.

Drew, Elizabeth. 1965. "The Quiet Victory of the Cigarette Lobby." *Atlantic Monthly* (September): 77.

Drope, Jeffrey and Raphael Lencucha. 2014. "Evolving Norms at the Intersection of Health and Trade." *Journal of Health Politics, Policy, and Law* 39: 591–31.

Druckman, James N. and Lawrence R. Jacobs. 2015. *Who Governs? Presidents, Public Opinion, and Manipulation*. Chicago: University of Chicago Press.

Edwards, George C. III. 2003. *On Deaf Ears: The Limits of the Bully Pulpit*. New Haven, CT: Yale University Press.

Elkin, L., G. Thompson, and N. Wilson. 2010. "Connecting World Youth with Tobacco Brands: YouTube and the Internet Policy Vacuum on Web 2.0." *Tobacco Control* 19: 361–66.

Elliot, Rosemary. 2005. "Soldiers." In *Tobacco in History and Culture: An Encyclopedia, Vol. 2*, edited by Jordan Goodman, 568–70. Detroit, MI: Charles Scribner's Sons.

Engs, Ruth Clifford. 2000. *Clean Living Movements: American Cycles of Health Reform*. Westport, CT: Praeger.

Enns, Peter K. 2015. "Reconsidering the Middle: A Reply to Martin Gilens." *Perspectives on Politics* 13: 1072–74.

——— and Christopher Wlezien. 2011. "Group Opinion and the Study of Representation." In *Who Gets Represented?*, edited by Peter K. Enns and Christopher Wlezien, 1–26. New York: Russell Sage Foundation.

Epstein, Lee and Andrew D. Martin. 2010. "Does Public Opinion Influence the Supreme Court? Possibly Yes (But We're Not Sure Why)." *Journal of Constitutional Law* 13: 263–81.

Erikson, Robert S. 2015. "Income Inequality and Policy Responsiveness." *Annual Review of Political Science* 18: 11–29.

———, Michael B. MacKuen, and James A. Stimson. 2002. *The Macro Polity*. New York: Cambridge University Press.

———, and Kent L. Tedin. 2015. *American Public Opinion*. Upper Saddle River, NJ: Pearson.

Ernster, Virginia L. 1985. "Mixed Messages for Women." *New York State Journal of Medicine* 85: 335–40.

Erskine, Hazel Gaudet. 1966a. "The Polls: Smoking." *Public Opinion Quarterly* 30: 140–52.

———. 1966b. "The Polls: Cancer." *Public Opinion Quarterly* 30: 308–14.

Evans, William N., Matthew C. Farrelly, and Edward Montgomery. 1999. "Do Workplace Smoking Bans Reduce Smoking?" *The American Economic Review* 89: 728–47.

Fallin, Amanda, Rachel Grana, and Stanton A. Glantz. 2014. "'To Quarterback Behind the Scenes': Third-Party Efforts, the Tobacco Industry and the Tea Party." *Tobacco Control* 23: 322–31.

"False And Misleading Advertising (Filter-Tip Cigarettes)—Twentieth Report by the Committee On Government Operations. Feb. 20, 1958." Washington, DC: U.S. Government Printing Office.

Fan, David P. 1988. *Predictions of Public Opinion from the Mass Media*. New York: Greenwood Press.

Farley, Shannon M., Micaela H. Coady, Jenna Mandel-Ricci, Elizabeth Needham Waddell, Christina Chan, Elizabeth A. Kilgore, and Susan M. Kansagra. 2015. "Public Opinions on Tax and Retail-Based Tobacco Control Strategies." *Tobacco Control* 24: e10–e13.

Farrelly, Matthew C., Terry F. Pechacek, and Frank J. Chaloupka. 2003. "The Impact of Tobacco Control Program Expenditures on Aggregate Cigarette Sales: 1981–2000." *Journal of Health Economics* 22: 843–59.

Farrelly, Matthew C., Terry Pechacek, Kristin Y. Thomas, and David Nelson. 2008. "The Impact of Tobacco Control Programs on Adult Smoking." *American Journal of Public Health* 98: 304–09.

Federal Trade Commission. 1964. *A Report on Cigarette Advertising and Output*. Washington, DC: Federal Trade Commission Bureau of Economics.

———. 1981. *Staff Report on the Cigarette Advertising Investigation*. Washington, DC: Federal Trade Commission.

Feldman, Stanley and Lee Sigelman. 1985. "The Political Impact of Prime-Time Television: 'The Day After.'" *Journal of Politics* 47: 556–78.

Ferrence, Roberta G. 1989.*Deadly Fashion: The Rise and Fall of Cigarette Smoking in North America.* New York: Garland Publishing.

Fichtenberg, Caroline M. and Stanton A. Glantz. 2000. "Association of the California Tobacco Control Program with Declines in Cigarette Consumption and Mortality from Heart Disease." *New England Journal of Medicine* 343: 1772–77.

———. 2002. "Effect of Smoke-Free Workplaces on Smoking Behavior: Systematic Review." *British Medical Journal* 325: 188–91.

Fisher, Edwin, Ross Brownson, Andrew Heath, Douglas Luke, and Walton Sumner II. 2002. "Cigarette Smoking." In *Handbook of Clinical Health Psychology*, edited by Thomas Boll, Vol. 2: 75–120. Washington, DC: American Psychological Association.

Fisher, R. A. 1957. "Dangers of Cigarette Smoking." *British Medical Journal* 2: 43.

———. 1958. "Lung Cancer and Cigarettes?" *Nature* 182: 168.

Foreman, Christopher H., Jr. 1994. *Plagues, Products, and Politics: Emergent Public Health Hazards and National Policymaking*. Washington, DC: Brookings.

Ford, Gary T., Debra J. Ringold, and Martha Rogers. 1990. "Cigarettes in the Popular Press, 1930–1960: Preliminary Research." *Advances in Consumer Research* 17: 467–73.

Ford, Henry. 1916. *The Case Against the Little White Slaver*. Dearborn, MI: Reprinted by the Historical Society of Michigan.

Freeman, B. and S. Chapman. 2009. "Open Source Marketing: Camel Cigarette Brand Marketing in the 'Web 2.0' World." *Tobacco Control* 18: 212–17.

Friedman, Kenneth Michael. 1975. *Public Policy and the Smoking-Health Controversy: A Comparative Study*. Lexington, MA: D.C. Heath and Company.

Friend, Karen and David T. Levy. 2002. "Reductions in Smoking Prevalence and Cigarette Consumption Associated with Mass-Media Campaigns." *Health Education Research* 17: 85–98.

Fritschler, A. Lee. 1969. *Smoking and Politics: Policymaking and the Federal Bureaucracy*. New York: Meredith Corporation.

———. 1983. *Smoking and Politics: Policymaking and the Federal Bureaucracy*. Englewood Cliffs, NJ: Prentice-Hall.

——— and Catherine E. Rudder. 2007. *Smoking and Politics: Bureaucracy Centered Policymaking*. Upper Saddle River, NJ: Pearson/Prentice Hall.

Furst, Peter T. 1976. *Hallucinogens and Culture*. Novato, CA: Chandler & Sharp.

——— 2005. "Shamanism." In *Tobacco in History and Culture: An Encyclopedia, Vol. 2*, edited by Jordan Goodman, 517–22. Detroit, MI: Charles Scribner's Sons.

Gamson, William A. and Andre Modigliani. 1987. "The Changing Culture of Affirmative Action." In *Research in Political Sociology, Vol. 3*, edited by R. A. Braumgart, 137–77. Greenwich: JAI.

Garfinkel, Lawrence and Steven D. Stellman. 1986. "Cigarette Smoking Among Physicians, Dentists, and Nurses." *CA: A Cancer Journal for Physicians* 36: 2–8.

Garner, Donald. 1977. "Cigarettes and Welfare Reform." *Emory Law Journal* 26: 269–335.

———. 1980. "The Cigarette Industry's Escape From Liability." *Business and Society Review* 33: 22–27.

———. 1980. "Cigarette Dependency and Civil Liability: A Modest Proposal." *Southern California Law Review* 53: 1423–26.

Gartner, Coral and Ann McNeill. 2010. "Options for Global Tobacco Control Beyond the Framework Convention in Tobacco Control." *Addiction* 105: 1–3.

Gately, Ian. 2001. *Tobacco: The Story of How Tobacco Seduced the World*. London: Simon & Schuster.

Gibson, Bryan and John Maurer. 2000. "Cigarette Smoking in the Movies: The Influence of Product Placement on Attitudes Toward Smoking and Smokers." *Journal of Applied Social Psychology* 30: 1457–73.

Gibson, Charles. 1964. *The Aztecs Under Spanish Rule*. Stanford, CA: Stanford University Press.

Gifford, Donald G. 2010. *Suing the Tobacco and Lead Pigment Industries: Government Litigation as Public Health Prescription*. Ann Arbor: University of Michigan Press.

Gilens, Martin. 2002. "An Anatomy of Survey-Based Experiments." In *Navigating Public Opinion*, edited by Jeff Manza, Fay Lomax Cook, and Benjamin I. Page, 232–50. New York: Oxford University Press.

———. 2005. "Inequality and Democratic Responsiveness." *Public Opinion Quarterly* 65: 778–96.

———. 2012a. "Two-Thirds Full? Citizen Competence and Democratic Governance." In *New Directions in Public Opinion*, edited by Adam J. Berinsky, 52–76. New York: Routledge.

———. 2012b. *Affluence and Influence: Economic Inequality and Political Power in America*. Princeton, NJ: Princeton University Press.

——— and Benjamin I. Page. 2014. "Testing Theories of American Politics: Elites, Interest Groups, and Average Citizens." *Perspectives on Politics* 12: 564–81.

Gilmore, Anna B., J. Robert Branston, and David Sweanor. 2010. "The Case for OFSMOE: How Tobacco Price Regulation is Needed to Promote the Health of Markets, Government Revenue, and the Public." *Tobacco Control* 19: 423–30.

Giovino, Gary A., Andrea C. Villanti, Paul D. Mowery, Varadan Sevilimedu, Raymond S. Niaura, Donna M. Vallone, and David B. Abrams. 2015. "Differential Trends in Cigarette Smoking in the USA: Is Menthol Slowing Progress?" *Tobacco Control* 24: 28–37.

Givel, Michael S. 2001. "Tobacco Lobby Political Influence on US State Legislatures in the 1990s." *Tobacco Control* 10: 124–34.

———. 2004. "The 'Global Settlement' With The Tobacco Industry: 6 Years Later." *Journal of Public Health* 94: 218–24.

———. 2005. "Philip Morris' FDA Gambit: Good for Public Health?" *Journal of Public Health Policy* 26: 450–68.

———. 2006. "Researching State Tobacco Policymaking: Issues, Data Sources, and Methods." *State Politics & Policy Quarterly* 6: 339–51.

———. 2007. "FDA legislation." *Tobacco Control* 16: 217–18.

———. 2008. "Assessing Material and Symbolic Variations in Punctuated Equilibrium and Public Policy Output Patterns." *Review of Policy Research* 25: 547–61.

——— and Stanton A. Glantz. 2000a. "Failure to Defend a Successful State Tobacco Control Program: Policy Lessons From Florida." *American Journal of Public Health* 90: 762–67.

——— and Stanton A. Glantz. 2000b. "Tobacco Control and Direct Democracy in Dade County, Florida: Future Implications for Health Advocates." *Journal of Public Health Policy* 21: 268–95.

——— and Andrew L. Spivak. 2013. *Heartland Tobacco War*. Lanham, MD: Lexington.

Glantz, Stanton A. and Edith D. Balbach. 2000. *Tobacco War—Inside the California Battles*. Berkeley, CA: University of California Press.

Glantz, Stanton A. and Michael Begay. 1994. "Tobacco Industry Campaign Contributions are Affecting Tobacco Control Policymaking in California." *JAMA* 272: 1176–82.

Glantz, Stanton A. and Patrick Jamieson. 2000. "Attitudes Toward Secondhand Smoke, Smoking, and Quitting Among Young People." *Pediatrics* 106: 1474–79.

Glantz, Stanton A., John Slade, Lisa A. Bero, Peter Hanauer, and Deborah E.Barnes. 1996. *The Cigarette Papers*. Berkeley, CA: University of California Press.

Glantz, Stanton A., Richard Barnes, and Sharon Y. Eubanks. 2009. "Compromise or Capitulation? US Food and Drug Administration Jurisdiction Over Tobacco Products." *PLoS Medicine* 6 (7): e1000118.

Godshall, William. 1999. "Giving 10% to Gain Eternity." *Tobacco Control* 8: 437–39.

Goldman, Lisa K. and Stanton A. Glantz. 1999. "The Passage and Initial Implementation of Oregon's Measure 44." *Tobacco Control* 8: 311–22.

Goldstein, Adam O. and Nathan S. Bearman. 1996. "State Tobacco Lobbyists and Organizations in the United States: Crossed Lines." *American Journal of Public Health* 86: 1137–42.

Gollust, Sarah E. and Julia Lynch. 2011. "Who Deserves Health Care? The Effects of Causal Attributions and Group Cues on Public Attitudes about Responsibility for Health Care Costs." *Journal of Health Politics, Policy and Law* 36: 1061–95.

Goodman, Jordan. 1993. *Tobacco In History: The Cultures of Dependence*. London: Routledge.

———. 1995. "Excitantia—Or, How Enlightenment Europe Took to Soft Drugs." In *Consuming Habits: Drugs in History and Anthropology*, edited by Jordan Goodman, Paul E. Lovejoy, and Andrew Sherratt, 126–47. London: Routledge.

———, Paul E. Lovejoy, and Andrew Sherrat. 1995. *Consuming Habits: Drugs in History and Anthropology*. London: Routledge.

Goodspeed, Thomas H. 1954. "The Genus Nicotina." *Chronica Botanica* 16: 1–536.

Gordillo, Jose Manuel Rodriguez. 2005. "Spanish Empire." In *Tobacco in History and Culture: An Encyclopedia, Vol. 2*, edited by Jordan Goodman, 585–93. Detroit, MI: Charles Scribner's Sons.

Gorovitz, Eric, James Mosher, and Mark Pertschuk. 1998. "Preemption or Prevention?: Lessons from Efforts to Control Firearms, Alcohol, and Tobacco." *Journal of Public Health Policy* 19: 36–50.

Gottlieb, Mark. 2014. "Overcautious FDA has Lost Its Way." *Tobacco Control* 23: 187–88.

Granovetter, Mark. 1978. "Threshold Models of Collective Behavior." *American Journal of Sociology* 83: 1420–43.

Gray, N., J. E. Henningfield, N. L. Benowitz, G. N. Connolly, C. Dresler, K. Fagerstrom, M. J. Jarvis, and P. Boylle. 2005. "Toward a Comprehensive Long Term Nicotine Policy." *Tobacco Control* 14: 161–65.

Grewal, Dhruv, Jerry Gotlieb, and Howard Marmorstein. 1994. "The Moderating Effects of Message Framing and Source Credibility on the Price-perceived Risk Relationship." *Journal of Consumer Research* 21: 145–53.

Gross, Cary P., Benny Soffer, Peter B. Bach, Rahul Rajkumar, and Howard Forman. 2002. "State Expenditures for Tobacco-Control Programs and the Tobacco Settlement." *New England Journal of Medicine* 347: 1080–86.

Grossman, M., J. L. Sindelar, J. Mullahy, and R. Anderson. 1993. "Policy Watch: Alcohol and Cigarette Taxes." *Journal of Economic Perspectives* 7: 211–22.

Guardino, Sara D. and Richard A. Daynard. 2005. "Punishing Tobacco Industry Misconduct: The Case For Exceeding A Single Digit Ratio Between Punitive And Compensatory Damages." *University of Pittsburgh Law Review* 67: 1–65.

Gruber, Jonathan. 2001. "Tobacco At the Crossroads: The Past and Future of Smoking Regulation in the United States." *Journal of Economic Perspectives* 15: 193–212.

———. 2002. "The Economics of Tobacco Regulation." *Health Affairs* 21: 146–62.

Hall, Wayne and Robert West. 2008. "Thinking About the Unthinkable: A De Facto Prohibition on Smoked Tobacco Products." *Addiction* 103: 873–74.

Haltom, William and Michael McCann. 2004. *Distorting the Law: Politics, Media, and the Litigation Crisis*. Chicago: University of Chicago Press.

Hamilton, J. L. 1972. "The Demand for Cigarettes: Advertising, The Health Scare, and the Cigarette Advertising Ban." *Review of Economics and Statistics* 54: 401–11.

Hammond, David. 2011. "Health Warning Labels on Tobacco Products: A Review." *Tobacco Control* 20: 327–37.

———. 2012. "Tobacco Packaging and Labeling Policies Under the U.S. Tobacco Control Act: Research Needs and Priorities." *Nicotine & Tobacco Research* 14: 62–74.

———, Geoffrey T. Fong, Ron Borland, Michael Cummings, Ann McNeill, and Pete Driezen. 2007. "Text and Graphic Warnings on Cigarette Packages." *American Journal of Preventative Medicine* 32: 202–09.

———, G. T. Fong, A. McNeill, R. Borland, and K. M. Cummings. 2006. "Effectiveness of Cigarette Warning Labels in Informing Smokers About the Risks of Smoking: Findings from the International Tobacco Control (ITC) Four Country Survey." *Tobacco Control* 15: iii19–25.

Hammond, E. C. and Daniel Horn. 1954. "The Relationship Between Human Smoking Habits and Death Rates: A Follow-Up Study of 187,766 Men." *JAMA* 155: 1316–28.

Hanauer, P. 1985. "Proposition P: Anatomy of a Nonsmokers' Rights Ordinance." *New York State Journal of Medicine* 85: 369–74.

———, G. Barr, and S. Glantz. 1986. "Legislative Approaches to a Smoke-Free Society." Berkeley, CA: American Nonsmokers' Rights Foundation.

Handa, Masuyuki. 2005. "Japan." In *Tobacco in History and Culture: An Encyclopedia, Vol. 1*, edited by Jordan Goodman, 277–81. Detroit, MI: Charles Scribner's Sons.

Hans, Valerie P. 2000. *Business on Trial: the Civil Jury and Corporate Responsibility*. New Haven, CT: Yale University Press.

Hanson, Jon D. and Kyle D. Logue. 1998. "The Costs of Cigarettes: The Economic Case for Ex Post Incentive-Based Regulation." *Yale Law Journal* 197: 1163–361.

Harkness, Jon M. 2007. "The U.S. Public Health Service and Smoking in the 1950s: The Tale of Two More Statements." *Journal of the History of Medicine and Allied Sciences* 62: 171–212.

Harley, David. 1993. "The Beginnings of the Tobacco Controversy: Puritanism, James I, and the Royal Physicians," *Bulletin of the History of Medicine*, 67: 28–50.

Harlin, Vivian. 1972. "The Influence of Obvious Anonymity on the Response of School Children to a Questionnaire About Smoking." *American Journal of Public Health* 62: 566–74.

Harris, Jeffrey E. 1983. "Cigarette Smoking Among Successive Birth Cohorts of Men and Women in the United States During 1900–1980." *Journal of the National Cancer Institute* 71: 473–79.

Harris, Jenine K., Sarah C. Shelton, Sarah Moreland-Russell, and Douglas A. Luke. 2010. "Tobacco Coverage in Print Media: The Use of Timing and Themes by Tobacco Control Supporters and Opposition Before a Failed Tobacco Tax Initiative." *Tobacco Control* 19: 37–43.

Harris Poll. 2000–2001. "The Power of Tobacco Addiction, #8 and #10." Available at archive.tobacco.org/news/51201.html

"The Health Consequences of Smoking—A Report of the Surgeon General." 2004. Rockville, MD: U.S. Department of Health and Human Services.

Henderson, James A., Jr. and Aaron D. Twerski. 2010. "Reaching Equilibrium in Tobacco Litigation." *South Carolina Law Review* 62: 67–103.

Herbst, Susan. 2002. "How State-Level Policy Managers "Read" Public Opinion." In *Navigating Public Opinion*, edited by Jeff Manza, Fay Lomax Cook, and Benjamin I. Page, 171–83. New York: Oxford University Press.

———. 2011. "Critical Perspectives on Public Opinion." In *The Oxford Handbook of American Public Opinion and the Media*, edited by Robert Shapiro and Lawrence Jacobs, 302–14. New York: Oxford University Press.

Hill, John F. January 16, 1908. "Temperance." *The Presbyterian Banner*.

Hilton, Matthew. 2000. *Smoking in British Popular Culture 1800–2000*. Manchester: Manchester University Press.

——— and Simon Nightingale. 1998. "'A Microbe of the Devil's Own Make': Religion and Science in the British Anti-Tobacco Movement, 1853–1908," In *Ashes to Ashes: The History of Smoking and Health*, edited by Stephen Lock, Lois Reynolds and E. M. Tansey, 41–77. Atlanta, GA: Rodopi.

Hilts, P. J. 1996. *Smokescreen: The Truth behind the Tobacco Industry Cover-up*. New York: Addison-Wesley.

Himmelfarb, Richard. 1995. *Catastrophic Politics: The Rise and Fall of the Medicare Catastrophic Coverage Act of 1988*. University Park, PA: Pennsylvania State University Press.

Hirshbein, Laura. 2011. "Scientific Research and Corporate Influence: Smoking, Mental Illness, and the Tobacco Industry." *Journal of the History of Medicine and Allied Sciences* 67: 374–97.

Hoang, Mai-Anh and Jonathan M. Samet. 2005. "Disease and Mortality." In *Tobacco in History and Culture: An Encyclopedia, Vol. 1*, edited by Jordan Goodman, 199–214. Detroit, MI: Charles Scribner's Sons.

Hoffman, Frederick. 1931. "Cancer and Smoking Habits." *Annals of Surgery* 93: 50–67.

Holford, Theodore R., Rafael Meza, Kenneth E. Warner, Clare Meernik, Jihyoun Jeon, Suresh H. Moolgavkar, and David T. Levy. 2014. "Tobacco Control and the Reduction in Smoking-Related Premature Deaths in the United States, 1964–2012." *JAMA* 311: 164–71.

Holmes, George. 1919. "Some Features of Tobacco History." *American Historical Association Annual Report* 1: 385–407.

Horn, Daniel. 1960. "Modifying Smoking Habits in High School Students." *Children* 7: 63–65.

———. 1963. "Behavioral Aspects of Cigarette Smoking." *Journal of Chronic Diseases* 16: 383–95.

———. 1968. "Current Smoking Among Teenagers." *Public Health Reports* 83: 458–60.

Howells, Geraint. 2011. *The Tobacco Challenge: Legal Policy and Consumer Protection*. Burlington, VT: Ashgate.

Hughes, Jason. 2003. *Learning To Smoke: Tobacco Use In The West*. Chicago: University of Chicago Press.

Hughes, John. 2000. "Reduced Smoking: An Introduction and Review of the Evidence." *Addiction* 95: S3–S7.

Hurt, Richard D. and Channing R. Robertson. 1998. "Prying Open the Door to the Tobacco Industry's Secrets About Nicotine." *JAMA* 280: 1173–81.

Hyland, Andrew, Joaquin Barnoya, and Juan E. Corral. 2012. "Smoke-Free Air Policies: Past, Present and Future." *Tobacco Control* 21: 154–61.

Ibrahim, Jennifer and Stanton A. Glantz. 2006. "Tobacco Industry Litigation Strategies to Oppose Tobacco Control Media Campaigns." *Tobacco Control* 15: 50–58.

———. 2007. "The Rise and Fall of Tobacco Control Media Campaigns, 1967–2006." *American Journal of Public Health* 97: 1383–96.

Ibrahim, Jennifer, T. H. Tsoukalas, and S. A. Glantz. 2004. "Public Health Foundations and the Tobacco Industry: Lessons from Minnesota." *Tobacco Control* 13: 228–36.

Institute of Medicine. 2007. *Ending The Tobacco Problem: A Blueprint For The Nation*. Washington, DC: The National Academies Press.

Ippolito, Richard A., R. Dennis Murphy, and Donald Sant. 1979. *Staff Report On Consumer Responses To Cigarette Health Information, Bureau of Economics, Federal Trade Commission*. Washington, DC: U.S. Government Printing Office.

Jacobs, Lawrence R. 1992. "The Recoil Effect: Public Opinion and Policymaking in the U.S. and Britain." *Comparative Politics* 24: 199–217.

———. 1993a. "Health Reform Impasse: The Politics of American Ambivalence Toward Government." *Journal of Health Politics, Policy and Law* 18: 629–55.

———. 1993b. *The Health of Nations*. Ithica, NY: Cornell University Press.

———, Eric D. Lawrence, Robert Y. Shapiro, and Steven S. Smith. 1998. "Congressional Leadership of Public Opinion." *Political Science Quarterly* 113: 21–41.

——— and Robert Shapiro. 2000. *Politicians Don't Pander: Political Manipulation and the Loss of Democratic Responsiveness*. Chicago: University of Chicago Press.

——— and Suzanne Mettler. 2011. "Why Public Opinion Changes: The Implications for Health and Health Policy." *Journal of Health Politics, Policy and Law* 36: 917–33.

Jacobson, Peter D., Jeffrey Wasserman, and Kristiana Raube. 1993. "The Politics of Anti-Smoking Legislation: Lessons from Six States." *Journal of Health Politics, Policy, and Law* 18: 787–819.

Jacobson, Peter D., Jeffrey Wasserman, and John R. Anderson. 1997. "Historical Overview of Tobacco Legislation and Regulation." *Journal of Social Issues* 53: 75–95.

Jacobson, Peter D. and Kenneth E. Warner. 1999. "Litigation and Public Health Policy Making: The Case of Tobacco Control." *Journal of Health Politics, Policy and Law* 24: 769–804.

Jacobson, Peter D. and Soheil Soliman. 2002. "Litigation as Public Health Policy: Theory or Reality?" *Journal of Law, Medicine & Ethics* 30: 224–38.

Jacoby, William G. 2000. "Issue Framing and Public Opinion on Government Spending." *American Journal of Political Science* 44: 750–67.

James, I. 1604. "A Counterblaste to Tobacco." London: Privately Printed.

Jamieson, Patrick E. and Dan Romer. 2010. "Trends in US Movie Tobacco Portrayal Since 1950: A Historical Analysis." *Tobacco Control* 19: 179–84.

———. 2015. "Portrayal of Tobacco Use in Prime-Time TV Dramas: Trends and Associations with Adult Cigarette Consumption-USA, 1955–2010." *Tobacco Control* 24: 243–48.

Jin, Jiyong. 2014. "Why FCTC Policies Have Not Been Implemented in China: Domestic Dynamics and Tobacco Governance." *Journal of Health Politics, Policy and Law* 39: 633–66.

Jones, David K., Katherine W. V. Bradley, and Jonathan Oberlander. 2014. "Pascal's Wager: Health Insurance Exchanges, Obamacare, and the Republican Dilemma." *Journal of Health Politics, Policy, and Law* 39: 97–137.

Jones, Raymond M. 1997. *Strategic Management in a Hostile Environment: Lessons From the Tobacco Industry*. Westport, NC: Quorum Books.

Judy, J. A. 1904. *Questionable Amusements and Worthy Substitutes*. Chicago: Western Methodist Book Concern.

Kagan, Robert A. and David Vogel. 1993. "The Politics of Smoking Regulation: Canada, France, and the United States." In *Smoking Policy: Law, Politics, and Culture*, edited by R. L. Rabin and S. D. Sugarman, 69–94. New York: Oxford University Press.

Kagan, Robert A. and Jerome H. Skolnick. 1993. "Banning Smoking: Compliance Without Enforcement." In *Smoking Policy: Law, Politics, and Culture*, edited by R. L. Rabin and S. D. Sugarman, 22–48. New York: Oxford University Press.

Kagan, Robert A. and William P. Nelson. 2001. "The Politics of Tobacco Regulation in the United States." In *Regulating Tobacco*, edited by Robert L. Rabin and Stephen D. Sugarman, 10–38. New York: Oxford University Press.

Karol, David. 2007. "Has Polling Enhanced Representation? Unearthing Evidence from the Literary Digest Issue Polls." *Studies in American Political Development* 21: 16–29.

Kelder, Graham E., Jr. and Richard A. Daynard. 1997a. "Judicial Approaches to Tobacco Control: The Third Wave of Tobacco Litigation as a Tobacco Control Mechanism." *Journal of Social Issues* 53: 169–86.

———. 1997b. "The Role of Litigation in the Effective Control of the Sale and Use of Tobacco." *Stanford Law & Policy Review* 63: 63–98.

Kell, Katharine T. 1965. "Tobacco in Folk Cures in Western Society." *The Journal of American Folklore* 78: 99–114.

Kellman, Jordan. 2005. "French Empire." In *Tobacco in History and Culture: An Encyclopedia, Vol. 1*, edited by. Jordan Goodman, 240–44. Detroit, MI: Charles Scribner's Sons.

Kelson, Saul, James Pullella, and Anders Otterland. 1975. "The Growing Epidemic." *American Journal of Public Health* 65: 923–38.

Kenkel, Donald S. 1991. "Health Behavior, Health Knowledge, and Schooling." *Journal of Political Economy* 99: 287–305.

Kessler, David. 1996. "The Food and Drug Administration's Regulation of Tobacco Products." *New England Journal of Medicine* 335: 988–94.

———. 2001. *A Question of Intent*. New York: Public Affairs Press.

Key, V. O. 1961. *Public Opinion and American Democracy*. New York: Knopf.

Khoo, Deborah, Yvonne Chiam, Priscilla Ng, A. J. Berrick, and H. N. Koong. 2010. "Phasing-Out Tobacco: A Proposal to Deny Access to Tobacco for Those Born from 2000." *Tobacco Control* 19: 355–60.

Kieren, V. G. 1991. *Tobacco: A History*. London: Hutchison.

Kim, Sei-Hill and James Shanahan. 2003. "Stigmatizing Smokers: Public Sentiment Toward Cigarette Smoking and Its Relationship to Smoking Behaviors." *Journal of Health Communication* 8: 343–67.

King, Karen Whitehill, Leonard N. Reid, Young Sook Moon, and Debra Jones Ringold. 1991. "Changes in the Visual Imagery of Cigarette Ads, 1954–1986." *Journal of Public Policy & Marketing* 10: 63–80.

Kirscht, John P., Don P. Haefner, S. Stephen Kegeles, and Irwin M. Rosenstock. 1966. "A National Study of Health Beliefs." *Journal of Health and Human Behavior* 7: 248–54.

Klaits, Joseph. 1985. *Servants of Satan: The Age of Witch Hunts*. Bloomington: Indiana University Press.

Kloepfer, William, Jr. 1985. "Report on Public Smoking Issue—Communications Committee." legacy.library.ucsf.edu/tid/ibd19a00. Accessed 7/14/2014.

Klooster, Wim. 2005. "Dutch Empire." In *Tobacco in History and Culture: An Encyclopedia, Vol. 1*, edited by Jordan Goodman, 219–22. Detroit, MI: Charles Scribner's Sons.

Kluger, Richard. 1997. *Ashes To Ashes*. New York: Vintage.

Knopf, S. Adolphus. 1929. "Effects of Cigarette Smoking." *Medical Journal and Record* 130: 488–89.

Koenig, Thomas and Michael Rustad. 1998. "'Crimtorts' as Corporate Just Deserts." *University of Michigan Journal of Law Reform* 31: 289–352.

Kohlmeier, Louis M., Jr. 1969. *The Regulators: Watchdog Agencies and the Public Interest*. New York: Harper & Row.

Kotnowski, Kathy and David Hammond. 2013. "The Impact of Cigarette Pack Shape, Size, and Openings: Evidence from Tobacco Company Documents." *Addiction* 108: 1658–68.

Kovach, Alexandra, 2009. "History of the Autopsy." In *Diagnoses From The Dead: The Book of Autopsy*, edited by Richard A. Prayson, 33–42. New York: Kaplan.

Kozlowski, Lynn T., Marvin E. Goldberg, Berwood A. Yost, Frank M. Ahern, Keith R. Aronson, and Christine T. Sweeney. 1996. "Smokers are Unaware of the Filter Vents Now on Most Cigarettes: Results of a National Survey." *Tobacco Control* 5: 265–70.

Krosnick, Jon A., LinChiat Chang, Steven J. Sherman, Laurie Chassin, and Clark Presson. 2006. "The Effects of Beliefs About the Health Consequences of Cigarette Smoking on Smoking Onset," *Journal of Communication* 56: S18–37.

Kull, Steven and I. M. Destler. 1999. *Misreading the Public: The Myth of a New Isolationism*. Washington, DC: Brookings Institution Press.

Kull, Steven and Clay Ramsay. 2002. "How Policymakers Misperceive U.S. Public Opinion on Foreign Policy." In *Navigating Public Opinion*, edited by Jeff Manza, Fay Lomax Cook, and Benjamin I. Page, 201–18. New York: Oxford University Press.

Kyriakoudes, Louis M. 2006. "Historians' Testimony on 'Common Knowledge' of the Risks of Tobacco Use." *Tobacco Control* 15: 107–16.

Ladd, Evertt Carl. 1998. "The Tobacco Bill and American Public Opinion." *Public Perspective* 9: 5–6.

LaFrance, Arthur B. 2000. "Tobacco Litigation: Smoke, Mirrors and Public Policy." *American Journal of Law & Medicine* 26: 187–203.

Landman, Anne, Daniel K. Cortese, and Stanton Glantz. 2008. "Tobacco industry sociological programs to influence public beliefs about smoking." *Social Science & Medicine* 66: 970–81.

Langer, William L. 1975. "American Foods and Europe's Population Growth, 1750–1850." *Journal of Social History* 8:51–66.

Laposata, Elizabeth, Allison P. Kennedy, and Stanton A. Glantz. 2014. "When Tobacco Targets Direct Democracy." *Journal of Health Politics, Policy and Law* 39: 537–64.

Lawton, M. Powell and Alfred E. Goldman. 1961. "Cigarette Smoking and Attitude toward the Etiology of Lung Cancer." *Journal of Social Psychology* 54: 235–48.

Lax, Jeffrey R. and Justin H. Phillips. 2012. "The Democratic Deficit in the States." *American Journal of Political Science* 56: 148–66.

Leland, Anne and Mari-Jana Oboroceanu. 2010."American War and Military Operations Casualties: Lists and Statistics." Washington DC: Congressional Research Service.

Levin, Morton, Hyman Goldstein, and Paul R. Gerhardt. 1950. "Cancer and Tobacco Smoking: A Preliminary Report." *JAMA* 143: 336–38.

Levy, David T., K. Michael Cummings, and Andrew Hyland. 2000. "Increasing Taxes as a Strategy to Reduce Cigarette Use and Deaths: Results of a Simulation Model." *Preventative Medicine* 31: 279–86.

Levy, David T., Elizabeth A. Mumford, and Boris Pesin. 2003. "Tobacco control policies and reductions in smoking rates and smoking related deaths." *Expert Review Pharmoeconomics Outcomes Research* 3: 457–68.

Levy, David T., and Karen B. Friend. 2003. "The effects of clean indoor air laws: what do we know and what do we need to know?" *Health Education Research* 18: 592–609.

Levy, David T., Frank Chaloupka, and Joseph Gitchell. 2004. "The Effects of Tobacco Control Policies on Smoking Rates: a Tobacco Control Scorecard." *Journal of Public Health Management and Practice* 10: 338–51.

Levy, David T., Leonid Nikolayev, Elizabeth Mumford, and Christine Compton. 2005. "The Healthy People 2010 smoking prevalence and tobacco control objectives: results from the *SimSmoke* tobacco control policy simulation model (United States)." *Cancer Causes and Controls* 16: 359–71.

Levy, David T., Andrew Hyland, Cheryl Higbee, Lillian Remer, and Christine Compton. 2007. "The Role of Public Policies in Reducing Smoking Prevalence in California: Results from the California Tobacco Policy Simulation Model." *Health Policy* 82: 167–85.

Levy, David T., Elizabeth A. Mumford, and Daniel A. Gerlowski. 2007. "Examining Trends in Quantity Smoked." *Nicotine & Tobacco Research* 9: 1287–96.

Levy, David T., Patricia L. Mabry, Amanda L. Graham, Tracy Orleans, and David B. Abrams. 2010. "Reaching Healthy People 2010 by 2013: A *SimSmoke* Simulation." *American Journal of Preventative Medicine* 38: S373–81.

Levy, David T., Jennifer L. Pearson, Andrea C. Villanti, Kenneth Blackman, Donna M. Vallone, Raymond S. Niaura, and David B. Abrams. 2011a. "Modeling the Future Effects of a Menthol Ban on Smoking Prevalence and Smoking-Attributable Deaths in the United States." *American Journal of Public Health* 101: 1236–39.

Levy, David T., Kenneth Blackman, John Tauras, Frank J. Chaloupka, Andrea C. Villanti, Raymond S. Niaura, Donna M. Vallone, and David B. Abrams. 2011b. "Quit Attempts and Quit Rates Among Menthol and Nonmenthol Smokers in the United States." *American Journal of Public Health* 101: 1241–47.

Levy, David T., Jennifer A. Ellis, Darren Mays, and An-Tsun Huang. 2013. "Smoking-Related Deaths Averted Due to Three Years of Policy Progress." *Bulletin of the World Health Organization* 91: 509–18.

Lewan, Todd. 1998. "Industry Watch: Dark Secrets of Tobacco Company Exposed." *Tobacco Control* 7: 315–19.

Lewit, Eugene M., Douglas Coate, and Michael Grossman. 1981. "The Effects of Government Regulation on Teenage Smoking." *Journal of Law and Economics* 24: 545–69.

Liberman, Jonathan. 2006. "The Future of Tobacco Regulation: A Response to a Proposal for Fundamental Institutional Change." *Tobacco Control* 15: 333–38.

Licari, Michael. 2005. "Taxation." In *Tobacco in History and Culture: An Encyclopedia, Vol. 2*, edited by Jordan Goodman, 603–09. Detroit, MI: Charles Scribner's Sons.

——— and Kenneth J. Meier. 1997. "Regulatory Policy When Behavior Is Addictive: Smoking, Cigarette Taxes and Bootlegging." *Political Research Quarterly* 50: 5–24.

———. 2000. "Regulation and Signaling: When a Tax is not Just a Tax." *Journal of Politics* 62: 875–85.

Lickint, Fritz. 1929. "Tabak und Tabakrauch als atiologisher Factor des Carcinoms." *Zeitschrift fur Krebsforschung* 30: 349–65.

Lieberman Research, Inc. 1986. "A Study of Public Attitudes toward Cigarette Advertising and Promotion Programs." New York: Privately Printed.

Lilienfeld, Abraham. 1959. "Emotional and Other Selected Characteristics of Cigarette Smokers and Nonsmokers as Related to Epidemiological Studies of Lung Cancer and Other Diseases." *Journal of the National Cancer Institute* 22: 259–82.

Lippman, Walter. 1925. *The Phantom Public*. New York: Simon & Schuster.

Littell, Robert. 1942. "Cigarette Ad Fact and Fiction." *Reader's Digest* (July): 5–8.

Livi-Bacci, Massimo. 2007. *A Concise History of World Population*. Oxford: Blackwell.

Lombard, Herbert L. and Carl R. Doering. 1928. "Cancer Studies in Massachusetts." *New England Journal of Medicine* 18: 481–87.

Loomis, B. R., M. C. Farrelly, J. M. Nonnemaker, and N. H. Mann. 2006. "Point of Purchase Cigarette Promotions Before and After the Master Settlement Agreement: Exploring Retail Scanner Data." *Tobacco Control* 15: 140–42.

Lum, K. L., R. L. Barnes, and S. A. Glantz. 2009. "Enacting Tobacco Taxes by Direct Popular Vote in the United States: Lessons from 20 Years of Experience." *Tobacco Control* 18: 377–86.

Lupia, Arthur. 1994. "Shortcuts Versus Encyclopedias: Information and Voting Behavior in California Insurance Reform Elections." *American Political Science Review* 88: 63–76.

——— and John G. Matsusaka. 2004. "Direct Democracy: New Approaches to Old Questions." *Annual Review of Political Science* 7: 463–82.

MacDonald, Heather, Stella Aguinaga, and Stanton A. Glantz. 1997. "The Defeat of Philip Morris' 'California Uniform Tobacco Control Act.'" *American Journal of Public Health* 87: 1989–97.

Madel, L. L. and S. A. Glantz. 2004. "Hedging Their Bets: Tobacco and Gambling Industries Work against Smoke-Free Policies." *Tobacco Control* 13: 268–76.

Magleby, David. 1989. "Opinion Formation and Opinion Change in Ballot Proposition Campaigns." In *Manipulating Public Opinion*, edited by Michael Margolis and Gary A. Mauser, 95–115. Pacific Groves, CA: Brooks/Cole.

———. 1995. "Governing By Initiative: Let the Voters Decide? An Assessment of the Initiative and Referendum Process." *University of Colorado Law Review* 1995: 13–46.

——— and Kelly D. Patterson. 1998. "Consultants and Direct Democracy." *PS* 31: 160–69.

Malone, Ruth E. 2002. "Tobacco Industry Documents: Comparing the Minnesota Depository and Internet Access." *Tobacco Control* 11: 285.

Malone, Ruth E. 2014. "Tobacco Endgames: What They Are and Are Not, Issues for Tobacco Control Strategic Planning and a Possible US Scenario." *Tobacco Control* 22: i42–i44.

———. 2015a. "FDA's Toothless Tiger and its 'Lost Pleasure' Analysis." *Tobacco Control* 25: 105.

———. 2015b. "Global Endgame Thinking: 'Pie in the Sky' or Essential Groundwork?" Available at www.ashscotland.org.uk/media/402501/Ruth-E-Malone.pdf.

——— and Edith D. Balbach. 2000. "Tobacco Industry Cocuments: Treasure Trove or Quagmire?" *Tobacco Control* 9: 334–38.

——— and Kenneth E. Warner. 2012. "Tobacco Control at Twenty: Reflecting on the Past, Considering the Present, and Developing the New Conversations for the Future." *Tobacco Control* 21: 74–76.

———, Q. Grundy, and L. A. Bero. 2012. "Tobacco Industry Denormalization as a Tobacco Control Intervention: A Review." *Tobacco Control* 21: 162–70.

———, P. A. McDaniel, and E. A. Smith. 2014a. "Tobacco Control Endgames: Global Initiatives and Implications for the UK." Available at www.cancerresearchuk.org/sites/default/files/policy_july2014_fullendgame_report.pdf.

———, Patricia McDaniel, and Elizabeth Smith. 2014b. "It Is Time to Plan the Tobacco Endgame." *British Medical Journal* 348: 1–2.

Mancall, Peter C. 2004. "Tales Tobacco Told in Sixteenth-Century Europe." *Environmental History* 9: 648–78.

Manza, Jeff and Fay Lomax Cook. 2002. "A Democratic Polity? Three Views of Policy Responsiveness to Public Opinion in the United States." *American Politics Research* 30: 630–667.

Markle, Gerald E. and Ronald J. Troyer. 1979. "Smoke Gets in Your Eyes: Cigarette Smoking as Deviant Behavior." *Social Problems* 26: 611–25.

Marmor, Theodore R. 2000. *The Politics of Medicare*. New York: Aldine DeGruyter.

———, Jonathan Oberlander, and Joseph White. 2009. "The Obama Administration's Options for Health Care Cost Control: Hope Versus Reality." *Annals of Internal Medicine* 150: 485–89.

——— and Jonathan Oberlander. 2011. "The Patchwork: Health Reform, American Style." *Social Science & Medicine* 72: 125–28.

Marshall, Thomas R. 1989. *Public Opinion and the Supreme Court*. London: Allen-Unwin.

———. 2008. *Public Opinion and the Rehnquist Court*. Albany, NY: SUNY Press.

———. 2012. "Public Opinion and Health Care Reform." In *Debates On U.S. Health Care*, edited by Jennie Jacobs Kronenfeld, Wendy E. Parmet, and Mark A. Zezza, 109–20. Los Angeles: Sage.

———. 2015. "The 1964 Surgeon General's Report and Americans' Beliefs about Smoking." *Journal of the History of Medicine and Allied Sciences* 70: 250–78.

Martyr d'Anghiera, Peter. 1516. *De Orbe Novo Decades*. Alcala de Henares, Spain: A. G. Brocar.

Matarazzo, Joseph D. and George Saslow. 1960. "Psychological and Related Characteristics of Smokers and Nonsmokers." *Psychological Bulletin* 57: 493–519.

Mather, Lynn. 1998. "Theorizing about Trial Courts: Lawyers, Policymaking, and Tobacco Litigation." *Law & Social Inquiry* 23: 897–940.

———. 2009. "Lawyers and Solicitors Separated by a Common Legal System: Anti-Tobacco Litigation in the United States and Britain." In *Fault Lines: Tort Law as Cultural Practice*, edited by David M. Engel and Michael McCann, 199–210. Stanford, CA: Stanford Law Books.

Matsusaka, John G. 2004. *For the Many or the Few*. Chicago: University of Chicago Press.

Matthews, J. Rosser. 2005. "Medical Evidence (Cause and Effect)." In *Tobacco in History and Culture: An Encyclopedia, Vol. 2*, edited by Jordan Goodman, 343–48. Detroit, MI: Charles Scribner's Sons.

Mayer, William G. 1992. *The Changing American Mind: How and Why American Public Opinion Changed between 1960 and 1988*. Ann Arbor: University of Michigan.

Mayhew, David R. 1974. *Congress: The Electoral Connection*. New Haven, CT: Yale University Press.

Mazur, Allan. 1981. "Media Coverage and Public Opinion on Scientific Controversies." *Journal of Communication* 31: 106–15.

McAuliffe, Robert. 1988. "The FTC and the Effectiveness of Cigarette Advertising Regulations." *Journal of Public Policy & Marketing* 7: 49–64.

McCann, Michael, William Haltom, and Shauna Fisher. 2013. "Criminalizing Big Tobacco: Legal Mobilization and the Politics of Responsibility for Health Risks in the United States." *Law & Social Inquiry* 38: 288–321.

McCullen, J. T., Jr. 1967 "Indian Myths Concerning the Origin of Tobacco." *New York Folklore Quarterly* 23: 264–73.

McCullough, David. 1977. *The Path Between the Seas: The Creation of the Panama Canal 1870–1914*. New York: Simon & Schuster.

McDaniel, P. A. and R. E. Malone. 2005. "Understanding Philip Morris' Pursuit of US Government Regulation of Tobacco." *Tobacco Control* 14: 193–200.

———. 2009. "The Role of Corporate Credibility in Legitimizing Disease Promotion." *American Journal of Public Health* 99: 452–61.

———. 2012. "'The Big WHY': Philip Morris's Failed Search for Corporate Social Value." *American Journal of Public Health* 102: 1942–50.

McDaniel P. A., E. A. Smith, and R. E. Malone. 2006. "Philip Morris' Project Sunrise: Weakening Tobacco Control by Working with It." *Tobacco Control* 15: 215–23.

McMillen, Robert C., Mark A. Gottlieb, Regina M. Whitmore Shaefer, Jonathan P. Winickoff, and Jonathan D. Klein. 2015. "Trends in Electronic Cigarette Use Among U.S. Adults: Use is Increasing in Both Smokers and Nonsmokers." *Nicotine & Tobacco Research* 17: 1195–202.

McNeill, Ann, David Hammond, and Coral Gartner. 2015. "Whither Tobacco Product Regulation?" *Tobacco Control* 21: 221–26.

"Medicine—Continuing Fight" *Time* (March 7, 1949): 75–76.

Melnick, R. Shep. 1999. "Tobacco Litigation: Good for the Body but Not the Body Politic." *Journal of Health Politics, Policy and Law* 24: 805–10.

Menard, R. R. 1980. "The Tobacco Industry in the Chesapeake Colonies, 1617–1730: An Interpretation." *Research in Economic History* 5: 109–77.

Menard, Russell. 1985. *Economy and Society in Early Colonial Maryland*. New York: Garland.

Mendez, David, Omar Alshanqeety, and Kenneth E. Warner. 2013. "The Potential Impact of Smoking Control Policies on Future Global Smoking Trends." *Tobacco Control* 22: 46–51.

———. 2005. "British Empire." In *Tobacco in History and Culture: An Encyclopedia, Vol. 1*, edited by Jordan Goodman, 96–101. Detroit, MI: Charles Scribner's Sons.

Meranto, Philip. 1967. *The Politics of Federal Aid to Education in 1965*. Syracuse, NY: Syracuse University Press.

Miles, Robert H. 1982. *Coffin Nails And Corporate Strategies*. Englewood Cliffs, NJ: Prentice-Hall.

Miller, Jon D. 1987. "The Challenger Accident and Public Opinion." *Space Policy* 3: 122–40.

———. 1998. "The Measurement of Civic Scientific Literacy." *Public Understanding of Science* 7: 203–23.

Miller, Karen S. 1992. *Smoking Up a Storm: Public Relations and Advertising in the Construction of the Cigarette Problem, 1953–1954. Journalism Monographs 136*. Austin, TX: University of Texas.

———. 1999. *The Voice of Business: Hill & Knowlton and Postwar Public Relations*. Chapel Hill, NC: University of North Carolina Press.

Miller, Leonard, Xiulun Zhang, Dorothy Rice, and Wendy Max. 1998. "State Estimates of Total Medical Expenditures Attributable to Cigarette Smoking 1993." *Public Health Reports* 13: 140–51.

Miller, Vincent P., Carla Ernst, and Francois Collin. 1999. "Smoking-Attributable Medical Care Costs in the USA." *Social Science & Medicine* 48: 375–91.

Mills, Clarence A. and Marjorie Mills Porter. 1950. "Tobacco Smoking Habits and Cancer of the Mouth and Respiratory System." *Cancer Research* 1: 539–42.

Mollenkamp, Carrick, Adam Levy, Joseph Menn, and Jeffrey Rothfeder. 1998. *The People vs. Big Tobacco: How the States Took On the Cigarette Giants*. Princeton, NJ: Bloomberg Press.

Monardes, Nicolás. 1571. *Segunda parte del libro, de las cosas que se traen de nuestraas Indias Occidentales, que sirven al use de medicina: Donde se trata del Tabaco, y de la Sassafras*. Seville: Alonso Escrivano.

Monardi, Fred and Stanton A. Glantz. 1998. "Are Tobacco Industry Campaign Contributions Influencing State Legislative Behavior?" *American Journal of Public Health* 88: 918–23.

Monk, Mary, Matthew Tayback, and Joseph Gordon. 1965. "Evaluation of an Antismoking Program Among High School Students." *American Journal of Public Health* 55: 994–1004.

Monroe, Alan. 1979. "Consistency between Policy Preferences and National Policy Decisions." *American Politics Quarterly* 7: 3–18.

———. 1998. "Public Opinion and Public Policy, 1980–1993." *Public Opinion Quarterly* 62: 6–28.

Moolgavkar, Suresh H., Theordore R. Holford, David T. Levy, Chung Yin Kong, Millenia Foy, Lauren Clarke, Jihyoun Jeon, William D. Hazelton, Rafeel Meza, Frank Schultz, William McCarthy, Robert Boer, Olga Gorlova, G. Scott Gazelle, Marek Kimmel, Pamela M. McMahon, Harry J. De Koning, and Eric J. Feuer. 2012. "Impact of Reduced Tobacco Smoking on Lung Cancer Mortality in the United States During 1975–2000." *Journal of the National Cancer Institute* 104: 541–48.

Moon, Robert W., Michael A. Males, and David E. Nelson. 1993. "The 1990 Montana Initiative to Increase Cigarette Taxes: Lessons for Other States and Localities." *Journal of Public Health Policy* 14: 19–33.

Moore, Mike. 1997. "The States Are Just Trying to Take Care of Sick Citizens and Protect Children." *ABA Journal* 83: 53.

Morley, C. P., K. M. Cummings, A. Hyland, G. A. Giovino, and J. K. Horan. 2002. "Tobacco Institute Lobbying at the State and Local Levels of Government in the 1990s." *Tobacco Control* 11: i102–i109.

Mullan, Fitzhugh. 1989. *Plagues and Politics—The Story of the United States Public Health Service*. New York: Basic Books.

Müller, Franz Hermann. 1939. "Tabakmissbrauch und Lungencarcinom." *Zeitschrift fur Krebsforschung* 49: 525–38.

Myers, Erin. 1998. "The Manipulation of Public Opinion by the Tobacco Industry: Past, Present, and Future." *Journal of Health Care Law and Policy* 2: 78–101.

Myers, Matthew L. 2013. "The FCTC's Evidence-Based Policies Remain a Key to Ending the Tobacco Epidemic." *Tobacco Control* 22: i45–i46.

———. 2014. "New Report Shows U.S. Lags Behind Much of the World in Requiring Graphic Cigarette Warnings—The FDA Must Act to Catch Up," Press Release (October 21). www.tobaccofreekids.org/press_releases/post/2014_10_14_warnings.

Nagler, Rebekah and Kasiosmayajula Viswanath. 2013. "Implementation and Research Priorities for FCTC Articles 13 and 16: Tobacco Advertising, Promotion, and Sponsorship and Sales to and by Minors." *Nicotine & Tobacco Research* 15: 832–46.

Nathanson, Constance A. 1999. "Social Movements as Catalysts for Policy Change: The Case of Smoking and Guns." *Journal of Health Politics, Policy, and Law* 24: 421–88.

———. 2007. "The Contingent Power of Experts: Public Health Policy in the United States, Britain, and France." *The Journal of Policy History* 19: 71–94.

National Association of Science Writers. 1958. "The Public Impact of Science in the Mass Media." Ann Arbor, MI: University of Michigan, Survey Research Center.

Nealey, Stanley M., Barbara Melber, and William Rankin. 1983. *Public Opinion and Nuclear Energy*. Lexington, MA: D.C. Health & Company.

Nee, Michael. 2005. "Origin and Diffusion." In *Tobacco in History and Culture: An Encyclopedia Vol. 2*, edited by Jordan Goodman, 397–402. Detroit, MI: Charles Scribner's Sons.

Nelson, Thomas E., Zoe M. Oxley, and Rosalee A. Clawson. 1997. "Toward a Psychology of Framing Effects." *Political Behavior* 19: 221–46.

Nelson, David E., Linda L. Pederson, Paul Mowery, Sarah Bailey, Varadan Sevilimedu, Joel London, Stephen Babb, and Terry Pechacek. 2015. "Trends in US Newspaper and Television Coverage of Tobacco." *Tobacco Control* 24: 94–99.

Neuberger, Maurine B. 1963. *Smoke Screen: Tobacco and the Public Welfare*. Englewood Cliffs, NJ: Prentice-Hall.

Nicholl, Jack. 1998. "Tobacco Tax Initiatives to Prevent Tobacco Use—A Study of Eight Statewide Campaigns." *Cancer* 83: 2666–79.

Nikogosian, Haik and Vera Luiza da Costa e Silva. 2015. "WHO's First Global Health Treaty: 10 Years in Force." *Bulletin of the World Health Organization* 93: 211–12.

Norr, Roy. 1952a. "Smokers are Getting Scared." *Christian Herald* (October): 19–20, 89–92.

———. 1952b. "Cancer by the Carton." *Reader's Digest* (December): 738–39.

Norton, Marcy. 2008. *Sacred Gifts, Profane Pleasures*. Ithica, NY: Cornell University Press.

Nuehring, Elaine and Gerald Markle. 1974. "Nicotine and Norms: The Re-Emergence of a Deviant Behavior." *Social Problems* 21: 513–26.

Oberlander, Jonathan. 2003. *The Political Life of Medicare*. Chicago: University of Chicago Press.

———. 2007a. "Learning from Failure in Health Care Reform." *New England Journal of Medicine* 357: 1677–79.

———. 2007b. "Through the Looking Glass: The Politics of the Medicare Prescription Drug, Improvement, and Modernization Act." *Journal of Health Politics, Policy and Law* 32: 187–218.

———. 2009. "Public Attitudes Toward Health Care Spending Aren't The Problem; Prices Are." *Health Affairs* 28: 1285–92.

———. 2010. "Long Time Coming: Why Health Reform Finally Passed." *Health Affairs* 29: 1112–16.

——— and Barbara Lyons. 2009. "Beyond Incrementalism? SCHIP And The Politics of Health Reform." *Health Affairs* 28: w399–w410.

O'Connell V. 2004. "New Laws Help Tobacco Makers with Big Judgments Amid Aggressive Lobbying." *Wall Street Journal* (July 19).

Ochsner, Alton and Michael DeBakey. 1941. "Carcinoma of the Lung." *Archives of Surgery* 42: 209–58.

Offen, Naphtali, Sarah R. Arvey, Elizabeth A. Smith, and Ruth E. Malone. 2011. "Forcing the Navy to Sell Cigarettes on Ships: How the Tobacco Industry and Politicians Torpedoed Navy Tobacco Control." *American Journal of Public Health* 101: 404–11.

O'Hegarty, Michelle, Linda Pederson, David Nelson, Paul Mowery, Julia Gable, and Pascale Wortley. 2006. "Reactions of Young Smokers to Warning Labels on Cigarette Packages." *American Journal of Preventative Medicine* 30: 467–73.

O'Keefe, M. Timothy. 1971. "The Anti-Smoking Commercials: A Study of Television's Impact on Behavior." *Public Opinion Quarterly* 35: 242–48.

Ong, Elisa K. and Stanton A. Glantz. 2000. "Tobacco Industry Efforts Subverting International Agency on Research on Cancer's Second-Hand Smoke Study." *The Lancet* 355: 1253–59.

———. 2001. "Constructing 'Sound Science' and 'Good Epidemiology': Tobacco, Lawyers, and Public Relations Firms." *American Journal of Public Health* 91: 1749–57.

Oreskes, Naomi and Erik M. Conway. 2010. *Merchants of Doubt*. New York: Bloomsbury Press.

Orey, Michael. 1999. *Assuming the Risk: the Mavericks, the Lawyers, and the Whistle-Bowers Who Beat Big Tobacco.* Boston: Little, Brown and Company.

Osypuk, Theresa L. and Dolores Acevedo-Garcia. 2010. "Support for Smoke-Free Policies: A Nationwide Analysis of Immigrants, US-Born, and Other Demographic Groups, 1995–2002." *American Journal of Public Health* 100: 171–81.

Outterson, Kevin. 2011. "Smoking and the First Amendment." *New England Journal of Medicine* 365: 2352–53.

Pacheco, Julianna. 2011. "The Polls: Trends—Public Opinion on Smoking and Anti-Smoking Policies." *Public Opinion Quarterly* 75: 576–92.

———. 2012. "The Social Contagion Model: Exploring the Role of Public Opinion on the Diffusion of Antismoking Legislation across the American States." *Journal of Politics* 74: 187–202.

———. 2013. "Attitudinal Policy Feedback and Public Opinion." *Public Opinion Quarterly* 77: 714–34.

——— and Graeme Boushey. 2014. "Public Health and Agenda Setting: Determinants of State Attention to Tobacco and Vaccines." *Journal of Health Politics, Policy and Law* 39: 565–89.

Page, Benjamin I. and Robert Y. Shapiro. 1982. "Changes in Americans' Policy Preferences, 1935–1979." *Public Opinion Quarterly* 46: 24–42.

———. 1983. "Effects of Public Opinion on Policy." *American Political Science Review* 77: 175–90.

———. 1984. "Presidents as Opinion Leaders: Some New Evidence." *Policy Studies Journal* 12: 649–61.

———. 1992. *The Rational Public*. Chicago: University of Chicago Press.

———. 2002. "The Semi-Sovereign Public." In *Navigating Public Opinion*, edited by Jeff Manza, Fay Lomax Cook, and Benjamin I. Page, 325–44. New York: Oxford University Press.

——— and Glenn R. Dempsey. 1987. "What Moves Public Opinion?" *American Political Science Review* 81: 23–43.

Parascandola, Mark. 1998. "Epidemiology: Second-Rate Science?" *Public Health Reports* 113: 312–20.

———. 2001. "Cigarettes and the US Public Health Service in the 1950s." *American Journal of Public Health* 91: 196–205.

———. 2004. "Skepticism, Statistical Methods, and the Cigarette." *Perspectives in Biology and Medicine* 47: 244–61.

———. 2005. "Warning Labels." In *Tobacco in History and Culture: An Encyclopedia Vol. 2*, edited by Jordan Goodman, 675–79. Detroit, MI: Charles Scribner's Sons.

Parmet, Wendy E. 1999. "Tobacco, HIV, and the Courtroom: The Role of Affirmative Litigation in the Formation of Public Health Policy." *Houston Law Review* 36: 1663–712.

——— and R. A. Daynard. 2000. "The New Public Health Litigation." *Annual Review of Public Health* 21: 437–54.

Patterson, James T. 1987. *The Dread Disease: Cancer and Modern American Culture*. Cambridge, MA: Harvard University Press.

Patwardhan, Pallavi, Robert McMillen, and Jonathan P. Winickoff. 2013. "Consumer Perceptions of the Sale of Tobacco Products in Pharmacies and Grocery Stores Among U.S. Adults." *BMC Research Notes* 6: 261–68.

Pearl, Raymond. 1938. "Tobacco Smoking and Longevity." *Science* (March 4): 216–17.

Pechmann, Cornelia and S. Ratneshwar. 1994. "The Effects of Antismoking and Cigarette Advertising on Young Adolescents' Perceptions of Peers Who Smoke." *Journal of Consumer Research* 21: 236–51.

Pertschuk, Michael. 2001. *Smoke in Their Eyes: Lessons in Movement Leadership from the Tobacco Wars*. Nashville, TN: Vanderbilt University Press.

Peters, E., D. Romer, P. Slovic, H. Jamieson, L. Wharfield, C. K. Mertz, and S. M. Carpenter. 2007. "The Impact and Acceptability of Canadian-Style Cigarette Warning Labels among U.S. Smokers and Nonsmokers." *Nicotine & Tobacco Research* 9: 473–81.

Peterson, Dan E., Scott L. Zeger, Patrick L. Remington, and Henry A. Anderson. 1992. "The Effect of State Cigarette Tax Increases on Cigarette Sales, 1955 to 1988." *American Journal of Public Health* 82: 94–96.

Peterson, Mark A. 1993. "Political Influence in the 1990s: From Iron Triangles to Policy Networks." *Journal of Health Politics, Policy and Law* 18: 395–438.

Peto, Richard and Alan Lopez. 2001. "Future Worldwide Health Effect of Current Smoking Patterns." In *Critical Issues in Global Health*, edited by C. Everett Koop, Clarence Pearson, and M. Roy Schwarz, 154–61. San Francisco: Wiley.

———, Jilliam Boreham, Michael Thun, Clarke Heath Jr., and Richard Doll. 1996. "Mortality from Smoking Worldwide." *British Medical Bulletin* 52: 12–21.

Petrone, Gerard S. 1996. *Tobacco Advertising: The Great Seduction*. Atglen, PA: Schiffer.

Pierce, John P. and Elizabeth A. Gilpin. 1995. "A Historical Analysis of Tobacco Marketing and the Uptake of Smoking by Youth in the United States: 1890–1977." *Health Psychology* 14: 500–08.

Pierce, J. P., E. Gilpin, and A. Farkas. 1998. "Can Strategies Used by Statewide Tobacco Control Programs Help Smokers Make Progress in Quitting?" *Cancer Epidemiology, Biomarkers & Prevention* 7: 459–664.

Pierce, John P., Won S. Choi, Elizabeth A. Gilpin, Arthur J. Farkas, and Charles C. Berry. 1998. "Tobacco Industry Promotion of Cigarettes and Adolescent Smoking." *JAMA* 279: 511–16.

Player, Tucker S. 1998. "After the Fall: The Cigarette Papers, the Global Settlement, and the Future of Tobacco Litigation." *South Carolina Law Review* (Winter): 311–41.

Pollay, Richard W. 1989. "Filters, Flavors . . . Flim-Flam, Too! On 'Health Information' and Policy Implications in Cigarette Advertising." *Journal of Public Policy and Marketing* 9: 30–39.

———. 1994a. "Exposure of US Youth to Cigarette Television Advertising in the 1960s." *Tobacco Control* 3: 130–33.

———. 1994b. "Promises, Promises: Self-Regulation of US Cigarette Broadcast Advertising in the 1960s." *Tobacco Control* 3: 134–44.

———, S. Siddarth, Michael Siegel, Anne Haddix, Robert K Merritt, Gary A. Giovino, and Michael P. Eriksen. 1996. "The Last Straw? Cigarette Advertising and Realized Market Share Among Youth and Adults, 1979–1993." *Journal of Marketing* 60: 1–16.

Pollock, David. 1996. "Forty Years On: A War to Recognize and Win." *British Medical Bulletin* 52: 174–82.

Porter, Roy. 1998. "Concluding Remarks." In *Ashes to Ashes: The History of Smoking and Health*, edited by Stephen Lock, Lois Reynolds and E. M. Tansey, 221–28. Atlanta, GA: Rodopi.

Pralle, Sarah. 2006. *Branching Out, Digging In*. Washington, DC: Georgetown University Press.

Price, Jacob M. 1995. "Tobacco Use and Tobacco Taxation: A Battle of Interests in Early Modern Europe." In *Consuming Habits: Drugs in History and Anthropology*, edited by Jordan Goodman, Paul E. Lovejoy, and Andrew Sherratt, 165–85. London: Routledge.

Pringle, Peter. 1998. *Cornered: Big Tobacco at the Bar of Justice*. New York: Henry Holt and Company.

Proctor, Robert N. 1997. "The Nazi War on Tobacco: Ideology, Evidence, and Possible Cancer Consequences." *Bulletin of the History of Medicine* 71: 435–88.

———. 1999. *The Nazi War on Cancer*. Princeton, NJ: Princeton University Press.

———. 2000. "Nazi Science and Nazi Medical Ethics: Some Myths and Misconceptions." *Perspectives in Biology and Medicine* 43: 335–45.

———. 2008. "Agnotology: A Missing Term to Describe the Cultural Production of Ignorance and Its Study." In *Agnotology: The Making and Unmaking of Ignorance*, edited by Robert N. Proctor and Londa Schiebinger, 1–36. Stanford, CA: Stanford University Press.

———. 2011. *Golden Holocaust: Origins of the Cigarette Catastrophe and the Case for Abolition*. Berkeley: University of California Press.

Quirk, Paul J. and Joseph Hinchliffe. 1998. "The Rising Hegemony of Mass Opinion." *Journal of Policy History* 10: 19–50.

Rabe, Barry George. 2013. "Political Impediments to a Tobacco Endgame." *Tobacco Control* 22: i52–i54.

Rabin, Robert L. 1992. "A Sociolegal History of the Tobacco Tort Litigation." *Stanford Law Review* 44: 853–78.

———. 1993. "Institutional and Historical Perspectives on Tobacco Tort Liability." In *Smoking Policy: Law, Politics, and Culture*, edited by Robert L. Rabin and Stephen D. Sugarman, 110–30. New York: Oxford University Press.

———. 1999. "The Uncertain Future of Tobacco Tort Litigation in the United States." *The Tort Law Review* 7: 91–95.

———. 2001. "The Third Wave of Tobacco Tort Litigation." In *Regulating Tobacco*, edited by Robert L. Rabin and Stephen D. Sugarman, 176–296. New York: Oxford University Press.

———. 2008. "Tobacco Control Strategies: Past Efficacy and Future Promise." *Loyola of Los Angeles Law Review* 41: 1721–67.

——— and Stephen D. Sugarman, eds. 2001. *Regulating Tobacco*. New York: Oxford University Press.

Rehnquist, William H. 1986. "Constitutional Law and Public Opinion." *Suffolk University Law Review* 20: 751–69.

Richards, John W., Jr., Joe B. Tye, and Paul M. Fischer. 1996. "The Tobacco Industry's Code of Advertising in the United State: Myth and Reality." *Tobacco Control* 5: 295–311.

Rigby, Elizabeth and Gerald C. Wright. 2010. "Whose Statehouse Democracy? How State Policy Choices Align with the Preferences of Poor, Middle-income, and

Wealthy Segments of the Electorate." In *Who Gets Represented*, edited by Peter Enns and Christopher Wlezien, 189–222. New York: Russel Sage.

Riis, Roger William. 1950. "How Harmful are Cigarettes?" *Reader's Digest* (January): 10–11.

Ringold, D. J. and J. E. Calfee. 1989. "The Informational Content of Cigarette Advertising: 1926–1986." *Journal of Public Policy and Management* 8: 1–23.

———. 1990. "What Can We Learn from the Informational Content of Cigarette Advertising? A Reply and Further Analysis." *Journal of Public Policy and Management* 9: 30–41.

Risse-Kappan, Thomas. 1991. "Public Opinion, Domestic Structure, and Foreign Policy in Liberal Democracies." *World Politics* 43: 479–512.

Robert, Joseph C. 1952. *The Story of Tobacco in America*. New York: Alfred A. Knopf.

Robicsek, Francis. 2005. "Mayas." In *Tobacco in History and Culture: An Encyclopedia, Vol. 1*, edited by Jordan Goodman, 339–43. Detroit, MI: Charles Scribner's Sons.

Robinson, Claude. 1932. *Straw Polls—A Study of Political Prediction*. New York: Columbia University Press.

Robinson, Michael J. 1976. "Public Affairs Television and the Growth of Political Malaise: The Case of 'The Selling of the Pentagon.'" *American Political Science Review* 70: 409–32.

Roeseler, April and David Burns. 2010. "The Quarter that Changed the World." *Tobacco Control* 19: i3–15.

Rogozinski, Jan. 1990. *Smokeless Tobacco in the Western World, 1550–1950*. New York: Praeger.

Roper Organization. 1978. *A Study of Public Attitudes Toward Cigarette Smoking and the Tobacco Industry: May 1978*. Available at www.industrydocumentslibrary.ucsf.edu/tobacco/docs/#id=fpyn0115.

Rosenberg, Gerald N. 1991, 2008. *The Hollow Hope: Can Courts Bring About Social Change*. Chicago: University of Chicago Press.

Rosenblatt, Milton B. 1964. "Lung Cancer in the 19th Century." *Bulletin of the History of Medicine* 38: 395–425.

Ross, Hana and Frank J. Chaloupka. 2003. "The Effect of Cigarette Prices on Youth Smoking." *Health Economics* 12: 217–30.

———. 2004. "The Effect of Public Policies and Prices on Youth Smoking." *Southern Economic Journal* 70: 796–815.

Rosten, Leo, ed. 1963. *Religions in America*. New York: Simon & Schuster.

Roviak, Liza S., Marilyn F. Johnson-Kozlow, and Melbourne F. Hovell. 2006. "Reducing the Gap between the Economic Costs of Tobacco and Funds for Tobacco Training in Schools of Public Health." *Public Health Reports* 121: 538–46.

Rowe, Harold B. 1935. *Tobacco Under the AAA*. Washington, DC: Brookings.

Rubert, Steven C. 2005. "Africa." In *Tobacco in History and Culture: An Encyclopedia, Vol. 1*, edited by Jordan Goodman, 23–31. Detroit, MI: Charles Scribner's Sons.

Rudder, Catherine E. and A. Lee Fritschler. 2009. "U.S.A. Tobacco Control: Six Lessons in Public Policy for Medical and Science Professionals." *World Medical & Health Policy* 1: 19–34.

Saad, Lydia. 1998. "A Half-Century of Polling on Tobacco: Most Don't Like Smoking But Tolerate It." *The Public Perspective* (August/September): 1–4.

Saiger, George L. 1960. "Errors of Medical Studies." *Journal of the American Medical Association* 173: 678–81.

Salber, Eva, R. B. Reed, and S. V. Harrison. 1963. "Smoking Behavior, Recreational Activities, and Attitudes Toward Smoking Among Newton Secondary School Children." *Pediatrics* 32: 911–18.

Samet, Jonathan M. 2001. "The Risks of Active and Passive Smoking," In *Smoking—Risk, Perceptions, & Policy*, edited by Paul Slovic, 3–28. Thousand Oaks, CA: Sage.

Samuels, Bruce E. and Stanton A. Glantz. 1991. "The Politics of Local Tobacco Control." *JAMA* 266: 2110–17.

Samuels, Bruce E., Michael Evans Begay, Anna Russo Hazan, and Stanton A. Glantz. 1992. "Philip Morris' Failed Experiment in Pittsburgh." *Journal of Health Politics, Policy and Law* 17: 329–51.

Santora, Patricia B. and Jack E. Henningfield. 2005. "Nicotine." In *Tobacco in History and Culture: An Encyclopeda, Vol. 2*, edited by Jordan Goodman, 387–92. Detroit, MI: Charles Scribner's Sons.

Sapolsky, Harvey M. 1980. "The Political Obstacles to the Control of Cigarette Smoking in the United States." *Journal of Health Politics, Policy and Law* 5: 277–90.

Sauer, Jonathan. 1993. *Historical Geography of Crop Plants*. Boca Raton, FL: CRC Press.

Schairer, Eberhard and Erich Schöniger. 1943. "Lungenkrebs und Tabakverbrauch." *Zeitschrift fur Krebsforshung* 54: 261–69.

Schauffler, Helen Halpin. 1993. "Health Insurance Policy and the Politics of Tobacco." In *Smoking Policy: Law, Politics, and Culture*, edited by Robert L. Rabin and Stephen D. Sugarman, 184–207. New York: Oxford University Press.

Schelling, Thomas C. 1971. "Dynamic Models of Segregation." *Journal of Mathematical Sociology* 1: 143–86.

———. 1992. "Addictive Drugs: The Cigarette Experience." *Science* 255: 430–33.

Schiltz, Michael E. 1970. *Public Attitudes Toward Social Security 1935–1965*. Washington, DC: U.S. Department of Health, Education, and Welfare.

Schlozman, Kay Lehman, Sidney Verba, and Henry E. Brady. 2012. *The Unheavenly Chorus: Unequal Political Voice and the Broken Promise of American Democracy*. Princeton, NJ: Princeton University Press.

Schmidt, David D. 1989. *Citizen Lawmakers*. Philadephia: Temple University Press.

Schrek, Robert, Lyle Baker, George Ballard, and Sidney Dolgoff. 1950. "Tobacco Smoking as an Etiologic Factor in Disease." *Cancer Research* 10: 49–58.

Schuman, Howard and Stanley Presser. 1981. *Questions and Answers in Attitude Surveys*. New York: Academic Press.

Schumpeter, Joseph. 1950. *Capitalism, Socialism, and Democracy*. New York: Harper.

Schwartz, Gary T. 1993. "Tobacco Liability in the Courts." In *Smoking Policy: Law, Politics, and Culture*, edited by Robert L. Rabin and Stephen D. Sugarman, 131–60. New York: Oxford University Press.

Segrave, Kerry. 2005. *Women and Smoking in America, 1880–1950*. Jefferson, NC: McFarland & Company.

Seldon, Barry J. and Khosrow Doroodian. 1989. "A Simultaneous Model of Cigarette Advertising Effects on Demand and Industry Response to Public Policy." *The Review of Economics and Statistics* 71: 673–77.

Shammas, Carole. 1994. "Changes in English and Anglo-American Consumption from 1550 to 1800." In *Consumption and the World of Goods*, edited by John Brewer and Roy Porter, 177–205. London: Routledge.

Shapiro, Robert Y. 2011. "Public Opinion and American Democracy." *Public Opinion Quarterly* 75: 982–1017.

——— and Lawrence R. Jacobs. 2011. "The Democratic Paradox." In *The Oxford Handbook of American Public Opinion and the Media*, 713–31. New York: Oxford University Press.

Shipan, Charles R. and Craig Volden. 2006. "Bottoms-up Federalism: The Diffusion of Antismoking Policies from U.S. Cities to States." *American Journal of Political Science* 50: 825–43.

Short, James J., Harry J. Johnson, and Harold A. Ley, Jr. 1938. "The Effects of Tobacco Smoking on Health." *Journal of Laboratory and Clinical Medicine* 1938: 586–89.

Siegel, Michael, Julia Carol, Jerie Jordan, Robin Hobart, Susan Schoenmarklin, Fran DuMelle, and Peter Fisher. 1997. "Preemption in Tobacco Control." *JAMA* 278: 858–63.

Silvette, H., P. S. Larson, and H. B. Haag. 1958. "Medical Uses of Tobacco, Past and Present." *Virginia Medical Monthly* 85: 472–84.

Simon, Julian L. 1968. "Doctors, Smoking, and Reference Groups." *Public Opinion Quarterly* 31: 646–47.

Singer, Eleanor, Theresa F. Rogers, and Mary Corcoran. 1987. "A Report: AIDS." *Public Opinion Quarterly* 51: 580–95.

Singer, Eleanor, Theresa F. Rogers, and Marc B. Glassman. 1991. "Public Opinion About AIDS Before and After the 1988 Government Public Information Campaign." *Public Opinion Quarterly* 55: 161–79.

Skocpol, Theda. 1992. *Protecting Soldiers and Mothers: The Policy Origins of Social Policy in the United States*. Cambridge, MA: Harvard University Press.

———. 1996. *Boomerang: Clinton's Health Security Effort and the Turn against Government in U.S. Politics*. New York: W.W. Norton.

Sloan, F. A., C. A. Mathews and J. G. Trogdon. 2004. "Impacts of the Master Settlement Agreement on the Tobacco Industry." *Tobacco Control* 13: 356–61.

Sloan, Frank A., Jan Ostermann, Gabriel Picone, Christopher Conover, and Donald H. Taylor, Jr. 2004. *The Price of Smoking*. Cambridge, MA: MIT Press.

Sloan, Frank A. and Justin G. Trogdon. 2004. "The Impact of the Master Settlement Agreement on Cigarette Consumption." *Journal of Policy Analysis and Management* 23: 843–55.

Sloan, Frank A., Emily Streyer Carlisle, John R. Rattliff, and Justin Trogdon. 2005. "Determinants of States' Allocations of the Master Settlement Agreement Payments." *Journal of Health Politics, Policy and Law* 30: 643–86.

Sloan, Frank A., Jennifer S. Allsbrook, Leanne K. Madre, Leah E. Masselink, and Carrie A. Mathews. 2005. "States' Allocations of Funds from the Tobacco Master Settlement Agreement." *Health Affairs* 24: 220–27.

Slovic, Paul. 1987. "Perception of Risk." *Science* 236: 280–85.

———. 1998. "Do Adolescent Smokers Know the Risks?" *Duke Law Journal* 47: 1133–41.

———, ed. 2000. *Smoking: Risk, Perception, and Policy*. Thousand Oaks, CA: Sage.

Smith, Elizabeth and Ruth Malone. 2003a. "Altria Means Tobacco: Philip Morris' Identity Crisis." *American Journal of Public Health* 93: 553–56.

———. 2003b. "Thinking the 'Unthinkable': Why Philip Morris Considered Quitting." *Tobacco Control* 12: 208–13.

Smith, Elizabeth, Virginia Blackman, and Ruth Malone. 2007. "Death at a Discount: How the Tobacco Industry Thwarted Tobacco Control Policies in US Military Commissaries." *Tobacco Control* 16: 38–46.

Smith, Elizabeth, Quinn Grundy, and Ruth E. Malone. 2015. "'It's Not a Priority When We're in Combat': Public Health Professions and Military Tobacco Control Policy." *American Journal of Public Health* 105: 660–64.

Smith, Eric R. A. N. 2002. *Energy, the Environment, and Public Opinion*. Lanham, MD: Rowman & Littlefield.

Smith, K. E., E. Savell, and A. B. Gilmore. 2013. "What is Known About Tobacco Industry Efforts to Influence Tobacco Tax?" *Tobacco Control* 22: 144–53.

Smith, Katherine Clegg, Melanie Wakefield, and Elizabeth Edsall. 2006. "The Good News About Smoking: How Do US Newspapers Cover Tobacco Issues?" *Journal of Public Health Policy* 27: 166–81.

Smith, Tom W. 1990. "The First Straw? A Study of the Origins of Election Polls." *Public Opinion Quarterly* 54: 21–36.

Smoking and Health: Summary of a Report of the Royal College of Physicians of London on Smoking in Relation to Cancer of the Lung and Other Diseases. 1962. London: Pitman Medical Publishing Co, Ltd.

Smoking and Health: Report of the Advisory Committee to the Surgeon General of the Public Health Service. 1964. Washington, DC: U.S. Department of Health, Education, and Welfare.

Smoking and Health: A Report on the Study of Smoking Behavior, Attitudes, and Knowledge of Public School Children in the State of Washington. 1969. Olympia, WA: Washington Superintendent of Public Education.

"Smoking and Lung Cancer," *Journal of the American Medical Association* (December 12, 1959): 2104.

Snegireff, Leonid S. and Olive M. Lombard. 1959. "Smoking Habits of Massachusetts Physicians: Five-Year Follow-up Study." *New England Journal of Medicine* 261: 603–04.

Snell, Clete. 2005. *Peddling Poison: The Tobacco Industry and Kids*. Westport, CT: Praeger.

Sobel, Robert. 1978. *They Satisfy: The Cigarette In American Life*. New York: Anchor Books.

Soroka, Stuart N. and Christopher Wlezien. 2005. "Opinion-Policy Dynamics: Public Preferences and Public Expenditure in the United Kingdom." *British Journal of Political Science* 35: 665–89.

———. 2009. *Degrees of Democracy: Politics, Public Opinion, and Policy*. New York: Cambridge University Press.

Spill, Rorie L., Michael J. Licari, and Leonard Ray. 2001. "Taking on Tobacco: Policy Entrepreneurship and the Tobacco Litigation." *Political Research Quarterly* 54: 605–22.

Starr, Paul. 1982. *The Social Transformation of American Medicine*. New York: Basic.

Steel, Paul. 1965. "Cigarette Smoking In School Children." *The Journal of the Medical Society of New Jersey* 63: 555–57.

Steinmo, Sven and Jon Watts. 1995. "It's the Institutions, Stupid! Why Comprehensive National Health Insurance Always Fails in America." *Journal of Health Politics, Policy and Law* 20: 329–71.

Stellman, Steven D. and Lawrence Garfinkel. 1986. "Lung Cancer Risk is Proportionate to Tar Yield: Evidence from a Prospective Study." *Preventative Medicine* 18: 518–25.

———. 1989. "Proportions of Cancer Deaths Attributable to Cigarette Smoking in Women." *Women & Health* 15: 19–28.

Sternthal, Brian, Lynn W. Phillips, and Ruby Dholakia. 1978. "The Persuasive Effect of Source Credibility: A Situational Analysis." *Public Opinion Quarterly* 42: 285–314.

Stewart, Grace G. 1967. "A History of the Medicinal Use of Tobacco 1492–1860." *Medical History* 11: 228–68.

Stimson, James A. 1991, 1999. *Public Opinion in America—Moods, Cycles, and Swings*. Boulder, CO: Westview.

———, Michael B. MacKuen, and Robert S. Erikson. 1995. "Dynamic Representation." *American Political Science Review* 89: 543–65.

Stone, Doris, ed. 1984. *Pre-Columbian Plant Migration*. Cambridge, MA: Harvard University Press.

Stratmann, Thomas. 2006. "Is Spending More Potent for or against a Proposition? Evidence from Ballot Measures." *American Journal of Political Science* 50: 788–801.

Streit, W. K. 1967. "Students Express Views on Smoking." *Journal of School Health* 37: 151–52.

"Students See Link between Smoking and Cancer." *Senior Scholastic* (February 17, 1960): 27.

Studlar, Donley T. 2002. *Tobacco Control: Comparative Politics in the United States and Canada*. Peterborough, Canada: Broadview Press.

———. 2014. "Cancer Prevention through Stealth: Science, Policy Advocacy, and Multilevel Governance in the Establishment of a 'National Tobacco Control Regime' in the United States." *Journal of Health Politics, Policy, and Law* 39: 503–45.

Sturm, Roland. 2002. "The Effects Of Obesity, Smoking, And Drinking On Medical Problems And Costs." *Health Affairs* 21: 245–53.

Sugarman, Stephen D. 1993. "Disparate Treatment of Smokers in Employment and Insurance." In *Smoking Policy: Law, Politics, and Culture*, edited by Robert L. Rabin and Stephen D. Sugarman, 161–83. New York: Oxford University Press.

Sulkin, Tracy. 2011. *The Legislative Legacy of Congressional Campaigns*. Cambridge: Cambridge University Press.

Susser, Mervyn. 1985. "Epidemiology in the United States after World War II: The Evolution of Technique." *Epidemiologic Reviews* 7: 147–77.

Sweda, Edward L., Jr. and Richard A Daynard. 1996. "Tobacco Industry Tactics." *British Medical Journal* 52: 183–92.

Talley, Colin, Howard Kushner, and Claire Sterk. 2004. "Lung Cancer, Chronic Disease Epidemiology, and Medicine 1948–1964." *Journal of the History of Medicine and Allied Sciences* 59: 329–74.

Tate, Cassandra. 1995. *The American Anti-Cigarette Movement, 1880–1930*. Ph.D. Dissertation. Seattle, WA: University of Washington.

———. 1999. *Cigarette Wars*. New York: Oxford University Press.

———. 2005. "Antismoking Movement Before 1950." In *Tobacco in History and Culture: An Encyclopedi, Vol. 1*, edited by. Jordan Goodman, 45–51. Detroit, MI: Charles Scribner's Sons.

Taylor, Andrew J. 2003. "Conditional Party Government and Campaign Contributions: Insights from the Tobacco and Alcoholic Beverage Industries." *American Journal of Political Science* 47: 293–304.

Taylor, Peter. 1984. *The Smoke Ring: Tobacco, Money, and Multinational Politics*. New York: Pantheon.

Tedin, Kent, Brandon Rottinghaus, and Harrell Rodgers. 2011. "When the President Goes Public: The Consequences of Communication Mode for Opinion Change across Issue Types and Groups." *Political Research Quarterly* 64: 506–19.

Teenage Smoking: National Patterns of Cigarette Smoking, Age 12 through 18, in 1968 and 1970. 1972. Washington, DC: National Clearinghouse for Smoking and Health.

"Teenage Smoking: New ACS Study Shows Young People's Beliefs and Behavior." 1968–1969. *Public Health Reports* 83: 3–7.

Tennant, Richard B. 1950. *The American Cigarette Industry: A Study in Economic Analysis and Public Policy*. New Haven, CT: Yale University Press.

Teret, S. P. and M. Jacobs. 1989. "Prevention and Torts: The Role of Litigation in Injury Control." *Law, Medicine & Health Care* 17: 17–22.

Terry-McElrath, Yvonne M., Sherry Emery, Melanie A. Wakefield, Patrick M. O'Malley, Glen Szczpka, and Lloyd D. Johnston. 2013. "Effects of Tobacco-Related Media Campaigns on Smoking Among 20–30-Year-Old Adults: Longitudinal Data from the USA." *Tobacco Control* 22: 38–45.

Thomas, Caroline Bedell. 1960. "Characteristics of Smokers Compared with Nonsmokers in a Population of Healthy Young Adults, including Observations on Family History, Blood Pressure, Heart Rate, Body Weight, Cholesterol, and Certain Psychological Traits." *Annals of Internal Medicine* 53: 697–718.

Thompson, George, Nick Wilson, and Richard Edwards. 2009. "At the Frontier of Tobacco Control: A Brief Review of Public Attitudes Toward Some-Free Outdoor Places." *Nicotine & Tobacco Research* 11: 584–90.

Thompson, George, Nick Wilson, Tony Blakely, and Richard Edwards. 2010. "Ending Appreciable Tobacco Use in a Nation Using a Sinking Lid on Supply." *Tobacco Control* 19: 431–35.

Thrasher, James F., Matthew C. Rousu, David Hammond, Ashley Navarro, and Jay R. Corrigan. 2011. "Estimating the Impact of Pictorial Health Warnings and 'Plain' Cigarette Packaging: Evidence from Experimental Auctions Among Adult Smokers in the United States." *Health Policy* 102: 41–48.

Thun, Michael, Richard Peto, Jillian Boreham, and Alan D. Lopez. 2012. "Stages of the Cigarette Epidemic on Entering its Second Century." *Tobacco Control* 21: 96–101.

Tilley, Nannie M. 1948. *The Bright-Tobacco Industry 1860–1929*. Chapel Hill, NC: University of North Carolina Press.

———. 1985. *The R. J. Reynolds Tobacco Company*. Chapel Hill, NC: University of North Carolina Press.

Tinkler, Penny. 2005. "Women." In *Tobacco in History and Culture: An Encyclopedia, Vol. 2*, edited by Jordan Goodman, 679–87. Detroit, MI: Charles Scribner's Sons.

"Tobacco Advertising Gone Mad." 1939. *Journal of the American Medical Association* 94: 8010.

Toch, Hans, Terrence Allen, William Lazer. 1961a. "The Public Image of Cancer Etiology." *Public Opinion Quarterly* 25: 411–14.

———. 1961b. "Effects of Cancer Scares: The Residue of News Impact." *Journalism & Mass Communication Quarterly* 38: 25–34, 126.

Traylor, Gregory W. 2010. "Big Tobacco, Medicaid-Covered Smokers, and the Substance of the Master Settlement Agreement." *Vanderbilt Law Review* 63: 1082–130.

Traynor, Michael P., Michael E. Begay, and Stanton A. Glantz. 1993. "New Tobacco Industry Strategy to Prevent Local Tobacco Control." *JAMA* 270: 479–86.

Traynor, Michael P. and Stanton A. Glantz. 1996. "California's Tobacco Tax Initiative: The Development and Passage of Proposition 99." *Journal of Health Politics, Policy, and Law* 21: 689–715.

Trichopoulos, Dimitrios, Anna Kalandidi, Loukas Sparros, and Brian MacMahon. 1981. "Lung Cancer and Passive Smoking." *International Journal of Cancer* 27: 1–4.

Troyer, Ronald J. and Gerald E. Markle. 1983. *Cigarettes: The Battle over Smoking*. New Brunswick, NJ: Rutgers University Press.

Tsoukalas, T. H. and S. A. Glantz. 2003. "Development and Destruction of the First State Funded Anti-Smoking Campaign in the USA." *Tobacco Control* 12: 214–20.

Tunney, Gene. 1941."Nicotine Knockout, or the Slow Count." *Reader's Digest* (December): 21–24.

Tursi, Frank V., Susan E. White, and Steve McQuilkin. 2000. *Lost Empire: the Fall of R. J. Reynolds Tobacco Company*. Winston-Salem, NC: *The Winston-Salem Journal*.

Ubelaker, Douglas H. 1992. "North American Indian Population Size: Changing Perspectives." In *Disease and Demography in the Americas*, edited by John M. Verano and Douglas H. Ubelaker, 169–76. Washington, DC: Smithsonian Institution Press.

Ura, Joseph Daniel and Christopher R. Ellis. 2008. "Income, Preferences, and the Dynamics of Policy Responsiveness." *PS: Political Science & Politics* 41: 785–94.

U.S. Congress. 1957. *False and Misleading Advertising (Filter-Tip Cigarettes): Hearings Before a Subcommittee of the Committee on Government Operations, House of Representatives, Eighty-Fifth Congress, First Session. July 18, 19, 23, 24, 25, and 26, 1957*. Washington, DC: U.S. Government Printing Office.

U.S. Surgeon General. 2014. *The Health Consequences of Smoking—50 Years of Progress: A Report of the Surgeon General, 2014*. Washington, DC: U.S. Department of Health and Human Services.

Use of Tobacco—Practices, Attitudes, Knowledge, and Beliefs—United States—Fall 1964 and Spring 1966. 1969. Washington, DC: U.S. Department of Health, Education, and Welfare.

Verano, John M. and Douglas H. Ubelaker, eds. 1992. *Disease and Demography in the Americas*. Washington, DC: Smithsonian Institution Press.

Viscusi, W. Kip. 1990. "Do Smokers Underestimate Risks?" *Journal of Political Economy* 98: 1253–69.

———. 1992. *Smoking: Making the Risky Decision*. New York: Oxford.

———. 1994. "Promoting Smokers' Welfare with Responsible Taxation." *National Tax Journal* 47: 547–58.

———. 2002. *Smoke-Filled Rooms: A Post-mortem on the Tobacco Deal*. Chicago: University of Chicago Press.

———. 2002/2003. "The New Cigarette Paternalism," *Regulation* (Winter): 58–64.

———. 2004. "The Blockbuster Punitive Damage Awards." *Emory Law Journal* 53: 1405–55.

——— and Benjamin J. McMichael. 2014. "Shifting the Fat-Tailed Distribution of Blockbuster Punitive Damages Awards." *Journal of Empirical Legal Studies* 11: 350–77.

Volanto, Keith. 2005. "New Deal." In *Tobacco in History and Culture: An Encyclopedia, Vol. 2*, edited by Jordan Goodman, 385–87. Detroit, MI: Charles Scribner's Sons.

Von Gernet, Alexander. 1995. "Nicotian Dreams: The Prehistory and Early History of Tobacco in Eastern North America." In *Consuming Habits: Drugs in History and Anthropology*, edited by Jordan Goodman, Paul E. Lovejoy, and Andrew Sherratt, 67–87. London: Routledge.

Voter Consumer Research. 1997. "Nationwide Segmentation Survey—A Survey Conducted for the Tobacco Institute." Bethesda, MD. legacy.library.ucsf.edu/tid/njk81d00

Wackowsky, Olivia and Christine Delnevo. 2015. "Smokers' Attitudes and Support for e-Cigarette Policies and Regulation in the USA." *Tobacco Control* 24: 574–81.

Wagner, Susan. 1971. *Cigarette Country: Tobacco in American History and Politics*. New York: Praeger.

Wagner, Wendy. 2007. "When All Else Fails: Regulating Risky Products Through Tort Litigation." *Georgetown Law Journal* 95: 693–732.

Walker, R. B. 1980. "Medical Aspects of Tobacco Smoking and the Anti-Tobacco Movement in Britain in the Nineteenth Century." *Medical History* 24: 391–402.

Wang, A. L., D. Roemer, I. Elman, B. I. Turetsky, R. C. Gur, and D. D. Lanleben. 2015. "Emotional Graphic Cigarette Warning Labels Reduce the Electrophysiological Brain Response to Smoking Cues." *Addiction Biology* 20: 368–76.

Ward, John W. and Christian Warren. 2007. *Silent Victories: The History and Practice of Public Health in Twentieth-Century America*. New York: Oxford University Press.

Warner, Kenneth E. 1977. "The Effects of the Anti-Smoking Campaign on Cigarette Consumption." *American Journal of Public Health* 67: 645–50.

———. 1979. "Clearing the Airwaves: The Cigarette Ad Ban Revisited." *Policy Analysis* 5: 435–50.

———. 1981. "State Legislation on Smoking and Health: A Comparison of Two Policies." *Policy Sciences* 13: 139–52.

———. 1989. "Effects of the Antismoking Campaign: An Update." *American Journal of Public Health* 79: 144–51.

———. 2006. "Tobacco Policy Research: Insights and Contributions to Public Health Policy." In *Tobacco Control Policy*, edited by Kenneth Warner, 3–86. San Francisco: Jossey-Bass.

———. 2013. "An Endgame for Tobacco?" *Tobacco Control* 22: i3–i5.

——— and Hillary A. Murt. 1983. "Premature Deaths Avoided by the Antismoking Campaign." *American Journal of Public Health* 73: 672–77.

———, Thomas Hodgson, and Caitlin Carroll. 1999. "Medical Costs of Smoking in the United States: Estimates, Validity, and Implication." *Tobacco Control* 9: 190–300.

——— and E. G. Martin. 2003. "The US Tobacco Control Community's View of the Future of Tobacco Harm Reduction." *Tobacco Control* 12: 383–90.

——— and David Mendez. 2010. "Tobacco Control Policy in Developed Countries: Yesterday, Today, and Tomorrow." *Nicotine & Tobacco Research* 12: 876–87.

——— and Jamie Tam. 2012. "The Impact of Tobacco Control Research on Policy: 20 Years of Progress." *Tobacco Control* 21: 103–09.

———, Donald W. Sexton, Brenda W. Gillespie, David T. Levy, and Frank J. Chaloupka. 2014. "Impact of Tobacco Control on Adult per Capita Cigarette Consumption in the United States." *American Journal of Public Health* 104: 83–89.

Warsh, Cheryl Krasnick. 2005. "Marketing." In *Tobacco in History and Culture: An Encyclopeda, Vol. 2*, edited by Jordan Goodman, 327–37. Detroit, MI: Charles Scribner's Sons.

Wassink, W. F. 1948. "Onstaansvoorwarden voor Longkanker." *Nederlands Tijdschrift voor Geneeskunde* 92: 3732–47.

Waxman, Henry. 2003. "Tobacco Industry Statements in the US Department of Justice Lawsuit." *Tobacco Control* 12: 94–101.

Weaver, R. Kent. 2002. "Polls, Priming, and the Politics of Welfare Reform." In *New Directions in Public Opinion*, edited by Adam J. Berinsky, 106–23. New York: Routledge.

Weinstein, Neil D. 1998. "Accuracy of Smokers Risk Perceptions." *Annals of Behavioral Medicine* 20: 135–40.

———. 1999. "What Does it Mean to Understand a Risk? Evaluating Risk Comprehension." *Journal of the National Cancer Institute Monographs* 25: 15–20.

———. 2001. "Smokers' Recognition of Their Vulnerability to Harm." In *Smoking—Risk, Perception, & Policy*, edited by Paul Slovic, 81–96. Thousand Oaks, CA: Sage.

———. 2005. "Smokers' Unrealistic Optimism About Their Risk." *Tobacco Control* 14: 55–59.

——— and Erika Waters. 2004. "Public Understanding of the Illnesses Caused by Cigarette Smoking." *Nicotine and Tobacco Research* 6: 349–55.

———, Paul Slovic, and Ginger Gibson. 2004. "Accuracy and Optimism in Smokers' Beliefs About Quitting." *Nicotine & Tobacco Research* 6: S375–80.

Weissert, Carol S. and William G. Weissert. 2002. *Governing Health: The Politics of Health Policy*. Baltimore, MD: Johns Hopkins University Press.

Whelan, Elizabeth. 1984. *A Smoking Gun: How The Tobacco Industry Gets Away With Murder*. Philadelphia, PA: Stickley.

White, Lawrence. 1988. *Merchants of Death: The American Tobacco Industry*. New York: Beech Tree Books.

White, Jenny and Lisa A. Bero. 2004. "Public Health Under Attack: The American Stop Smoking Intervention Study (ASSIST) and the Tobacco Industry." *American Journal of Public Health* 94: 240–50.

Whyte, Gregor, Philip Gendall, and Janet Hoek. 2014. "Advancing the Retail End-game: Public Perceptions of Retail Policy Interventions." *Tobacco Control* 23: 160–66.

Wilbert, Johannes. 1987. *Tobacco and Shamanism in South America*. New Haven, CT: Yale University Press.

———. 1991. "Does Pharmacology Corroborate the Nicotine Therapy and Practices of South American Shamanism?" *Journal of Ethnopharmacology* 32: 179–96.

Wilbur, Phillip. 1996. "'Weekly Reader' and 'Current Events': Case Studies in Journalistic 'Objectivity' Run Amok." *Tobacco Control* 5: 97–98.

Williams, Tannis M. 1971. *Summary and Implications of Review of Literature Related to Adolescent Smoking*. Washington, DC: U.S. Department of Health, Education, and Welfare.

Wilson, Karen M., Michelle Torok, Robert McMillen, Susanne Tanski, Jonathan D. Klein, and Jonathan P. Winickoff. 2014. "Tobacco Smoke Incursions in Multiunit Housing." *American Journal of Public Health* 104: 1445–53.

Wilson, N., G. Thomson, M. Tobias, and T. Blakely. 2004. "How Much Downside? Quantifying the Relative Harm from Tobacco Taxation." *Journal of Epidemiology and Community Health* 58: 451–54.

Winickoff, Jonathan P., Joan Friebely, Susanne E. Tanski, Cheryl Sherrod, George E. Matt, Melbourne F. Hovell, and Robert C. McMillen. 2009. "Beliefs About the Health Effects of 'Thirdhand' Smoke and Home Smoking Bans." *Pediatrics* 123: e74–79.

Winickoff, Jonathan P., Robert C. McMillen, Donna M. Vallone, Jennifer L. Pearson, Susanne E. Transki, Janelle H. Dempsey, Cheryl Healton, Jonathan D. Klein, and David Abrams. 2011. "US Attitudes About Banning Menthol in Cigarettes: Results From a Nationally Representative Study." *American Journal of Public Health* 101: 1234–36.

Winickoff, Jonathan P., Robert McMillen, Susanne Tanski, Karen Wilson, Mark Gottlieb, and Robert Crane. 2015. "Public Support for Raising the Age of Sale for Tobacco to 21 in the United States." *Tobacco Control* 24: published on-line April 15 as 10:1136/toaccocontrol-2014–052126.

Winkler, John K. 1942. *Tobacco Tycoon: The Story of James Buchanan Duke*. New York: Random House.

Winter, Joseph, ed. 2000. *Tobacco Use by Native North Americans*. Norman: University of Oklahoma Press.

———. 2005. "Native Americans." In *Tobacco in History and Culture: An Encyclopedia, Vol. 2*, edited by Jordan Goodman, 375–82. Detroit, MI: Charles Scribner's Sons.

Withey, Stephen B. 1959. "Public Opinion About Science and Scientists." *Public Opinion Quarterly* 23: 382–88.

Wlezien, Christopher. 1995. "The Public as Thermostat: Dynamics of Preferences for Spending." *American Journal of Political Science* 39: 981–1000.

———. 2004. "Patterns of Representation: Dynamics of Public Preferences and Policy." *Journal of Politics* 66: 1–24.

——— and Stuart N. Soroka. 2011. "Inequality in Policy Responsiveness?" In *Who Gets Represented?*, edited by Peter K. Enns and Christopher Wlezien, 285–310. New York: Russell Sag Foundation.

Wolfson, Mark. 2001. *The Fight Against Big Tobacco: The Movement, the State, and the Public's Health*. New York: Adine De Gruyter.

"Women and Cigarettes." 1932. *Printers' Ink* 158 (February 18): 25–27.

Wood, Robert S. 2006. "Tobacco's Tipping Point: The Master Settlement Agreement as a Focusing Event." *The Policy Studies Journal* 34: 419–36.

Worsham, Jeffrey. 1998. "Wavering Equilibriums." *American Politics Quarterly* 26: 485–512.

———. 2006. "Up in Smoke: Mapping Subsystem Dynamics in Tobacco Policy." *Policy Studies Journal* 34: 437–53.

Wright, John. 2004. "Campaign Contributions and Congressional Voting on Tobacco Policy, 1980–2000." *Business and Politics* 6: 1–26.

Wynder, Ernest L. and Evarts A. Graham. 1950. "Tobacco Smoking as a Possible Etiologic Factor in Bronchiogenic Carcinoma." *JAMA* 143: 329–36.

Wynder, E. L., E. A. Graham, and A. B. Croninger. 1953. "Experimental Production of Carcinoma with Cigarette Tar: Part One." *Cancer Research* 13: 855–64.

Xu, Xin, Ellen E. Bishop, Sara M. Kennedy, Sean A. Simpson, and Terry F. Pechacek. 2015. "Annual Healthcare Spending Attributable to Cigarette Smoking—An Update." *American Journal of Preventive Medicine* 48: 326–33.

Yang, J. S. and R. E. Malone. 2008. "'Working to Shape What Society's Expectations of Us Should Be': Philip Morris' Societal Alignment Strategy." *Tobacco Control* 17: 391–98.

Yang, Joshua S. and Thomas E. Novotny. 2009. "Policy Coherence in US Tobacco Control: Beyond FDA Regulation." *PLoS Medicine* 6: 1–5.

Youth and Tobacco—Preventing Tobacco Use Among Yong People. 1992. U.S. Department of Health & Human Services. Washington, DC: U.S. Government Printing Office.

Zagona, Salvatore and M. Russell Harter. 1966. "Credibility of Source and Recipient's Attitude: Factors in the Perception and Retention of Information on Smoking Behavior." *Perceptual and Motor Skills* 23: 155–68.

Zeller, Mitch. 2012. "Three Years Later: An Assessment of the Implementation of the Family Smoking Prevention and Tobacco Control Act." *Tobacco Control* 21: 453–54.

Index

About the Author

Thomas R. Marshall is professor of political science at the University of Texas at Arlington where he teaches classes in American government, public opinion, and campaigns and elections. He received his PhD from the University of Minnesota. He is the author of three prior books and of numerous articles and book chapters. His recent work focuses on public opinion and health care policy.

Lightning Source UK Ltd.
Milton Keynes UK
UKOW04n0139201217
314771UK00001B/106/P

9 781498 504324